THE JEWS OF HARLEM

The Jews of Harlem

The Rise, Decline, and Revival of a Jewish Community

Jeffrey S. Gurock

NEW YORK UNIVERSITY PRESS
New York

NEW YORK UNIVERSITY PRESS
New York
www.nyupress.org

Library of Congress Cataloging-in-Publication Data
Names: Gurock, Jeffrey S., 1949– author.
Title: The Jews of Harlem : the rise, decline, and revival of a Jewish community / Jeffrey S. Gurock.
Description: New York : New York University Press, [2016] | Includes bibliographical references and index.
Identifiers: LCCN 2016018950 | ISBN 9781479801169 (cl : alk. paper)
Subjects: LCSH: Jews—New York (State)—New York—History. | Harlem (New York, N.Y.)—History. | African Americans—New York (State)—New York—Relations with Jews.
Classification: LCC F128.9.J5 G868 2016 | DDC 974.7/004924—dc23
LC record available at https://lccn.loc.gov/2016018950

New York University Press books are printed on acid-free paper, and their binding materials are chosen for strength and durability. We strive to use environmentally responsible suppliers and materials to the greatest extent possible in publishing our books.

Manufactured in the United States of America

10 9 8 7 6 5 4 3 2 1

Also available as an ebook

For Elise and Michael

CONTENTS

ACKNOWLEDGMENTS

It is a pleasure to thank the many people who have encouraged and assisted me in the writing of this book. Forty years ago, Professor Kenneth T. Jackson of Columbia University—the nation's foremost urban historian—sparked my interest in writing about the Jews of Harlem. I shall always be his student even as today he sees me as a colleague, especially as a Fellow of the New York Academy of History, an organization that he has championed to give due recognition to the sagas of the many races and religions that make up Gotham's saga. I hope that through this book I am continuing to do justice to that mission. Grateful thanks are also extended to Professor David Rothman of Columbia University, who helped sharpen my arguments in writing initially about the uptown community, and to Dr. Naomi W. Cohen, professor emerita of Hunter College, who was my first and foremost teacher and mentor in the field of American Jewish history.

I am grateful that NYU Press shared my enthusiasm to revisit Jewish Harlem and to update its important history to the present day. Special thanks are due to my editor Jennifer Hammer who has gracefully challenged me to broaden the scope of this work while assuring me constantly that the book was mine to write. Similarly, I am thankful that my colleague and friend of long-standing Professor Deborah Dash Moore of the University of Michigan took time out from her own busy schedule to carefully read and comment on the penultimate draft of this work. Her perspectives on Gotham's history were of invaluable help in complementing my own visions of New York Jewish history. As with all of my scholarly endeavors, I rely on the advice and counsel of my friend and colleague Professor Benjamin R. Gampel of the Jewish Theological Seminary.

In the search for sources and materials, the outstanding library staff at Yeshiva University, including John Moryl, Zvi Erenyi, Rabbi Moshe Shapiro, and the indefatigable Mary Ann Linahan, assisted me as always.

David Khabinsky of Yeshiva University's Public Affairs Department did excellent work in providing me with visuals for this book. Most importantly, I am warmed by the enthusiasm that my home institution has shown for my labors, beginning with our president, Richard M. Joel, and our provost and fellow historian, Dr. Selma Botman. Beyond Yeshiva, I am also grateful that Harlem music historian John Reddick invited me into his world. I should also thank Professor Ronald Miller and the Berman Jewish Data Bank of the Jewish Federations of North America for providing me with and for crunching demographic data on the presence of Jews in Harlem over the past few decades. Of course, any errors of fact or interpretation that appear in this book are mine alone.

I am blessed with a wonderful, supportive family. Forty years ago, I dedicated my Harlem book to Pamela for keeping alive the vision of a completed project. She continues, as always, to be the bedrock of the Gurocks. Our three children and their spouses and our seven grandchildren inspire me in countless ways whether or not they will ever read my books. Most recently, Elise has joined our crew, contributing additional warmth and charm to our family. I am so pleased to dedicate this book to her and to my son Michael and I know that *The Jews of Harlem* will find a special place in their hearts and on their coffee table.

Jeffrey S. Gurock

THE JEWS OF HARLEM

116th Street in a gentrified, present-day Harlem (photo courtesy of Yeshiva University Office of Communications and Public Affairs).

Introduction

Forty Years with the Jews of Harlem—the Old and the Renewed

In the spring of 2002, David Dunlap, architecture columnist for the *New York Times*, came to my office to discuss an article he was composing about a lost and forgotten Jewish community. The subject of his investigation was Harlem. I was taken aback by the idea that a New York Jewish settlement that once had housed close to 175,000 Jews was not remembered. After all, I had written my first book, *When Harlem Was Jewish, 1870–1930*, in 1978. And for more than the next quarter century, I had reminded everyone who would hear me out—fellow academicians and the general public alike—how important the community had been in the history of Gotham. I argued everywhere that the saga of immigrant Jewish life and advancement in the metropolis during the early decades of the prior century was incomplete without considering Harlem. One of the prime intellectual conceits was that a complex set of forces motivated Jewish relocation from one area of the city to the next and greatly influenced the types of group identifications that were maintained. Prior historians had not been sensitive to the reality that downtown—that is, the Lower East Side—and uptown alike were home, at least after 1900, to both poor and more affluent Jews. Previous scholars also had not discussed how these two sibling communities likewise included both acculturated Jews and those who were just starting to learn American ways. Indeed, the fact was that more immigrants and their children moved to Harlem, or were pushed out of the so-called "ghetto," before they achieved financial success than as a sign that they had begun to make it in America. The key to comprehending where Jews ended up residing was inexorably tied to their presence in a dynamic and ever-changing city. Training as an urban historian had taught me that improvements in rapid transit, slum removal efforts, and booms and busts in real estate markets—

among many other transformative phenomena—that affected the lives of all New Yorkers were fundamental parts of the Jewish experience in Gotham as well.

In addition, as a student of the history of African American–Jewish relations—a field of study that was only beginning to come into its own in the late 1970s—I argued that this crucial inter-group encounter could not be fully told without reference to where and when large numbers of both groups first lived in close proximity to each other in a twentieth-century neighborhood. Other writers were focusing on the statements that black and Jewish leaders were making about one another and had not paid particular attention to examining how the men and women on the street related to each other, with a particular concern with identifying the dynamics that had led Jews to exit the part of Gotham that became the African American mecca. As it turned out, one of the listeners to my stock-in-trade presentation agreed so heartily with these interests and conceptualizations that he began his own fruitful exploration of the great degree to which Jews and African Americans collaborated in the musical and theatrical worlds uptown from the turn of the twentieth century through the 1930s. Still, I had to agree with David Dunlap that some eighty years had passed since Jewish Harlem's heyday. And close to forty years had gone by since I had first made much of the neighborhood's transcendent significance.[1]

Anxious to accommodate Dunlap's desire to see physical remnants of the old neighborhood, we jumped into my car and fifteen minutes after we left my university office in Washington Heights we were standing near the corner of 116th Street and Fifth Avenue. That wide street from east to west was, to my mind, the most important thoroughfare of Jewish Harlem. As we stood on the steps of the Harlem Baptist Temple Church at 18 West 116th Street, which once had been home to Congregation Ohab Zedek, a renowned synagogue, I evoked for Dunlap the sight of thousands of Jewish men, women, and children promenading up and down that street on the High Holidays—perhaps attending services or maybe just strolling to see and be seen by their neighbors. One of this congregation's greatest attractions during the 1910s was its famous cantor, Yossele Rosenblatt, perhaps known to film aficionados as the voice that chanted "Kaddish" in the original *The Jazz*

Singer, which starred Al Jolson. Although the cantor and the actor who played the son of a cantor did not know one another, I mused that they both had Harlem connections. Rosenblatt's link was obvious; his counterpart's was somewhat notorious. As a youth, Jolson was captivated by the sounds of black music played in the uptown neighborhood. Later on, he knew of, and frequented, many of the after-hours clubs in Harlem in the 1920s and 1930s where he enjoyed the company of both African American and Jewish entertainers and patrons. I did not mention that it was at Bloodgood's house of assignation—somewhere in the neighborhood and late in the 1910s—that Jolson heard, for the first time, George Gershwin's "Swanee," a song that he would adopt as a signature piece. Jolson's embrace of that composition would soon make it the songwriter's first great hit.

Ohab Zedek and its cantor also were the venue and the voice for a public expression of grief at the passing of a very different type of Harlem Jewish celebrity of that era. The great Yiddish writer Sholem Aleichem, renowned as the "Jewish Mark Twain," lived for two years in the uptown neighborhood before he moved up to the Bronx. When he died on May 13, 1916, at the age of fifty-seven, he was memorialized with a citywide funeral that began on Kelly Street in the Bronx. The cortege's first stop in Manhattan was Rosenblatt's synagogue, where the cantor recited the memorial prayer in front of a throng that lined the wide thoroughfare. From Harlem, the mourners traveled to the Lower East Side and ultimately to Sholem Aleichem's burial place in Mount Neboh Cemetery on the Brooklyn-Queens border.[2]

Looking to the right of the former Ohab Zedek, to the northeast corner of 116th Street, I pointed out another church—The Church of the Lord Jesus Christ of the Apostolic Faith. Like the Harlem Baptist Temple Church, it stood out amid a group of rundown apartment buildings that, generations earlier, had been new, expensive residences, homes to affluent immigrant Jews and their children. In the early twentieth century, when Jews predominated on that street, the Mount Morris Theatre occupied the space, which eventually was made suitable for a Christian house of worship. That locale had its own Jewish religious history. It was there in the mid-1910s that an ambitious rabbi held what he called "monster rallies," effectively Jewish revival meetings aimed at "retrieving" Jews who were not attending Ohab

Zedek or for that matter his own, competing congregation situated down the block close to Lenox Avenue and 116th Street. The calling card of Rabbi Herbert S. Goldstein's Institutional Synagogue was its offer of a multitude of ancillary cultural and recreational activities to the youth of the neighborhood. He hoped that those who came during the week for art and music classes, used the library, and, most importantly, repaired to the pool and gymnasium, would return for services on Sabbath and holidays. The concept—that those who "came to play would stay to pray"—did not originate with Goldstein. His professor at the Jewish Theological Seminary of America, Mordecai M. Kaplan, had hatched the idea some years earlier. And in time, the value of secular ancillary activities within Jewish religious space would find its greatest expression in communities both near and far from Harlem. But the first full-fledged experiment in creating what became known as the "Synagogue Center" project began on 116th Street. As I boasted that "there are steps in the evolution of the American synagogue here," I trusted that Dunlap comprehended that so much of New York and larger American Jewish history had been played out on just this one Harlem street, worthy of remembering for posterity.

As the conversation about Jewish Harlem moved on inevitably to the history of its decline, Dunlap posed a not uncommon question: Which one of the more than one hundred congregations was "the last synagogue in Harlem"? I responded that that distinction—at least as it applied to the shuls that east European immigrants and their children established and attended during its Jewish peak years from 1900 through World War I—belonged to Congregation Tikvath Israel, housed in a narrow brownstone on 112th Street, east of Lexington Avenue in "El Barrio," Spanish Harlem. The designation of Tikvath Israel was complemented by a personal story. In 1974, when I was working on my book, I became aware of the congregation's existence and decided to attend services on a Sabbath. I went to East Harlem not knowing whether the shul was operating. When I arrived, I was greeted warmly by a Rabbi Golub, who exclaimed that my presence was "like a miracle," for without me they had but nine men, one short of the quorum for prayers in this Orthodox synagogue. I was moved when Rabbi Golub requested that I chant the prophetic portion of the week—the Haftarah. As I descended down the rickety steps from the reader's desk after my recitation, I shook hands with the other worshippers, elderly gentlemen who lived in the housing project across the street and merchants who came in from their little stores in the area. Before I left, Rabbi Golub allowed that divine powers assisted his synagogue's survival on an ongoing basis. It seemed fitting that his shul's name in English means "Hope of Israel." He explained that "every time we have services, someone unexpected shows up and makes it possible." But a few years later, when I drove down on a Sunday to 112th Street, I saw that the synagogue's hope was now gone. It had become the Christ Apostolic Church of U.S.A. David Dunlap liked the story so much that he included the tale of my miraculous appearance in East Harlem in his *Times* piece. And when he launched his comprehensive guide to Manhattan's houses of worship, he was sure to recount that incident as one of the more intriguing sagas that he had come across in his work.[3]

But the assertion that there were "no synagogues in Harlem" touched off a basically friendly, if public, disagreement with the leaders of the Old Broadway Synagogue of 126th Street, a congregation that is situated off Broadway and right down the hill from Morningside Heights. Soon after Dunlap's article appeared the synagogue's president, Dr. Paul Radensky, contended that his institution was "the last and only (perhaps for now) functioning mainstream synagogue in Harlem" and that they had been there since 1923. He was proud that the Old Broadway Synagogue had "been placed on the State and National Registry of Historic Places," assuring that his building could never be torn down.[4]

I rejoined the discussion about Jewish Harlem's congregational longevity when another *Times* writer interviewed me in the fall of 2003. Newspaper "stringer" Francine Parnes was crafting a story about Radensky's efforts to increase membership and asked for a sense of the congregation's place in history. I made clear that "Old Broadway was at least three blocks west of Jewish Harlem, whose western boundary was Morningside Avenue." In other words, Radensky's synagogue was really not part of the community's scene when Harlem was Jewish. Rather it served Columbia, Barnard, and Jewish Theological

Seminary students who—primarily under the long-term leadership of Rabbi Jacob Kret (1950–1997)—walked down from Morningside Heights to attend services. The Old Broadway Synagogue's Hebrew name, the Chevrah Talmud Torah Anshe *Maarovi* (The Congregation of the People Who Study the Torah in the *Western* [part of uptown]), has an interesting backstory. But its founders did not call themselves a Harlem institution and neither would I. How people who lived in an area defined its geographical boundaries is always the best indicator of where a neighborhood starts and ends. And Harlem's Jewish history was almost over by 1930, when those who founded the "western" congregation in what is St. Nicholas Heights were just getting started.[5]

A decade after the discussion with David Dunlap about Jewish Harlem's past "on location," I started conducting walking tours of the old neighborhood, which had been renewed and almost completely transformed. Among my tourists was a BBC World Service reporter who eventually broadcasted the walk and talked to audiences across the globe, as well as a correspondent for Swiss public radio who translated my remarks into German for her audience. With gentrification both in the air rights and on the ground, the story of when Harlem was Jewish was back in vogue. Standing on the corner of 116th Street and Fifth Avenue, I pointed out to listeners both in front of me and far away that the Harlem Baptist Temple Church and the Church of the Lord Jesus Christ were the only buildings on the south and east sides of 116th Street that still remained from the old days of Harlem. Every other structure on that block was either a new apartment complex or an upscale emporium or business office.

For a while in 2012, I was concerned that the Harlem Baptist Temple Church was doomed to be demolished and with that destruction the Hebrew writing on the front of the church—the last archeological proof that the street was once Jewish—would be effaced. I did not look forward to pointing out to future groups and radio audiences the building that would take Ohab Zedek's and Harlem Baptist's place and lamenting, "That's where a major synagogue used to be. You cannot see any physical evidence that it once existed. You will have to take my word on this!" Fortunately, some "initial funds were found to get the work started to repair the main roof . . . sealing and repair of structural cracks on east and west bearing wall" among other necessary improvements.[6] As of autumn 2014, the building remained standing, with repairs ongoing, making it possible to tell the story of Harlem's Jewish history in front of an artifact of its past. But in a real sense this accounting of the survival of that old church next door to the Harlem Physical Therapy Center—with that health center's bright purple awning, and the large electronics store with its large red frontage—was also a fitting segue to talking about the area's future.

Actually, my own personal orientation to a new Harlem and, more importantly, a renewed uptown Jewish community, began in 2008, when a young Jewish couple who had bought a brownstone in the western reaches of the neighborhood read *When Harlem Was Jewish* and contacted me to unabashedly proclaim that "Jews were back uptown."

Their basic family saga—which was ultimately recounted in some detail within my later book *Jews in Gotham*—was the story of a young real estate principal and his wife who resided in a cramped midtown Manhattan apartment and desired a home with a backyard along a street where their youngsters might eventually play. As they contemplated a search for space, Shoshana Borgenicht was pregnant with their first child. She and Yoel found their dream house at 341 West 122nd Street, between Manhattan and Morningside Avenues in the western reaches of Harlem, just one block east of Morningside Park, down the hill from Morningside Heights and Columbia University. A generation earlier, this part of town had been crime riddled. The park was effectively off-limits to the law abiding. But times had changed. The Borgenichts were fortunate enough—and prescient enough about Harlem becoming ever more attractive to middle-class families—to buy an aging three-story house that just a few years earlier had been a single-room occupancy rooming house, home then to the poor and transient. As late as the 1990s, some ten people had shared the living space. The Borgenichts retained, for a while, one artifact of 341's prior history, a pair of lights outside of the brownstone that when illuminated had told potential customers that rooms were available. When they moved in, they worked hard to make the residence livable according to twenty-first-century middle-class standards, including updating the hundred-year-old plumbing and constructing a modern kitchen. I got to know the Borgenichts quite well as the family grew to five—Rex came along in 2006, Theo in 2008, and Delia followed in 2009—and they seemed quite happy on a street that is becoming increasingly gentrified.[7]

I have often thought about why Shoshana and Yoel were in touch. Perhaps, through reading my book carefully, they recognized that they were exemplars of a repeating pattern in the history of Jews in Harlem. A century earlier, east European Jewish immigrants on the make financially, invested and settled in Central Harlem. In the 1870s and 1880s, similar decision-making about housing had obtained among central European Jews who felt cramped in the city. Back then—100 and 125 years ago—as now, advertisements and word of mouth drew aspiring Jews in a chain migration to a region of Manhattan that was conveniently situated close to midtown and downtown work places.

Though proud that Jews had returned to Harlem, the Borgenichts were not especially excited that incipient manifestations of Judaism had returned as well. If anything, their very awareness that a Chabad (Lubavitch) outpost had been created just five blocks away from their home was pure happenstance. One Saturday, Yoel bumped into two "Orthodox Jews" who were walking towards him on Manhattan Avenue. After stopping to greet them, Yoel discovered that the renowned Orthodox Jewish outreach movement had recently set up shop in the community. Had this chance encounter led to an extended conversation, the Hasidim undoubtedly would have told their fellow Jew how, in 2005, their leader, Rabbi Shaya Gansbourg, had come to seek out Jews in the neighborhood. The tale that his followers would relate over and over again to those who might be interested "started on a M60 bus ride from LaGuardia Airport down 125th Street" where Gansbourg was struck by Harlem's street scape and thought "something must be happening here." He "saw Staples . . . Old Navy" and thought "maybe this is a place to look at." In time, the ambitious rabbi, in the spirit of Rabbi Goldstein of almost a century earlier, looked to involve—to "retrieve," so to speak—what he believed to be the two thousand unaffiliated Jews in Harlem in Jewish religious activities. Hard numbers on Jewish population are hard to come by.

His work took on two dimensions. He sought out Jewish students for cultural and religious activities at the City College of New York (CCNY), which is situated on the campus bluff of St. Nicholas Heights that overlooks Harlem. Jewish students who once predominated at a school that was known as "the *cheder* [the Jewish school house] on the hill" were returning in noticeable numbers to this inexpensive mecca of higher education that was reacquiring a reputation as a quality college. For Gansbourg, with CCNY becoming a school of choice for Jews, there was a need to recreate Jewish life on campus. The enrollment of Jews at "City" had dropped precipitously in the 1980s–1990s when the school was tarred in many quarters as an institution that had lost its former robust academic standards. But now, its low tuition and especially its fine engineering and biomedical programs made sense to them.[8]

And then there was Gansbourg's larger dream of establishing the first twenty-first-century synagogue in Harlem proper. Shaya and his wife, Goldie, opened their center in 2006 with funding from a real estate developer named Baruch Singer. But the Borgenicht family did not pick up on the invitation to attend the services and classes that were being offered in a modest, first-floor apartment. Chabad of Harlem's only physical marker was a small handwritten sign that was hung in a window.[9]

Over time, Chabad of Harlem has made its presence better known through a series of public events that highlighted that a synagogue was growing in the neighborhood. In November 2012, for example, the *New York Times* and the *Daily News*, among other general-interest outlets, publicized the dedication of the first Torah Scroll in Harlem in seventy-five years. The media asked me to authenticate the dating of this ritual revival. I commented enthusiastically that "it's very exciting. There's a lot of growth potential in Harlem. . . . Having a Torah is a sign of permanence for a community." Not only that, when the Torah ceremony took place, my wife and I made sure to be there and danced with our fellow Jews, a unique form of participant-observation for a hardboiled academic such as myself.[10]

On an ongoing basis, Chabad has made itself known to Jews and gentiles through its erection of a sukkah in Morningside Park and its Lag B'Omer (Jewish field day) picnics and barbecues. Sadly, Shaya Gansbourg passed away in February 2013 at the age of fifty-seven, but in all of their activities, he and later his family emphasized to Jews and gentiles alike that "Harlem is a safe place to live and raise children." Remember that twenty years earlier, Morningside Park was a very scary place. Looking ahead, the Gansbourg family has been talking about "a complete Jewish infrastructure . . . with kosher restaurants, a mikveh, Jewish education and a synagogue with activities around the clock."[11]

An African American promoter of Harlem noted Chabad's optimistic take on the neighborhood's contemporary scene quite approvingly. Publisher Daniel Bretton Tisdale wrote in his *Harlem World Magazine* in March 2012 that "across the street from a once-abandoned building where squatters lived until recent years and drug deals and muggings kept the sidewalks empty after dark, a few dozen people sat and sang and schmoozed for several hours. When they walked out later that night, they joined other people strolling outside, passing a brick-façade doorman apartment building that had just risen across the street."[12]

The Jews who as of the mid-2010s were linked to the Harlem Chabad community were a diverse group. Congregants included "a professional poet, a dermatologist and a public school teacher." These and other members hailed "from Mexico, the Dominican Republic, France and Great Britain." One worshipper—of a traditional bent—found the Gansbourgs online when he "was looking for someone to check his mezuzah and tefillin [phylacteries]." Others who were not especially committed to Jewish ritual were recruited by the energetic Hasidic couple and later other family members through phone conversations and chance meetings in local cafés. For most families, Chabad's program for small children was a prime attraction, along with their desire for a "sense of community." Notably, one participant in this incipient revival of Jewish life in Harlem reflected publicly that he was "returning to a neighborhood as important to American Jewish history as the Lower East Side. It's a place where the Jewish community left a footprint."[13]

We will never know whether the ever-increasing Jewish action on the streets near their home, or in the safe and rehabilitated park where their children and their neighbors played, would eventually have enticed the Borgenichts to check out the Chabad outpost. For in 2012, the family, notwithstanding Yoel's frequent assertion that he and his loved ones "still loved Harlem" and his continuing to work in real estate and construction in the neighborhood, departed for even "greener pastures." The Borgenichts relocated to Montclair, New Jersey. For them, "the lure of suburbia" with its promise of "better public schools" for their three youngsters was all too compelling. Perhaps, as they packed up for their move, Yoel and Shoshana might have contemplated for a moment that they were reliving another major part of Harlem's earlier Jewish story. So many Jews did not stay long in that uptown part of town as they were attracted—as it was said back in the pre–World War II period—to "more salubrious settings." Back then, the Grand Concourse in the Bronx, the Upper West Side and Washington Heights in Manhattan, and neighborhoods in Brooklyn—most notably Flatbush, Boro Park, and Bensonhurst—and parts of Queens like Astoria and Long Island City beckoned. Jews of that era did not reside either in Jackson Heights or in Forest Hills, which were restricted. Social anti-Semitism kept them out. In our present day, the Borgenichts were off to settle beyond the George Washington Bridge. But Yoel would be back, on an ongoing basis, to make his deals and to check out his construction work, not unlike Jews who maintained businesses in Harlem long after they stopped living in the community.[14]

Interestingly enough, had the Borgenichts tarried in the city a year or so longer, the family might have found that a new public school in Harlem was a perfect fit for their children's educational needs. When Yoel and Shoshana first settled in the neighborhood their prime concern was finding the right kind of Jewish-multicultural preschool program for their older boy. As it turned out, in 2013, thanks to funding from a major Jewish philanthropic foundation, the Harlem Hebrew Language Academy Charter School was established at 147 St. Nicholas Avenue, a mere six blocks from the Borgenichts' brownstone. That school teaches the Hebrew language to children of all racial backgrounds but stays clear of promoting the Jewish religion among its pupils. The financial supporters' far from hidden agenda included developing "understanding for Israel . . . and Jewish culture among non-Jews." But as important, it promised that the institution would be a vehicle for "cultural respect in general." Given the values that Yoel and Shoshana desired to inculcate in their youngsters, Rex, Theo, and Delia would have been very much at home within a student body that was "one third white . . . 44% black and 10% Latino."[15]

As Harlem's Jewish historian, I have had a forty-year relationship with this neighborhood. From this unique vantage point, I recognize not only how history is repeating itself in the neighborhood but also how different the Jewish scene is today from what it was eighty years or a century ago. It is from that experience and perspective that I write about Harlem and its Jews, certain that a new generation of readers, beginning with those who have once again moved "uptown," desires to know not only how Jewish Harlem rose, what life was like on its streets and in its institutions, how Jews got along with their neighbors, and when and why Jewish Harlem declined, but also what is contributing to its ongoing reemergence.

To tell the community's once and present story, of course, requires us to delve into the interrelated histories of the metropolis, with its own rises and declines; of its Jews, with their multiple identities and commitments to this city; and of New York's African American community, with its unique burdens and challenges. This present volume benefits from the wealth of new knowledge that has emerged since I wrote *When Harlem Was Jewish* back in 1978. While still focused on social and political relationships, this work also synthesizes cultural and intellectual trends within and among groups who shared neighborhood space. Essentially, the book first explores Harlem Jewry's life as it rose to prominence within the metropolis. It points out how this community's innovations in attempting to address the problems of group identification eventually contributed so much to American Jewish life beyond its neighborhood and city. From there, the volume looks at Jews, as friends and as foes, to African Americans, during the years after 1920 when Harlem became the black mecca. It accounts for how in the 1960s the name of that neighborhood came to symbolize all that was wrong in inter-racial relations in Gotham. Finally, this book explores and interprets the present-day beginnings of Jewish return to Harlem within a dynamic city undergoing demographic and economic transformations, and it interrogates the question of what gentrification means for varying classes of neighborhood people. So here is Harlem's Jewish story told anew—from its very beginning—knowing that its history is not over, but rather a work in progress.

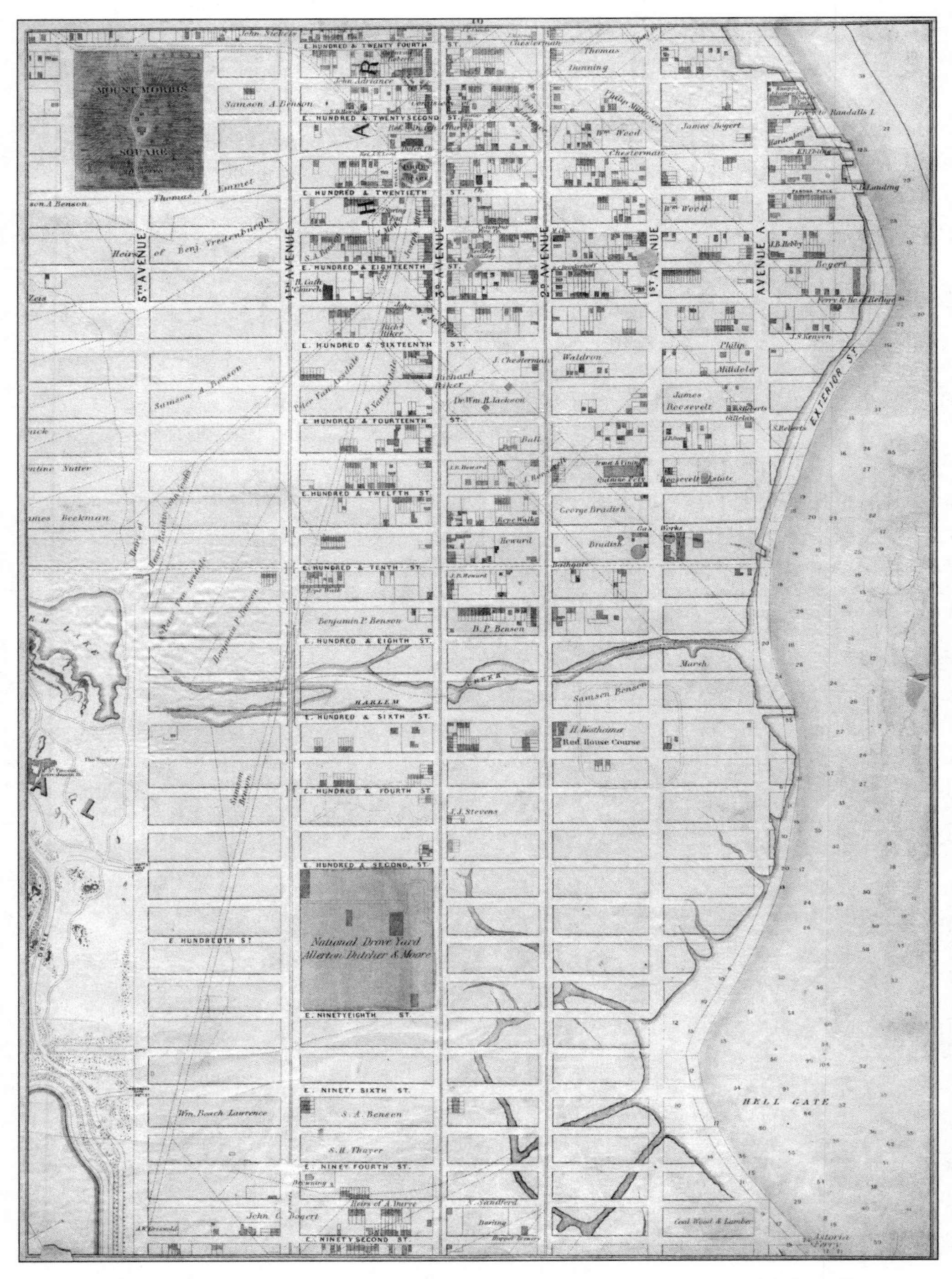

Harlem, “a Village on the Outskirts of the City,” circa 1870 (map courtesy of Lionel Pincus and Princess Firyal Map Division, New York Public Library).

1

A Jewish Outpost in Harlem, 1870–1880

It was the kind of decision that young Jewish couples would make frequently during the next half century and then again at the turn of the new millennium. In the years immediately after the Civil War, Israel and Emma Stone, who had grown up on the Lower East Side, considered leaving the immigrant hub where their families lived. By 1870, they had determined to reside in Harlem, a remote outpost within the northern reaches of Manhattan Island. Israel's parents had brought him to America as a one-year-old in 1850. He was born in Scotland as Solomon and Jennetta traveled to the United States from their native Prussia. The family settled in downtown's Tenth Ward, where Solomon found work as a glazier, a skilled laborer. There within a neighborhood known as Kleindeutschland, they took part in the social and cultural life of the Jewish and gentile newcomers from central Europe. If they behaved like most of their fellow Jewish immigrants, the focus of their leisure time conviviality was a lodge—a *verein*—where folks could spin tales of what it had been like on the other side, share news about what life continued to be in Germany, and discuss the issues of the day in America, including their quest to advance in this country. Often these gatherings took place in modest beer halls. The flow of libations contributed to the warmth and hyperbole of the storytelling. These societies were also places where young people might congregate, and parents were pleased when their sons and daughters found a suitable marriage partner from a similar background.[1]

While still a teenager, Israel met and fell in love with Emma, whose family likewise hailed from Prussia. And in 1869, they were blessed with the birth of Celia. She would be one of three daughters. Despite his tender age and whatever his educational achievements may have been, to support his wife and young child, Israel Stone aspired to be an entrepreneur. Such seems to have been a common goal of second-generation Kleindeutschlanders. Meanwhile, as a glazier, with steady work as a skilled artisan, Solomon Stone may well have been in the economic position to help his son get started. We know nothing about Emma's family's economic status. Perhaps they were able to assist as well. But where would Israel set up his retail clothing store?[2]

There was always the option of trying his luck in the highly competitive world of commerce downtown. But could he succeed in making his mark? After all, since the end of the 1850s, so many central European immigrants had "made the transition from dry-goods peddler to clothing merchant that they took over most of New York's dry goods market." Beyond the hub, as of the mid-1860s, potential customers conceivably could be found primarily among the affluent Jewish immigrants and their children who were leaving "an increasingly poor and rapidly growing Lower East Side for more suitable and commodious housing north of 42nd Street." There they settled comfortably among the gentiles next door and down the block. A new neighborhood in the East 50s, on and near Lexington Avenue, for example, was becoming home to thousands of three story row houses, many with brownstone fronts, ideal for prosperous business people and their often extended families. The development of previously unimproved land on Lexington Avenue, north of 42nd Street a decade earlier, permitting traffic north- and south-bound, had opened up that thoroughfare for residential construction. And then there were the rich and the famous customers who owned the landmark mansions that made Fifth and Madison Avenues, also north of 42nd Street, fashionable, as these streets remain today. Although many of the Jews who settled in midtown were not especially interested in synagogue life, enough of them were disposed to relocate their congregations from south of 14th Street to this new district. A substantial community had been brought into existence; people who might frequent Stone's store for their suits, dresses and other dry goods. Israel Stone, however, looked further uptown and focused on the financial potentialities that existed in Harlem, a locality that was situated several miles north towards the very tip of Manhattan. He hoped to find his niche far away from the bustling, crowded, and, perhaps most importantly, highly competitive developing city.[3]

So disposed, when this "clothier"—as the city directory of the day identified him—set up his first modest emporium on Third Avenue and 127th Street, he wisely situated his business only two blocks north of the neighborhood's emerging main commercial thoroughfare. At that point in its history, 125th Street was described as Harlem's "Broadway where we all went to do our shopping" by residents of "a village on the outskirts of the city." In other words, Stone sought out a clientele among patrons who though legally residing in New York City were essentially in their own "rural retreat" made up of "the aristocratic New Yorkers [with] its chief charm its well-bred seclusion." And, while the business strip was then still on "a lane, in fact, all the thoroughfares were lanes," 125th Street, east to west, was destined to become Harlem's major crosstown and congested commercial center.[4]

Stone could only hope that the owners of some of the grand estates that in the mid-1850s began "starting up like mushrooms on spots which five years ago were part of the dense and tangled forest" would become enamored of his establishment. These were people who were not inclined to spend the money for carriage travel downtown and/or had the time to take the horse car for the one-and-a-half-hour trip down to City Hall. Besides which, straphanging on these conveyances meant dealing with little less than "a perfect bedlam of wheels." In 1864, the *New York Herald* spoke for suffering commuters when it observed, "modern martyrdom may be succulently described as riding in a New York omnibus. The discomforts, inconveniences and annoyances of a trip in one of these vehicles are almost intolerable." Mid-nineteenth-century Gotham had a long way to go before it could boast of possessing a comprehensive and commendable rapid transit system. Perhaps a more genteel way of getting downtown was the steamboat option that linked 125th Street with Peck Slip near the Battery. But that marine transportation was unreliable even during the summer months that it operated. Essentially Stone aspired to cater to an upscale clientele that lived and worked near him because, as the *New York Evening Post* put it in 1867, "the upper part of the island is . . . almost useless to persons engaged in daily business of any kind in the city." His competitive advantage against clothiers downtown was that he was prepared to settle in Harlem for his customers. Israel and Emma Stone packed up Celia and their belongings and off they went uptown. Early on, the family lived just a few steps west of Israel's store.[5]

It is too much to assert that Israel and Emma Stone recognized how their decision to move in search of consumers was—in microcosm—so very reminiscent of the larger American Jewish narrative of their time. Still, their story fits a well-trod pattern of group behavior among central European Jewish immigrants and their children. From the 1820s to well beyond the 1870s, the origins of Jewish communities throughout the United States were tied to the arrival of ambitious peddlers who brought their products to clients who resided away from the major cities. These entrepreneurial pioneers often stayed, set up the first dry goods stores in town, and ultimately succeeded in establishing Jewish economic and religious life. Harlem, of course, was not a Midwestern, Southern, or far Western outpost. But effectively its denizens lived apart from the city, remote from its emporia. And people like Israel Stone stepped up to service their consumer needs.[6]

Israel Stone also fit the model of a community builder on a frontier. Given where he and his family lived and worked, Israel and Emma certainly had the option of distancing themselves completely from Jewish life. Perhaps growing up they had both heard from their immigrant parents about people whom they knew who had moved away from their faith and backgrounds when they arrived in this land of freedom. But the young couple was of a traditional religious bent and began attempting very early in their time uptown to cope with their isolation from downtown synagogues and schools. They grasped the ironic reality that the same remoteness from the city that was a boon to their business opportunities simultaneously undermined their connections to their faith. Unquestionably, the Stones shared these sentiments with their neighbors Adolf and Celina Zabinskie. An older couple—in 1870, Adolph was fifty, Celina was forty-four—the Zabinskies were Prussian Jews too who had lived on Grand Street on the Lower East Side where Adolf was a retail dealer of boots and shoes. In the late 1860s, Adolf and Celina relocated themselves, their five children, and their business to Harlem, where two of the older youngsters helped out in the store.[7] The elder Zabinskies concurred that their—and even more importantly their youngsters'—religious identification was imperiled. What chance would their next generation have to maintain even a modicum of their faith's commitments growing up as they were in a remote, outlying area bereft of contact with Jewish educational and spiritual organizations? So in 1869, these two families and a handful of other Harlem Jews, recognizing that "they were too far away to attend the city synagogues, even if they were willing to ride" to services on the Sabbath and holidays which, reportedly, "they were not," organized Congregation Hand-in-Hand. At the first, the synagogue was "little more than a *chevra*—a religious association" that conducted "divine services above a printing store on Third Avenue." In subsequent years, the members—"few [in numbers], the means sparse"—rented space on 116th Street and Second Avenue and then at the Harlem Savings Bank on Third Avenue and 124th Street before settling down—for at least a decade—when they leased space from the Grace Episcopal Church on 116th Street and Third Avenue. It was a proud early moment when the Rev. Henry S. Jacobs of Congregation B'nai Jeshurun, the second-oldest New York synagogue, came uptown to participate in the dedication of the new home. Congregants were even happier when they were able to eventually purchase the building.[8]

While still at the Harlem Savings Bank, the Stones, Zabinskies, and other community builders, small-time merchants all, were heartened by the arrival in their midst of Solomon and Sarah Carvalho. They were a couple that was known in American and Jewish circles well beyond Harlem. And Solomon knew all about the difficulties of creating religious life on a frontier. What he had to tell his fellow congregants before, after, and during services about how he garnered large-scale public attention had to have fascinated his listeners who had led much more prosaic lives.

In 1853, explorer John Charles Fremont convinced this painter and daguerreotype artist, who hailed from Charleston, South Carolina, to accompany him—and to take photographs—on what turned out to be a quixotic adventure to find a western railroad route to California through the Rocky Mountains. Sadly, the expedition was a total failure. The group of adventurers ended up trapped in the Rockies and a Mormon family saved Carvalho from death through exposure. The unfortunate Jewish traveler recorded all of his misadventures in what became a national best-selling book, *Incidents of Travels and Adventures in the Far West*. But Carvalho did succeed in making it eventually to California, where he was instrumental in organizing Los Angeles's first Jewish institution, the Hebrew Benevolent Society of Los Angeles. Reportedly, upon arrival in town and after setting himself up with a photo shop on the second floor of a building owned by Samuel and Joseph Labbatt, he heard from these brothers of the absence of "any organization in the small Jewish community." In short order, the society was formed to provide religious services, a school, and a variety of mutual aid benefits.[9]

Possessed of the desire to help out in Harlem too and having sufficient resources to finance a crucial initiative—Solomon had pioneered a new process for hot-water heating—after returning back east, the Carvalhos in 1874 founded a free Jewish religious school in the neighborhood. Indeed, rather than wait for the congregation to inaugurate instruction for the children, they decided to establish a small school in their own home, which served initially some forty-five youngsters. In 1876, the Carvalho school was named the Shangarai Limud Sunday School Society—sometimes called the "Hebrew School Society"—when the congregation's ladies auxiliary took control of educational activities. The school's constitution specifically provided that only women could be active members of the educational society. It did, however, grant the all-male congregational school committee advisory status, and more importantly financial control over the society, making the chairman of the school committee an ex-officio member of the women's board of managers. The women, led by Sarah Carvalho, who served as school superintendent, were to provide a staff of unpaid volunteer instructors, while their husbands controlled the purse strings. It is not known how skilled the instructors were as transmitters of just the very basics of the Jewish heritage. The school met for two hours on Sundays, and after the "weekly recitation of the Ten Commandments in assembly," Sarah Carvalho led "a discussion of the weekly [Torah] portion." Still, with the establishment of the school in their own neighborhood, it became possible for religiously committed Harlem parents to avoid facing the dilemma common to many Jewish families—to this day—in settlements or towns remote from the major centers of Jewish education. How were they to provide for the inculcation of even a minimum of Jewish teachings in their youngsters beyond merely through mimetic observation or participation in family religious ritual?[10]

But how truly committed were most early uptown Jews? They clearly wanted a synagogue and a school, but signs of ambivalence towards sustained identification were also apparent. Indeed, to the Carvalhos' and their colleagues' frustration, while many of their Jewish neighbors were pleased to have a school for their youngsters—and a free institution at that—parental interest in the actual goings on in the classroom often wavered. Israel Stone and Adolf Zabinskie's brother, George, were among some two score men listed as "founders and subscribers" to the institution as of 1877. They were part of a committed core of strongly involved Jews in early Harlem. Yet many more showed only episodic interest in religious life and were often oblivious to ancestral traditions. The so-called "apathy of the parents and guardians of the 200 children who have been receiving gratuitous instruction" came to a head early in 1880 when "not a single parent or guardian attended the annual meeting for the election of officers." Chagrined beyond the angry words that they spoke to a reporter from the *American Hebrew*, a newly established Anglo-Jewish newspaper in New York, "the few ladies and gentlemen who have devoted their energies" to Shangarai Limud threatened to walk away from their efforts, "to disband and the school to be dismissed" if parents did not show greater enthusiasm for Jewish education. Chastised by this public critique, a respectable number of area residents attended a second gathering a week later and to the pleasure of the newspaper reportedly "the Harlem brethren have awakened from their lethargy and have determined to support and maintain their school."[11]

This diversity of Jewish interest, knowledge, and commitment was also readily apparent when the Harlem Young Men's Hebrew Association was established in 1879. Five years earlier, the city's first Jewish "Y" was opened on 21st Street off Sixth Avenue with the expressed mission to "promote a better feeling and higher culture among young men and to unite them in a liberal organization which shall tend to their moral, intellectual and social improvement." The problem that the organization sought to ameliorate was, frankly, the bad behavior of Americanized children of central European immigrants. Too many youngsters, it was perceived and said publicly, were caught up in a mid-nineteenth-century version of the contemporary twenty-first-century "club scene" where they "dabbl[ed] . . . in silly fashions, drink, and gamble, swear and make bets." The Y offered instead a liquor-free and almost smokeless environment with a welter of cultural and recreational activities of which the community could be proud. And four years into its existence, the association was popular enough that it moved to larger quarters on 42nd Street and Sixth Avenue, where it could boast of a reading room, gymnasium, bowling alley, club, and classrooms. Evidently, young Harlem Jews' pastime pursuits likewise troubled their parents' generation. And again given their remoteness from Jewish life in the city, uptown leaders determined to emulate the midtown Y's mission and program.[12]

Ever the institutional joiner, Solomon Carvalho was the first secretary of the new Y and early on may have influenced it to hold a social benefit ball in 1880 to support the Sunday School initiative. Generally speaking, those who supported the shul and school also backed the cultural association, but many of those who frequented the Y did not attend services. Truth be told, the leaders of Hand-in-Hand were troubled by the attitude of those who "think that all Judaism requires is to join the YMHA and attend its entertainments." However, people like Solomon Carvalho and others who were religiously inclined had to have been red-faced a year later, when the *Jewish Messenger*, another New York weekly, upbraided the Y for showing an unconscionable lack of concern for Jewish tradition by scheduling a boat ride up the Hudson River on the fast day of Tisha B'av. Apparently, those who cared about Judaism at the Jewish Y were not doing due diligence about its activities. The fundamentally secular Jewish organization was reminded that it was a *Hebrew* (the word was emphasized in the original) association and directed to consult a Jewish calendar before arranging for an entertainment on a day of Jewish national mourning.[13]

In some quarters within American Jewry of the era, there would have been no inconsistency in a Jewish association—even a religious one—hosting an outing on the day that commemorates the destruction of the Holy Temple in Jerusalem and other calamitous events in their people's history. Reform Judaism of that day saw the end of the ancient Jewish state in 70 C.E. not as God's punishment for their sins, but as a turning point in the Jews' fulfilling a divine mission to spread ethical monotheism to the world. The idea that Jews had been thus liberated from a geographical and cultic-based locale to spread morality to the world may have been preached—and perhaps even celebrated—in midtown Reform temples. But no such teaching informed the Y's calendar makers, as ignorance rather than dissent from traditional practice seems to have obtained. Still an outpost, the community in the 1870s had no rabbi, Reform or otherwise. The services at Hand-in-Hand were led by a series of undistinguished "readers" who knew the liturgy better than the others who made up the minyan. Isaac Schickler, whom a city directory described only as a "teacher," was their first cantor at a salary of $100 per annum. Rev. Max Rubin, late of the Norfolk Street Synagogue, followed him in 1880. But Rubin did not last long due to "the uncertainty of collecting his salary" of $600 annually. A Mr. I. Lindner then took over at lower compensation "in order to reduce expenses."[14]

Since they were bereft of professional congregational leadership, it was left to those lay people who cared about synagogue ritual to determine exactly how traditional their services should be. Many other Harlem Jews—as we have just seen—did not really concern themselves with what practices prevailed in a shul that they only occasionally attended. No matter; congregational lore has it that initially, the Stones, Zabinskies, and their fellows "made a virtue out of a necessity" as they "did not send the women to the gallery for reason that there was no gallery" in their rented spaces. But otherwise the "ritual was Orthodox." So-called "mixed seating" was a very common practice nationwide among congregations of that era which viewed themselves as Orthodox. But in Harlem, deviation from a traditional norm seemed to be architecturally determined rather than theologically ordained. However, while still in its first decade of existence, a majority of voters within this small congregation opted to make more ritual alterations. As early as 1876, when a confirmation ceremony was held at the synagogue, a newspaper report noted that "the management of congregation composed of such diverse"—but unspecified—"elements has peculiar obstacles of its own." And crucially when, in 1877, a decision was made to introduce an organ to complement prayers on holy days—a more substantial change in ritual—many members broke with Hand-in-Hand and attempted to establish their own competing synagogue, Congregation Tents of Israel, in a nearby hall. One year later a second group left the synagogue over a new proposed reform—precisely what was intended is not known—leaving Hand-in-Hand with a membership of only seventy as of 1880. Very likely, it was this splintering of ranks that caused Hand-in-Hand to renege on its agreement with Rev. Rubin and to opt for the less expensive Mr. Lindner.[15]

When Rubin was hired, it was reported that with "his first class choristers" accompanying him—surely a pleasant development for those who wanted a more modern ritual—the congregation looked forward to an "increase in its effectiveness making it a center of influence for the good." But Hand-in-Hand's inability to reach a consensus on the nature of "divine services" dampened these hopes as controversy undermined its limited dues base. In succeeding decades, even with a rabbi at its helm, the congregation—renamed Temple Israel of Harlem in 1887—would continue to debate how much of the old ways and ritual was relevant as it eventually became the landmark Reform congregation in Harlem.[16]

In the meantime, while Harlem's first Jewish settlers continued to work towards creating a community uptown, these entrepreneurs seemed to be making out quite well economically and to their great pleasure were respected for their contribution to the neighborhood. Surely, the Jews had to have felt that they belonged when a contemporary chronicler of uptown life publicly admired what Jewish merchants were doing for Harlem's commercial growth. Speaking from the rostrum of the Harlem YMHA to a crowd that included "many descendants of the early settlers," Colonel Alonzo B. Caldwell identified by name several Jewish storekeepers who "try to please their customers by competing with downtown merchants" and directed the audience to patronize local businessmen, stating "it is better for the purchasers to leave his dollars in Harlem . . . you can trade now in nearly all things as cheap in Harlem as elsewhere." Caldwell also emphasized the importance of tolerance and cooperation between Christians and Jews, calling upon all those who resided uptown to "continue cultivating the friendliness as of yore in 'ye ancient village' and leave animosities and contentions to other localities."

Israel Stone and Adolph Zabinskie had to have been particularly moved by Caldwell's remarks. They were among the storekeepers mentioned by name as worthy of local patronage. Caldwell advised his listeners—and readers, as the talk was later published in pamphlet form—to "go and buy . . . your clothing at Stone's . . . your shoes at Zabinskie's." At least five other members of Hand-in-Hand were praised and promoted along with merchants named Callahan, Jarvis, and Robinson.[17]

Israel Stone's family was doing quite well. As of 1880, while Israel was still a "clothier"—as he was enumerated in the federal census—they were affluent enough to have in their employ Irish immigrant Mary Egan, who worked as a live-in household servant. Emma Stone was recorded as "keeping house" as she watched over her two daughters who were of school age. And they had to be pleased to live now in a brownstone located just a few steps east of Lenox Avenue. They moved out of their first uptown place, a noisy, dirty dwelling located right under the Third Avenue El, between 125th and 126th Streets. From their stoop, west of Fifth Avenue, they could see—and most certainly frequented—the newly laid out and beautiful Mount Morris Park that was located only a block away. Their sight lines to this bucolic preserve were almost perfect; their home was but one of three buildings on their street in what was still a rural-like section of Harlem. And less than a mile away was the northern end of Central Park, also perfect for a family outing. America's first landscaped park, opened just a decade before the Stone's ventured uptown, it would prove to be a rustic refuge for Harlem dwellers for generations to come. The only dark spot on the lives of Israel and Emma was that their first born, Celia, was not listed on the 1880 census form. She may well have died before her eleventh birthday.[18]

In the decade that followed, the extension of fast, cheap, and efficient rapid transit lines to the tip of Manhattan ended Harlem's history as a remote, sparsely populated, almost rural settlement. For the Stone family and the neighborhood's other Jews, the drawing of their area into the orbit of city life brought with it both complexities and opportunities. On the one hand, there was the worry—as Col. Caldwell implied—that uptown customers would now opt to shop in midtown emporia, a potential danger to their business. Caldwell hoped, of course, that shoppers would continue to support the community's local merchants. Alternatively, for Stone and other entrepreneurs, the filling in of Harlem east of Third Avenue with residences and occupants of all sorts once the new, elevated railroads became a fixture in the neighborhood meant an increase in potential customers. And since many of the new denizens of Harlem were central European Jews—like themselves—there was a chance for a substantial growth in Jewish life uptown. As it turned out, different classes of Jews would settle in varying sections of an expanding uptown, based on their abilities to pay differing levels of housing costs. Some of the more affluent newcomers would join hands with Stone's congregation—and lived near him too—as it grew to become Harlem's most famous early synagogue. Indeed, by 1890, the Carvalhos would not be the only famous Jews to sit in the pews of Temple Israel of Harlem. Some of these members would involve themselves in local political and social activities. Other newcomers—of more modest means and social interests—opted for different sorts of religious and communal life. As it grew beyond its era as an outpost, Jewish Harlem would encompass a diversity of community life and experience that would long be its trademark.

Benjamin Franklin Peixotto (top right), Cyrus Sulzberger (left), Oscar Hammerstein I (bottom right) (photos courtesy of Jacob Rader Marcus Center of the American Jewish Archives).

2

Brownstone Jewish Bourgeoisie and Workers in Tenements, 1880–1900

In 1868, New York City seemed poised to finally solve its long-troubling rapid transportation problem. For generations during the nineteenth century, the absence of conveyances that would possess their "own right of way and . . . not compete for space with other vehicles" had vexed city officials as it stymied metropolitan growth. But now, with the calamitous Civil War at an end, "the nation was bending its energies again to industrial pursuits." In the city, it was a moment of "large anticipations born of contemplated improvements." Indeed, the issue of rapid transit "had been narrowed to a choice between plans." And there were many aspirants ready to do the job of linking downtown with the upper reaches of the island. The general view was that "no reason existed for doubting that before long Harlem on both sides of the island would be as near to the City Hall as 42nd street was by means of horse cars and omnibuses." Prototypical sections of elevated railways were constructed in 1868 to show to all concerned the "feasibility of this new method of locomotion." Although some naysayers carped at "the disfigurement of the city" from these high rising structures over streets and avenues, the future, it seemed, lay with those who advocated utility over appearances. In the half decade that followed, notwithstanding several fits and starts in construction, substantial linkages were achieved crisscrossing much of the midtown area, north to 59th Street.[1]

But even as plans continued to be hatched and construction of those elevated ("El") lines that were already underway did not completely cease, the big jump to Harlem was stalled in 1873 when an economic depression of unprecedented magnitude—the Panic of 1873—hit the city and the nation. Concisely put, America's, and indeed the world's, financial markets, were plunged into a precipitous decline when financing outlets of all sorts were overextended as investors speculated on the quick building of the Northern Pacific Railroad, a route that promised to link the Great Lakes with the West Coast. When these firms ran out of capital and went bankrupt, the country's entire financial system was undermined. And since America was "more globally integrated than ever before," the international capitalist system was brought to the brink. In New York City, the traumas that were first felt on Wall Street spread rapidly up and down the island. Speculators—including those who bought up lands along the projected up-to-Harlem El routes—were, reportedly "swept out of sight [by the] momentous and unprecedented crisis." Construction starts were halted and with that stoppage went the grand plans for "the boom on the metropolitan frontier." As in all such depressions, poor and working-class people suffered grievously. Approximately one quarter of New Yorkers lost their jobs and those who held on found their wages cut by one third. Homelessness became a way of life for many of the dispossessed and shanties, where other unfortunates found temporary refuge, pockmarked the major downtown districts.[2]

Poor Jews were not immune to this financial calamity—even if uptown's well-heeled Jewish financiers, like Joseph Seligman and August Belmont, joined many Christian moguls in capitalizing on the situation. From downtown to as far north as Yorkville on the Upper East Side of Manhattan, the indigent needed "money to pay rent, to support neglected little children and to relieve temporary wants." Such were the exigencies that in 1874 led the Hebrew Benevolent and Orphan Asylum Society, the Hebrew Benevolent Fuel Association, the Hebrew Relief Society, the Ladies Benevolent Society (Gates of Prayer), and the Yorkville Ladies Benevolent Society to come together as the United Hebrew Charities. It is not known how Harlem Jews were faring during this most difficult time. But there is one indication that all was not going well in their quarters too. As late as 1880—at a time when the city and country was slowly digging out of economic decline—Hand-in-Hand was unable to contribute even ten dollars to a United Hebrew Charities Burial Society appeal.[3]

In the decade that followed, the fate and face of New York City and Harlem would be altered dramatically. Within these years of growth and transformation, the fortunes and status of Jews uptown would change as well. Finally in 1879, with the nation's economy slowly recovering, finances were available to bring the first elevated railroads up to Harlem. The Third Avenue El started out at South Ferry at the southernmost tip of Manhattan and proceeded northbound to 42nd Street and Fourth Avenue. From there, it moved eastward to Third Avenue and then turned left and north to its terminus at 129th Street. A year later the Second Avenue line followed suit from its first stop at Chatham Square at the foot of the Bowery to 129th Street. These long-awaited rapid transit improvements cut travel time between Harlem and City Hall nearly in half, facilitating greater uptown participation in a variety of city activities. At five cents a ride during special "commission [rush] hours" of 5:30–7 a.m. and 5–7 p.m., the forty-five-minute trip was cheaper than the existing horse-drawn railways or omnibuses. The private carriage service would remain the province of those with much time on and money in their hands. Initially, people like Harlem booster Col. Caldwell were apprehensive about the fate of their favored uptown stores with midtown shops now much more accessible. But their worries proved totally unfounded. Rather, the new system of transportation sparked a then-unprecedented wave of residential construction that brought tens of thousands of new residents to Harlem as large expanses of previously undeveloped land were covered over. The newcomers had the option of shopping in the neighborhood or downtown, where many of them commuted to for work. By 1885, when the focus of real estate development shifted to the West Side and Morningside Heights sections of Manhattan—where communities sprung up within walking distance of their own Eighth and Ninth Avenue elevated lines, west of Central Park—nearly half the East Harlem lands south of 125th Street and east of Fifth Avenue were home to tenements, brownstone flats, and private houses.[4]

Even at this early stage of its emergence as a growing urban neighborhood, Harlem became home to varying classes of people who resided in very different types of living quarters. Some—like those who owned homes—would have abundant resources to shop at the best stores in the neighborhood. Others—particularly those who lived in tenements—would struggle to make ends meet. Initially, Harlem builders focused their attention primarily on those properties near or adjoining the elevated lines. During 1881—the year of the decade's most pronounced construction activity—more than two thirds of the buildings completed in Harlem arose within the streets and avenues east of Third Avenue and north of 100th Street. This section would be the province of members of "the great working population" that found their way uptown, many of whom had been billeted previously on the Lower East Side. For these newcomers, the change in addresses did not constitute a complete alteration in their way of life. For they—like so many downtowners—ended up in dumbbell-shaped tenements that contributed to the "covering of all vacant space." These multiple dwellings were hardly the healthiest of settings. Indeed, when these poorly ventilated, five-story walk-ups with their "steep rickety steps and narrow doors," shared toilet facilities, and "flimsy, death trap fire escapes" appeared uptown, they caught both the eye and ire of Frederick Law Olmstead. Comparing the state of affairs uptown with much of the worst housing situations downtown, he declared that "the elevated railroads and the uptown movement lead as yet to nothing better for even . . . five or six miles away from the center of population, there are new houses of the ridiculous, jammed–up pattern, as dark and noisome . . . as if they were parts of a besieged fortress." The only type of housing that was worse for the masses were the hideous "railroad flats," basically box cars piled up on top of one another with almost no light or ventilation, and lacking plumbing—privies were outside—which also could be found on some uptown streets. In other words, for Olmstead, the renowned architectural landscaper and social commentator, Harlem—once a bucolic frontier—was fast becoming another slum quarter of the city, while real estate speculators were garnering immense profits in the uptown district.[5]

The Els themselves contributed more than their share to the noise in the area. Author and literary critic William Dean Howells, who lived and worked near the elevated lines—even if he resided south of Harlem—complained of "nineteen hours and more of incessant rumbling day and night." He said: "no experience of noise can enable you to conceive of the furious din that bursts upon the sense when at some corner two cars encounter on the parallel tracks. . . . The noise is not only deafening, it is bewildering." Another, less prominent critic—an unnamed writer for the *Real Estate Record and Builders Guide*—was similarly dismayed. He wrote in 1883 that Harlem was becoming "one of the most depressing quarters of New York. There is in its streets, the thoughtless and conventional repetition of forms intrinsically bad which makes up the bulk of the architecture of this island."[6]

Still, for working-class families downtown who "during the prevalence of [the] hard times" of the Panic of 1873, "'doubled up' so to speak in boarding and lodging houses," or were trapped in the most uninviting, oldest tenements—life in Harlem, even in a dumbbell, was an improvement in the physical conditions of their existences. Perhaps, in the end, in many cases, the decision to move uptown may well have been predicated on the willingness of workers—with a long laboring day ahead to commute back and forth from a downtown job—to afford their family the chance to reside in a relatively less crowded district. And then again, there were other more fortunate workers who found employment in the burgeoning construction industry in their own neighborhood, essentially working on buildings like those within which they lived. Such family choices—which were closely linked to rapid transit improvements—would long be a part of Harlem's working-class experience.[7]

Easier and happier choices were the lot of those families who could afford to rent or purchase the much better quality brownstones that were constructed on Park and Madison Avenues, close to the Els but away from the noise and the dirt that sprayed from the tracks. Early in 1880, for example, twelve three-story and basement brownstones, characterized as "houses for the middle class," were constructed at 110th—111th Streets between Madison and Fourth (Lexington) Avenue. Reportedly, "not a single one of them built on the old stereotypical style [which] must be regarded as among the most notable East Side improvements." These dwellings, it was predicted, would attract to Harlem "the army of clerks and bookkeepers and others who now that rapid transit is a reality will look for houses in the area and not in New Jersey or Brooklyn." Similarly, late in 1879, a promotional piece boasted about the seven houses that were completed on 116th Street, west of Lexington Avenue, that all had "the parlors and various chambers being gotten up in a manner which would do credit to houses of greater pretension." The presence of "modern plumbing" on the premises was duly emphasized. And the very location of 116th Street was also a selling point. The thoroughfare was described as "wide and well-paved and lined on each side with handsome shade trees."[8]

As fate would have it, both for themselves and for the destiny of the city, the workers and the burghers who left the downtown area for new quarters uptown at the close of the 1870s did so at just the right time. For in 1881—almost immediately after El lines made their way to the northern reaches of the island—the metropolis became the destination for tens of thousands of Jewish immigrants from eastern Europe. These newcomers came to the shores of America because of the long-term religious persecution that they had suffered and the absence of worthwhile occupational opportunities in their home countries. For some, pogroms had made their lives even more unbearable. Disembarking through Castle Garden at the foot of Manhattan, many of these poor immigrants began their American lives on the Lower East Side. And there was room for them in this quarter of the city—though indigence forced them to cope with dumbbell tenements and worse—because those earlier Irish and central European newcomers who had advanced economically were making their way out of the neighborhood. Simultaneously, New York City was able to absorb tens of thousands of Italian immigrants who had begun to arrive several years earlier. They settled en masse west of the Bowery within what had been previously an overwhelmingly Irish American neighborhood. Of course, when these so-called "new immigrants" from eastern and southern Europe entered the mix downtown, there were still plenty of poor Irish and central Europeans around in the neighborhood. Nonetheless, the ethnic future of Manhattan south of 14th Street lay with those who would occupy so-called "Little Italy" and what was dubbed the Jewish "Ghetto" of the Lower East Side.[9]

Indeed, within the Jewish section, the demographic transformation was so remarkably quick and complete that by 1890, New York's Tenth Ward, bordered by Grand, Norfolk, and Division Streets and the Bowery, right in the heart of the former central European quarter, had become 70 percent east European. By that date, comparable concentrations could be found in such "Jewish streets" as Rivington, Monroe, and Catherine in the Seventh and Thirteenth Wards. Reflecting on what took place at that time, a contemporary amateur historian who lived in the hub would characterize the wide thoroughfare of East Broadway as a central avenue of a "Russian-American colony . . . a mammoth wheel with its numerous spokes of congested streets." Meanwhile, west of the Bowery in and around Thompson, Sullivan, Grand, Broome, and Houston Streets, all within the Sixth and Fourteenth Wards, Italian Americans predominated.[10]

Amid this redistribution of the city's population, Harlem became one of several safety valve neighborhoods for the thousands of Irish and central Europeans, among them many Jews, whose last known addresses had been downtown. The central Europeans who settled in the heart of Yorkville between 72nd Street and 96th Street east of Park Avenue helped make it—even more than before—a "German" neighborhood. With its signage, food stores, and beer halls, it would retain that ethnic character for more than the next half century. The Irish would gain control of the West Side's Twenty-Second Ward, settling along the route of the Eighth and Ninth Avenue Els. The Irish would also hold on to their part of town, which included parts of the notorious "Hell's Kitchen," likewise for more than a half century. And both the central Europeans and the Irish settled in large and almost equal numbers in the newly built-up sections of Harlem. By 1890, these two groups, and again among the Germans were many Jews, well exceeded the area's families of long and distinguished standing whose lineages in their "village" often dated back generations.[11]

Still, for all of the commotion born of the new locomotion, Harlem did not totally lose its character as "a neighborhood very genteel." But the locus of that segment of the community known for its "people of taste and wealth," like Col. Caldwell, shifted west to between Sixth and Eighth Avenue. West of Fifth Avenue and north of 110th Street—where some fortunate residences might overlook Central Park. This area would become home to even more expensive brownstones than those on Madison and Fifth Avenues and some grand estates. The old-time, American-born Harlemites were joined in the 1880s by a second "army of downtowners" who were far more affluent than the aforementioned "clerks and bookkeepers'" who were "making their way in this delightful section." Chafing also at the overcrowded and dirty inner city, they looked to be part of "a suburban colony but with all the advantages of city life." One young man who grew up in a home on 125th Street between Fifth and Lenox Avenue would recall that for his mother and father, their Harlem was "a prosperous residential haven in Manhattan" that spared them from "such uncouth citizens as might be found downtown, in the shanty towns of the Bronx, or the unspeakable wastes of Brooklyn." Living a healthy walk away from elevated railroads to the east and west of them—if such was their daily or occasional need—these members of elite New York society were able to think of themselves as residents "of a district . . . distinctly devoted to the mansions of the wealthy [and] the homes of the well-to-do." Their contact with the less affluent element would be at "the places of business of the tradespeople who minster to their wants."[12]

In their part of uptown, the best of the brownstones were "veritable castles of respectability," while on "some of the shaded streets" there were "mansion[s] of some merchant prince or beer baron" replete with "handsome lawns covered with sportive cast-iron animals." It was said that the "best of these homes were on 138th and 139th Streets, west of Seventh Avenue." Among the distinguished New Yorkers who started calling Harlem their home in the last decades of the nineteenth century were not only successful entrepreneurs but politicians like Chauncey Depew, an attorney for Cornelius Vanderbilt's railroad interests and the president of the New York Central Railroad System, who in 1899 became a United States senator from New York, and Tammany Hall's own Mayor Thomas Gilroy, political machine boss Richard Croker, and the New York postmaster, Charles Dayton.[13]

In step with their gentile counterparts, Jews who possessed significant wealth, and who could boast of their own noteworthy connections and lineages, also made their homes in the still open spaces of western Harlem. Indeed, one of New York Jewry's most elite—and extended—new families resided in the fancy part of the neighborhood. In the late nineteenth century, Benjamin Franklin Peixotto was one of the most famous Jews in America. A scion of one of the first families to settle in North America—his grandfather was a longtime cantor at New York's Congregation Shearith Israel, America's oldest Jewish congregation—Peixotto was a successful merchant, then an attorney, later a diplomat and a respected Jewish community leader. He was best known for his appointment by President Ulysses S. Grant, in 1870, as the American consul to Romania, where he lodged frequent protests with the Bucharest government over its reneging on its promise of emancipation for Jews to which it had agreed in the Treaty of Paris of 1856. Later, from 1887 to 1885, Peixotto was U.S. consul in Lyons. In the last years of his life—while still engaged in Republican Party politics—he moved to Harlem and resided at the corner of 130th Street and Fifth Avenue.[14]

Less than a half mile away, Peixotto's niece Rachel Peixotto Sulzberger resided with her husband, Cyrus Sulzberger, in a "redbrick town house opposite Mount Morris Park," that untrammeled stretch of land that ran from 118th to 122nd Street east of Fifth Avenue. Rachel and Cyrus's son, Arthur Hays Sulzberger, would marry Iphigene Ochs, a daughter of the family that had gained control of the *New York Times*. Arthur was very proud of his maternal lineage and would emphasize that he was a descendent of the *Hays* Sulzberger clan. They were of the Sephardic stock that had arrived in America in the first quarter of the eighteenth century and were in New York in time for an ancestor, David Hays, to fight both in the French and Indian War and in the Revolutionary War. Arthur's paternal side, by contrast, were relative newcomers to America. Cyrus was the son of Ashkenazic parents who had come to the United States from Sulzberg after the Revolution of 1848. Reportedly, Rachel did not let her husband forget his family's humble immigrant roots and that he had "married up." In any event, as a youngster, Arthur's great uncle, Daniel P. Hays, who also lived in the classy section of Harlem, undoubtedly reminded him that he was part of a great "First American Jewish Family." He could have regaled his nephew with the story of Esther Hays, David's wife and the daughter of Asser Etting, who was another early New York Jew. In 1779, Esther, a hero of the struggle for American freedom, suffered the loss of her home when Tories burned it to the ground because she refused to divulge the positions of patriotic forces. Arthur's mother surely did more than just talk about her family's virtuous ties to the rise of the United States. She became a member of the nativist Daughters of the American Revolution and demanded that her son similarly join its male counterpart organization. Thus, for at least a decade, until Cyrus and Rachel moved their growing family to even more commodious accommodations on West 87th Street, the Peixotto-Sulzberger-Hays relatives were, arguably, the most famous Jews in Harlem.[15]

But if that distinguished clan included the most renowned Jews living uptown, newspaper publisher Oswald Ottendorfer was the most noticeable. Having made a fortune as president of the *New Yorker Staats Zeitung*, the most important German-language weekly in town, he transformed a property on West 136th Street near Broadway into "a huge and ostentatious pagoda and a Moorish pavilion with a Jewish star in the dome in the garden." [16]

And then there was the real estate builder and entertainment mogul Oscar Hammerstein I, who did much to transform the face of both the poor and affluent sections of uptown. In many ways an American "rags to riches" success, Hammerstein arrived almost penniless from Germany in 1847, having fled his tyrannical, abusive (and rich) father, who was a stockbroker and construction magnate. The young man found his first job working in a tobacco factory and later rolled cigars before hitting on an invention that would speed up production. In his lifetime, he would be credited with "about a hundred patents." With some capital from his discovery of how to make "a mold that would produce a dozen uniformed sized cigars at a time," Hammerstein invested in the burgeoning real estate market of Harlem in the 1880s. He made money both in the tenement district and in the brownstone and luxury private homes area. For himself and his family, he first bought a row house on West 115th Street in 1887, only to resell that property just a year later to afford a move to what he called "my Moorish Castle," at 142nd Street and Seventh Avenue. Quickly thereafter—and almost a generation ahead of the local real estate curve—Hammerstein became among the first to invest in large-scale apartment buildings. His vision of Harlem as a desirable first-class community—and also befitting his personal interest in high culture—led this entrepreneur in 1889 to construct the Harlem Opera House. In time, even as his entertainment endeavor experienced financial ups and downs, the offerings first at his grand venue and then at his even larger Columbus Theatre built in 1890 on 125th Street satisfied his ambition to make the Harlem opera scene competitive with the renowned Metropolitan Opera House at Broadway and 39th Street. It was his hope that his uptown attractions would be so compelling that music buffs would travel up to Harlem at night. When these devotees did just that after rush hour, they began a pattern of peregrinations into the neighborhood by those in search of music of all sorts that would be part of Harlem's history for generations.[17]

Notwithstanding the increase in the Jewish presence in Harlem during the 1880s, and despite the growing visibility of such high-profile families and operators in the neighborhood at a time in America when social prejudice often undermined their status, Jews generally received a favorable reception among the Christians around them. For example, in 1886, Jews were accorded a prominent role in a community-wide Independence Day celebration organized under the auspices of the local post of the Grand Army of the Republic. David N. Carvalho and David Rutsky—both early members of Hand-in-Hand—served on the Committee of Management. Carvalho was chairman of the Press Committee. And they, as well as Daniel P. Hays and Israel Stone, very likely by then the Harlem Jewish resident of longest standing, were listed as financial supporters of the event. They were surely touched by the remarks of the president of the Independence Day Association, who asserted that in organizing this joyful occasion "we took not into consideration whether the citizens were white or black, Democrat or Republican, naturalized or native-born."[18]

Similarly, as Democrats and Republicans, Jews found their places in local clubs of both parties. Peixotto and Rutsky cast their lots with the nascent GOP uptown when its association was founded in 1888. Thirteen Jews, including the Carvalhos, Cyrus Sulzberger, Daniel P. Hays, and the young Jacob Cantor—a newspaperman and attorney who was destined to become both a state senator and Manhattan borough president—gained acceptance within the powerful Tammany-dominated Democratic machine in the neighborhood. In 1891, Hays made it to the short list as a potential appointee for a judgeship on the Court of Common Pleas. Peixotto was also very happy to pay the substantial $100 initiation fee to join the prestigious Harlem Club, whose clubrooms were located four blocks from his home. It was the surest sign that he was an elite member of uptown society.[19]

However, at almost the same time, in 1889 Jacob Cantor felt the sting of exclusionary anti-Semitism when he was temporarily blackballed from that elite men's association. Given his growing reputation as a respected professional and public servant, Cantor's election should have been a mere formality. However, several members attempted to stop his election "solely on the ground of his being Jewish." Ultimately, Cantor was elected because, according to one Jewish observer, "the electors were too refined and had too much of an American sense to judge a man on his religion alone." As it turned out, this evaluation about the state of tolerance in the club did not last forever. In 1907 reportedly "rather than admit Jewish members"—at a time when Jews were becoming the predominant religious group uptown—the Harlem Club "disbanded."[20]

The opening of Harlem to large-scale residential construction in the last decades of the nineteenth century, and its absorption of downtown migrants of many social and economic stations, altered the fate of early neighborhood Jewish institutions. For Harlem's oldest synagogue, it meant a new era of growth and development as it attracted to its membership rolls many of the newly settled affluent Jews who lived west of Fifth Avenue. By the mid-1880s, congregational old timers like the Stones and the Zabinskies could have shared a pew with the Peixottos, Hayses, and Suzlbergers. It will be recalled that by the 1880s, Israel Stone, who was doing quite well in his clothing store, was able to move his family to Fifth Avenue. These neighbors would have prayed side by side; that is, if the very distinguished newcomers did not grab all of the front row seats for their families. In 1886, newly elected vice president Daniel Hays certainly sat up front. Four years later, he would be elected president of the congregation now known as Temple Israel. He would preside for more than a decade in that lay leadership post in the synagogue's new home on 125th Street and Fifth Avenue, the crossroads—as we have already seen—of uptown's business, entertainment, and now its Jewish religious life. The choice of venue was dictated by "the movement of the [affluent] Jewish community to the west side of Harlem," which was "now building up and was becoming a choice centre for private residences." The prior edifice—that former church on 116th Street and Third Avenue—had become "too small and too far east" for the congregation's growing constituency; so much so that prospective affiliates "paid their membership dues though there were no seats to offer them."[21]

Dr. Maurice H. Harris, the synagogue's first full-time rabbi, led the congregation's relocation to its new home. The English-born Harris began his association with Hand-in-Hand in 1881 while still a student at Columbia University and the Temple Emanu-El Theological Seminary. He initially served the congregation as a "volunteer nominally-paid part time preacher." He was paid $300 a year until he completed his rabbinical studies and seems to have been ordained by Rabbi Gustav Gottheil of Temple Emanu-El since the school—which was really a rabbinical "prep school"—did not ordinarily ordain its students. In fact, at that point in the United States, only Cincinnati's Hebrew Union College ordained rabbis and it graduated its first class just a year before Harris assumed his pulpit in Harlem. Whatever the degree of validity of his rabbinical diploma, Harris would serve with distinction at Temple Israel for a full forty years.[22]

No one questioned the rabbi's qualifications, but not all congregants concurred with Harris's religious approach. As with so many synagogues of that era, the laity harbored a vast variety of feelings about what aspects of the traditions—both within temple and personal life—they wished to maintain. Cyrus Sulzberger's family, for example, tended towards Orthodox behavior in their home, albeit with one noteworthy deviation. Friday night dinner in their brownstone was a time for the "recitation of Hebrew prayers," kiddush (sanctification of wine), and *ha-motzi* (the blessing over bread) that began the repast. Reportedly, Rachel Hays Sulzberger "oversaw the meal with the meticulousness of a kashruth rabbi." However, she also sneaked out of the eating area for "short sessions of smoking behind the dining-room screen." Lighting up on the Sabbath is a clear violation of Biblical Sabbath law. We do not know what Daniel Hays's personal religious values were. But it seems that, notwithstanding the traditionalism of his Shearith Israel heritage, he was supportive of his rabbi's efforts to keep moving the congregation away from Orthodoxy.[23]

Harris described himself as a "moderate reformer" as he guided the congregation further from its original Orthodox moorings by introducing additional English-language prayers and more importantly by replacing the traditional siddur with the *Minhag Jastrow*. Of course, by the time he first ascended the pulpit, men and women sat together during prayers that were accompanied by an organ. His moderation certainly may be seen through the choice of a modern prayer book. While this reordering of Jewish ritual provided worshippers with a service that was considerably shorter than the Orthodox one, on the ideological level its teachings did not "anticipate the disappearance of the national aspirations of the Jewish people" as was then preached by radical Reformers. Along those same lines, the congregation continued to observe "the second day of festivals," which theologically speaking bows to the primacy of life in the Land of Israel as opposed to the Diaspora.[24]

However, almost predictably, Harris's laity were not totally in step with their rabbi's initiatives. Early on, it will be remembered that while still known as Hand-in-Hand, disagreements over ritual had led to the splintering of congregational ranks. Such was generally the pattern nationally when cooler heads could not bridge controversy over traditions and changes. But at Temple Israel, the membership and rabbi stayed together after a remarkable "peace conference" reconciled synagogue factions. Both Rabbi Kaufmann Kohler, a leading spokesman for an ideologically strong Reform movement, and the traditionalist Myer S. Isaacs, who on most days had much to say against his interlocutor's religious viewpoints, trimmed their theological sails that day in Harlem. The two men addressed a reconciliation meeting and succeeded in convincing both sides that "the necessity of peace in synagogue life transcended all other ritual and personal considerations." These eminences called upon worshippers to settle their differences harmoniously and "to support their present executive and minister."[25]

By the mid-1890s, Harris steered Temple Israel into the Reform camp. He became an early member of its Central Conference of American Rabbis and the congregation adopted the Union Prayer Book, which the rabbi would later recall as "an advance towards a more complete reform." Still, an "acrimonious" issue remained: the question of worship with an uncovered head. Apparently the majority, including Rabbi Harris, wished to pray without hats or yarmulkes. For Harris, it was "strange that this particular ceremonial which makes a difference between occidental and oriental rather than between Jews and gentiles should have been the cause of such severe theological contention." However, "in deciding to adopt the occidental practice"—by which he meant no head coverings—"Temple Israel always made a provision that anyone who had conscientious scruples about removing a hat could keep his head covered during services." Such would be the policy both on 125th Street and long after 1903, when Temple Israel followed its most affluent members further west and south to even grander surroundings at 120th Street and Lenox Avenue.[26]

Meanwhile, in keeping with the emphasis of Reform teaching of the time, Harris preached strongly about the importance of his flock participating in good works to succor the poor and unfortunates as a "duty of Jews in full accordance with the spirit of Mosaic legislation." Such had been a core teaching of the Pittsburgh Platform that many of the rabbi's colleagues promulgated as a Jewish social gospel mission in 1885, four years after Harris came to Temple Israel. Accordingly, the congregation participated in a variety of Reform charitable activities in the city. The most noteworthy link was its Sisterhood of Personal Service founded in 1891. It was modeled after the Temple Emanu-El Sisterhood that had come into existence several years earlier. Rabbi Harris pointed to the good work done by Emanu-El's women when he proposed the creation of the Harlem Sisterhood. "A congregation," he declared, "can and must be the center for a large amount of good. A society has been formed in this city—that I would like you to make your ideal—whose only dues are personal service."[27]

The women of Temple Israel responded affirmatively to the rabbi's appeal. Interest and ability in good works, it was said at the time, was a particularly feminine proclivity. The uptown sisterhood sponsored a sewing circle for the poor of East Harlem, a Perseverance Club for uptown working young women, and a free kindergarten for needy tenement children. In 1894, the sisterhood became the uptown affiliate of the United Hebrew Charities. Fourteen years earlier—it will be recalled—before Temple Israel's most affluent members arrived uptown, Hand-in-Hand was too poor to support a citywide campaign. Later in that decade, as poor east European Jews began settling in larger numbers amid Third Avenue's tenement district, Temple Israel surrendered part of its district-wide charitable responsibilities to two smaller women's organizations, the Amelia Relief Society and the Deborah Relief Society, which operated in the Yorkville–Lower Harlem vicinity. These cooperating groups would expand their activities when additional indigent Jews migrated uptown after the turn of the twentieth century.[28]

While the 1880s–1890s witnessed Temple Israel grow in numbers, wealth, and the expansion of its contacts with institutions south of Harlem, the closing of the travel gaps between uptown and downtown hastened the decline of the early Harlem Y and the Harlem Lodge of the B'nai B'rith. By 1885, with Harlem emerging as just another residential neighborhood in increasing contact with an expanding metropolis, organizational leaders realized that uptown-bound members could still retain their active affiliation with midtown and downtown branches and older Harlem residents could now readily participate in all citywide activities. Thus, anticipating the relocation of the midtown Y to 58th Street and Lexington Avenue—accessible by the Third Avenue El—the fifty-one members of the Harlem Y liquidated their assets and pooled their funds with the larger Manhattan group. In 1900, New York's first Y would move even closer to Harlem when it built a large and enduring facility on 92nd Street and Lexington Avenue. Similarly, in 1886 the B'nai B'rith, which maintained several branches in the neighboring Yorkville area, consolidated its Harlem affiliate with Lebanon Lodge No. 9. More than two decades would elapse before both of these organizations would remerge—under totally different contemporary circumstances—as important parts of the Harlem social scene.

During this same era, late in the nineteenth century, some of the working-class Jews of central European extraction who settled in Harlem brought their religious institutions with them. Such was the case, for example, with Chevrah Ansche Chesed, founded in 1877 at Beekman Place, near 50th Street. Harlem was the final stop on a long congregational odyssey that saw a small group of families who desired to live and worship together migrate first to Yorkville and eventually to 112th Street, east of Lexington Avenue. Soon they would amalgamate with a second congregation late of Yorkville, Temple Mount Zion, and together Chevrah Ansche Chesed's membership would serve the Jews of the tenement district into the first decade of the twentieth century.[29]

Concomitantly, however, before Congregation Shaare Zedek could begin its own religious work among the middle-class Jews who settled near its sanctuary on 118th Street west of Fifth Avenue, its lay leaders had to settle their differences with fellow Jews who remained downtown. And the struggle over relocation turned out to be fraught with acrimony and long-term bad feelings. The downtown congregation dated back to 1837, when a group of Jews "primarily from Posen"—a part of Poland that in the nineteenth century was controlled by Prussia—arrived in the United States and desired to pray according to the Orthodox ritual of their home province. After holding services in a series of temporary homes in the 1840s, the members were able to secure a permanent place at 38 Henry Street in the heart of Kleindeutschland.[30] The question of its permanence in the district was, however, called into question in 1897, and in a most problematic way, when a group of synagogue leaders, headed by real estate operators Bernard Galewski and Aaron Levy, attempted surreptitiously to sell the downtown synagogue and use the proceeds to establish their congregation in Harlem. Galewski, for one, had come a long way economically since his arrival downtown late in the 1870s. He had started out as a "shoemaker and in an alley-way on Orchard Street"—he could not afford shop rent—and began "repairing shoes at from five to twenty cents a pair." But as of 1902, his work-a-day era was behind him. He was known on the Lower East Side to be "worth several hundred thousand [dollars] with his residential destination Harlem." And he wanted his shul to go with him. Other trustees, upon hearing of the projected move, quickly went to court and received an injunction blocking final real estate negotiations until board members could have the opportunity to vote on the sale and relocation. When the board of trustees finally considered the Galewski-Levy initiative, a majority voted to maintain the congregation where it was, on the Lower East Side.[31]

Galewski, Levy, and their minority of dissenters continued to press their fellow congregational leaders for assistance in establishing a new Shaare Zedek presence in Harlem. Finally in May 1899, uptown and downtown factions agreed to an appropriation of $6,000 to construct a synagogue for Harlem-bound members in return for their official resignation from the downtown congregation and their forfeiture of all mutual benefit privileges, including the important right of burial in the cemetery plot maintained by the downtowners. The uptown group was to become a completely separate entity with no official ties whatsoever with the Henry Street congregation. Those on the move willingly accepted their exile and used the severance payout to build their 118th Street sanctuary. They also hired Rabbi Leopold Zinsler away from downtown in the hope of garnering greater prestige for the Harlem synagogue.

Although officially divorced, Harlem Shaare Zedek congregants maintained close contact with downtown members because residents of the Lower East Side were constantly abandoning the old neighborhood for uptown, a chain migration that continued well into the first decade of the twentieth century. Finally, in 1910, the last remaining leaders of the downtown faction agreed to the disposal of the Henry Street property and officially moved the congregation to Harlem. Still—as bad blood continued to boil—they steadfastly refused to negotiate amalgamation with the uptown group, preferring to hold their own services in a local public hall. Finally in 1914, the long-enduring dispute ended when all factions were reunited in the 118th Street sanctuary.[32]

Meanwhile, starting in the late 1880s, amid this era of increased Jewish presence and visibility in Harlem, small groups of east European Jewish immigrants established their own outpost uptown. A very rough estimate of their numbers would place approximately thirteen hundred Russian and Polish pioneers, residing in almost equal numbers east and west of the Third Avenue El. Like the Hand-in Hand settlers of the early 1870s, whose part of the neighborhood they began to take over, these newcomers' arrival began almost imperceptibly. The Yiddish newspapers of the day hardly mentioned this uptown presence. For example, from 1888 to 1892, the *Yiddishes Tageblatt* (Jewish Daily News), which had been around since 1884, published only a few handfuls of articles about the colony of uptown east European Jews and advertisements about neighborhood opportunities. One "want-ad" looked for "operators to make children's jackets and pants." Another entrepreneur searched "for good operators and fine finishers of a good costume house" and warned "only good people should apply." And a butcher was on the lookout for a partner who possessed $200 to invest—"a must." A real estate ad announced "rooms at 221 East 102nd Street," in the tenement section of the district. One option was a "three room apartment painted from $7 a month and up." Those interested were advised to "inquire with the janitor."[33]

At the same time—and very likely to the great chagrin of the established central European community of Harlem Jews—one of the very first mentions of their east European brethren in the local neighborhood press was an account of the malfeasance of a rabbi. The Rev. Samuel Distillator, who regularly advertised in the *Tageblatt* his multiple talents as a performer of marriage ceremonies, mohel ("certified proficient by the best doctors"), and ritual slaughterer was arrested in 1892, wrote the *Harlem Local Reporter*, "for killing a number of chickens in a butcher shop . . . which is in violation of the Health Code when done without a permit." Ultimately of greater significance was the establishment of the first Russian Jewish congregation, Nachlath Zvi, in 1891 and the Uptown Talmud Torah a year later. That Jewish school in particular eventually would be both a landmark and somewhat controversial communal institution as it joined a network of organizations that would attempt to meet the needs of a large, ever-expanding population of east European Jews. Indeed, during the next two decades—roughly from 1895 to 1917—immigrants and their children who hailed from Russia and Poland along with newcomers from Romania and Hungary would become the largest Jewish group in the neighborhood. And after 1900, thousands from the Ottoman Empire would join these uptown migrants as the Jewish ethnic mix in Harlem's streets was completely transformed.[34]

An elegant parlor in Harlem, 1912 (photo courtesy of Museum of the City of New York).

3

Uptown Homes for Jewish Immigrants, 1895–1917

In 1907, muckraking journalist Burton J. Hendrick alerted his readers in *McClure's* magazine to a massive takeover underway in the streets of uptown Manhattan. The "invaders" of Harlem were "the capitalists of the East Side"—"East Side Jews" who occupied lands that "had been the former country seats of well-known Knickerbocker families." Within this "territory . . . extending from the northern boundary of Central Park"—at 110th Street—continuing "north-west to the Harlem River"—around 155th Street—"a community of 75,000 strong" had built up "colonies" from "Fourth to Lenox Avenues." After "buying up the old estates, parceling them out to each other and realizing enormous profits," Hendrick explained, "Jewish builders are already at work putting up acre after acre of apartments and tenement houses." And "into them is crowding a Jewish population."[1]

Hendrick was surely overwrought in his description of a previously untrammeled Harlem privileged estate community now caught in the throes of unprecedented, rapid transformation. After all, for a quarter century, the neighborhood had steadily been moving away from its longtime rural character. Still, a new era of construction and substantial increase in population was indeed well underway. The difference now was that the occupiers of homes and properties were not scions of old American clans—including some renowned colonial Jewish families—or primarily central European immigrants on the make and on the move, even if at least one of them, Israel Stone, was participating in the takeover of Harlem lands. As of 1900, this former, small-time clothes merchant had become a builder and could be found residing on the corner of Seventh Avenue and 133rd Street. Five years later, state census takers noted that he was engaged in real estate, an occupation that permitted Israel and Emma, their growing extended family, and their servant to live quite well on 130th Street, west of Eighth Avenue. Nonetheless, Hendrick was right that the bulk and excitement of transactions centered on the activities of east European Jews who were making their mark in the rapid turnover of lands. It was, he lamented, as if "an area especially rich in historical associations . . . extending from the northerly boundary of Central Park to the Harlem River," which had been "the path of Washington's retreat" during the Revolutionary War was becoming "occupied by thousands of Russian Jewish exiles." This "bourgeoisie" that was now settling uptown "was made up entirely of East Siders who have outgrown their station." For Hendrick, in a highly competitive market, "Russian Jewish landholders . . . now control almost every parcel . . . because they have shown themselves the fittest to survive."[2]

Actually, explained Abraham Cahan, the immigrant community's best-known literary figure and a keen reporter on downtown life, these newly successful men—"and women too who were ardently dabbling in real estate"—had come up through the ranks of working-class Jews. For the editor of the Yiddish daily *Forward*, those who were profiting from real estate speculation as "builders of tenements or frame-dwellings" had begun their lives in America as "carpenters, house painters, bricklayers or installment peddlers," if they were not merely small trades people of the slums. Rather, these "all-rightniks," to use the parlance of the day—prosperous upstarts who tended to be quite smug and were frequently overbearing about their achievements when they interacted with those less fortunate than they—had been in this land of opportunity just long enough to cobble together sufficient resources to make their deals in a local café over "a glass of tea or sorrel soup" or to elbow their way into a transaction on Harlem's "Real Estate Curb" on 116th Street and Fifth Avenue. "In some cases," Cahan reported additionally, "written agreements to buy or sell were drawn up. Agents had commissions. In many cases, the written contract was resold prior to the glass of tea being finished and several thousand dollars made."[3]

For Cahan, who was also the author of the classic immigrant novel *The Rise of David Levinsky*, the fictionalized character "Max" personified the pride and exuberance of those who were rising economically, many of whom were settling in Harlem: "Max who but years ago was a poor operator, lean, bent and worn out with work, who stepped aside for every man and wore a ragged old coat. Now his face is beaming, a large diamond sparkles on his shirt front and his face wears that peculiar expression which tells you without words that Max has a large bank book in his pocket." Progressive writer Edward A. Steiner most certainly agreed with Cahan's understanding of how a poor immigrant could make it with alacrity to a fancy apartment on Fifth Avenue north of Central Park. He observed: "From a presser the man may become a cutter, then a designer, and at last open a shop in Harlem, and his wife wears diamonds. Harlem is the goal and the further uptown he moves the larger, one may be sure, is his bank account." And, for what it was worth, at the same time that Cahan and Steiner were describing the lifestyles of these new uptown residents, a sociologist doing field work in the neighborhood reported that some "families speak apologetically and at times are embarrassed when their former residence in the lower parts of the city are mentioned."[4]

In many respects, David A. Cohen was a real life all-rightnik, a Jewish "rags to riches" phenom, complete with mixed feelings about, and troubling behavior towards, his old neighborhood. Once praised as one "of the leading representatives of the Jewish race in Harlem," he was born in Suwalk, Russo-Poland, in 1854 and migrated to the United States in 1880. Beginning at the bottom of the economic ladder as a housewares peddler, in a very short time, Cohen emerged as a rising downtown entrepreneur. By the 1890s, he owned both a tinware business and a clothing factory. Later in the decade, he entered the real estate profession and became president of Golde and Cohen Realtors. Soon thereafter, he gravitated to the construction industry and became a major stockholder in the Universal Construction Company. This firm, which initially did much work on the Lower East Side, was founded by members of Congregation Kehal Adath Jeshurun of Eldridge Street, a synagogue where many of the newly affluent downtown Jews prayed. In the 1890s, Cohen served several terms as president of the Eldridge Street Synagogue.[5]

After 1900, Cohen relocated his family to Harlem, settling in the better part of uptown on 113th Street, half a block west of Fifth Avenue, and acquiring several large tracts of uptown land. One was situated along Seventh Avenue at 114th Street. Another was located at 136th Street and Lenox Avenue. Probably his best-known Harlem business transaction was his selling of a parcel lying at 114th Street at the corner of Seventh Avenue to Congregation Ansche Chesed for $108,000 in 1907. His customers in this sale included many of those central European Jews of long-standing in the neighborhood who had moved beyond their own working-class "stations" in East Harlem and were dwelling in this grand part of the neighborhood.[6]

Very likely, Cohen gained entrée for this important transaction because of his growing reputation in the neighborhood as a socially responsible investor who directed a considerable portion of his profits back into the uptown community and helped sponsor a variety of Harlem social and cultural organizations. The Cohen family, in addition, seemed quite comfortable interacting with the members of Ansche Chesed and even of Temple Israel. Elias A. Cohen, David's son, became a member of the Board of Trustees of the 114th Street congregation and was secretary of the Harlem Federation, a settlement house that Maurice Harris's congregants supported. It seems that the Cohens and others of east European heritage who were doing quite well gained acceptance among the affluent elite of Jewish Harlem.[7]

There was, however, a dark side to David Cohen's activities that unquestionably caused some of the Jews he had left behind downtown to denigrate him as possessed of some of the worst characteristics of an all-rightnik. Beginning in 1908, the word on the street, among three of the Yiddish newspapers, and within the congregation where he once worshiped was that Cohen was overbearing, disingenuous, and manifestly uncaring about the Lower East Side community from which he had aggressively distanced himself. Some of his harshest critics might have opined in their angriest moments that while Cohen maintained strict Orthodox Jewish ritual practices—unlike many other all-rightniks who rapidly abandoned adherence to the traditions—somehow as he rose in society, he had lost touch with the faith's emphasis on benevolence and charity.[8]

The cause célèbre that circled around Cohen seemingly started innocently enough in April 1903, when he told the board of trustees of the Eldridge Street Synagogue that several members "were thinking of establishing a branch of our shul uptown, for the benefit of our congregation." But since those who wanted the congregation to have a presence in Harlem had yet to present "actual plans," Cohen's proposal was quietly tabled. Four years later, in April 1907, the would-be uptown contingent came back to the other trustees with a concrete plan and the board agreed in principal to create an uptown center and "that our shul should contribute to its initial expenses." Again the plan did not move with alacrity. However, in November 1908, a committee of the board—that Cohen headed—recommended the purchase of a building on 113th Street and Fifth Avenue. And on November 18, 1908, a congregational majority agreed that "the matter of the branch to be a benefit for our congregation."

But in the months that followed the proposal went sour and in a series of subsequent meetings, bad blood emerged between the "brothers," as members were referred to in the minute books. Indeed, at a showdown meeting in August 1909, it was determined that "no mortgage was to be taken out on the shul" that the brothers who had moved uptown had purchased. And, in fact, in a vote indicative of where sentiments stood, the downtowners asserted—by a vote of six in favor and forty-five opposed—that Cohen and his colleagues did not have the right "to use the same name" of Kehal Adath Jeshurun.

At the root of this dramatic shift, with all of the attendant anger and congregational warfare that followed, was the downtowners' ever-increasing sense that the Harlem-bound contingent wanted more than mere financial assistance and formal approbation. Rather, the perception was that David Cohen and his friends were intent on building their uptown Fifth Avenue synagogue at the expense of the Eldridge Street Synagogue community.

Cohen's problematic goals were unquestionably confirmed in the minds of his erstwhile congregational brothers when soon after the August turndown, he secured an injunction against his old-home synagogue blocking it from merging with a smaller religious group, the Anshe Lubtz, whose members were from the Polish town of Lubtz, several hundred miles northwest of Warsaw. In the nasty court proceedings that followed, Cohen contended that, in violation of synagogue bylaws, "himself and others similarly situated" were not duly informed that an amalgamation was afoot. In response, Vice President Abraham Feinberg presented evidence before Justice John J. McCall in New York State Supreme Court that Cohen knew all about the plans and that his new adversary—a fellow Jew who once sat with him in the front rows of the sanctuary—was in court to cynically undermine his financially strapped synagogue. They had brought in the Anshe Lubtz to bolster their dues base, helping it to continue to serve downtown Jews. In other words, to

Cohen's dismay and a subsequent anger, his request for funds had not been approved because a new leadership cadre born out of the merger was not about to commit funds to an uptown initiative. And Cohen was out to delegitimize those who were now in power on Eldridge Street and to reassert his control even though he lived in Harlem.

For Abraham Cahan's newspaper, the socialist *Forward*, Cohen's actions were all-rightnik behavior, if not synagogue imperialism, at its very worst. For the newspaper, it was a class struggle in a religious venue. In its view, "the old Adath Jeshurun attempted very hard to take in the Lubtz *chevrah* because without them, the shul could no longer exist." It was "the plan of the uptown rich Jews to take out money from the Eldridge Street shul and to apply it towards the Harlem one. When the new Lubtzer members refused, the rich Jews proceeded to try to evict the Lubtzer and use the money for their purposes." Happily for Feinberg's side—cheered on by the *Forward*—Justice McCall agreed with their position. He determined that after the August 1909 rebuff, Cohen, a man whom the judge described "as the moving spirit in the proceedings," sought the court's help to undo the present majority rule.

Left unsaid in McCall's verbally restrained decision—characteristic of a magistrate who admitted, on the record, that he would have preferred not to have to deal with intra-Jewish battles—was that Cohen pressed the Eldridge Street Synagogue to follow his lead uptown because a Harlem branch was clearly an integral element of a master plan to create his own center of religious life in the new Jewish quarter. By the time of this dispute, and actually as early as 1905, Cohen had already been instrumental in transforming the Uptown Talmud Torah from a small *cheder*—a Jewish one-room school house—on 104th Street into a "modern educational institute with all its accessories" on 111th Street and Lexington Avenue, just a few blocks away from his newly purchased synagogue property. Looking ahead, Cohen envisioned the timely relocation of the Yeshiva Rabbi Isaac Elchanan, a school for the training of Orthodox rabbis in America then ensconced on the Lower East Side, to a site not far from his own home on West 113th Street and within a short walking distance from the "uptown" Kehal Adath Jeshurun. Indeed, in the course of the adjudication of the injunction, Cohen, as the rabbinical school's new president, actually moved his board towards purchasing two houses a few steps west of 115th Street.

Cohen was so determined to have his synagogue complement his other endeavors that two weeks after the new controlling group at Eldridge Street turned his request down, he personally paid $26,000 of his own money to purchase the 113th Street property. Thus, for this aggressive all-rightnik, a victory in court would have carried significant financial implications but also was inextricably connected to issues of personal pride, power, and prestige within both the uptown and downtown communities. But, as fate would have it, David Cohen's large scale plans would not come to full fruition as, just a week after the McCall ruling, he passed away at the age of fifty-seven. Four years later, Cohen's widow conveyed the 113th Street property to a financially solvent congregation that for the next decade held services in what became one of Harlem's landmark synagogues.[9]

But if the Cohens and their friends moved to Harlem at least in part to get away from the poor of the Lower East Side, ironically, they could not help but notice that only a few blocks east of where they resided on Madison, Fifth, Lenox, or Seventh Avenues, indigent and working-class brethren from the old neighborhood were living en masse in the tenements along Second and Third Avenues starting at 96th Street. In fact, the Jewish history of Harlem of the 1870 and 1880s effectively repeated itself around the turn of the twentieth century when east European Jews came to predominate on the local scene as two socially and economically diversified immigrant communities lived side by side or avenue by avenue. As before, the calculus of affordable housing and availability of employment and the daunting question of commutation—getting to work on time—loomed large in the Jews' feelings and decisions about moving up to Harlem.

Although the neighborhood had a small group of east European Jews and their first institutions, a shul named Nachlath Zvi and a school—the Uptown Talmud Torah—whose first instructor, Rabbi Joseph Leib Sossnitz, advertised his multiple talents in the Yiddish press in the early 1890s as a "pedagogue and teacher," the era of mass migration uptown did not commence until after 1895.[10] Prior to that time, most Russian and Polish immigrants wishing to escape the overcrowded Lower East Side or to explore new economic opportunities beyond downtown looked to the new Jewish settlement in the then outlying Brownsville neighborhood in Brooklyn. Crucially, in that locale, needle trades workers, which was the skilled occupation that employed more immigrant Jewish laborers than any other, found jobs in better surroundings because some of their bosses moved their sweatshops across the river. Jewish construction workers—painters, plasterers, bricklayers, paper hangers—and other skilled and semi-skilled people also found work in a variety of locally based shops and industries. Very few Brownsville Jews had to commute back to the Lower East Side to earn their livelihoods.[11]

Harlem of the early 1890s offered far fewer occupational opportunities. No Harlem Jew rivaled Brownsville's Elias Kaplan, who moved his large factory and his legion of garment workers to the new neighborhood. In fact, throughout its Jewish history, the uptown Manhattan neighborhood was never home to a large needle trades industry. While there were certainly many small, independently owned, tailor shops—Edward Steiner noticed them and sometimes employers advertised for assistants to help run the business—Harlem did not house great garment factories. Thus, while some of these low-salaried sweatshop workers, much like Harlem's central European Jewish laborers of a generation earlier, were willing to ride the Els back and forth, to and from the Lower East Side, morning and evening, not to mention pay the daily car fare, many more tailors, pressers, operators, and fitters were not. Their families would stay put where they were downtown, coping as best they could with slum conditions.[12]

Similarly, in the 1890s, the cigar-making industry, which then also gave employment to thousands of downtown workers, had only begun to shift its large operations from the Lower East Side to Yorkville and East Harlem. Consequently, here again, commutation time and cost of travel figured in the decisions of most of those skilled workers to stay in the hub with their families. And then there were the difficulties Jewish construction workers faced in securing jobs in that depressed Harlem industry. Building activity that had peaked in the mid-1880s had been in decline for years and Jewish workers who hoped to live where they worked found that they had to compete with members of other ethnic groups for the scarce jobs that existed.[13]

Migration to Harlem thus remained an option only for the fortunate few: tailors who set up their own local shops or fellow garment workers who were talented or valuable enough to arrive later than the average worker; lucky building trades people who found work uptown;

small shopkeepers and peddlers who risked to live and sell in Harlem away from their regular clientele; and the early business success stories who had risen out of the working class and could create their own time schedules.

And even for the most exceptional east European immigrant, the paucity of decent, available housing reduced the attractiveness of many Harlem addresses. The twenty-five-year-old, now densely populated tenement district near the Els that rose in the 1880s offered only the prospect of rapidly deteriorating dumbbell tenements and railroad flats, like those downtown. By the 1890s, an observer of the local scene "from the windows of the elevated train going north after leaving the 89th Street station," could find "row after row, block after block of tenements," not to mention "two great breweries, the towering chimney of the electric power-house, the extensive repair shop of the elevated railway, the great round gas tanks and here and there a factory building breaking in spots these solid rows." While that uptown area remained appreciably less congested than the Lower East Side, these accommodations were hardly a great inducement to migrate. Those with considerable money could, of course, look west to the brownstones and apartment buildings on Madison and Fifth Avenue. But such residences, in addition to their expense, were by the early 1890s in short supply.[14]

It remained for the decade that bridged 1895–1905 for large numbers of east European Jews to move uptown. They arrived amid the real estate booms and busts that occurred during this era that were so closely linked to the fits and starts in municipal plans to once again improve rapid transit to Harlem. Many would be attracted during the years when types of housing superior to what was available on the Lower East Side and at rents comparable to, if not lower than, those downtown were made available. Meanwhile, for Jewish construction workers, in particular, the spikes in building developments offered possibilities for sustained employment. The center of the new work sites was the previously underdeveloped segments of East and Central Harlem. The impetus for real estate speculation in what remained of the Harlem "village" scene was the expectation that the long-awaited construction of a subway system linking the neighborhood with downtown would become a reality. But as in the previous endeavor of a generation earlier—when the Els were built—the gears of municipal life moved very slowly.

Central Harlem's residents had been agitating for a subway system for many years. One neighborhood weekly began as early as 1890 to criticize city officials for not recognizing that "New York and especially Harlem is losing population and growth constantly because of the lack of facilities for quick and comfortable transit between the north and south ends of Manhattan Island." The beneficiaries of the city's lethargy were real estate developers in Brooklyn and even west of the Hudson in New Jersey.[15]

The municipal government responded half-heartedly, creating in 1891 a permanent commission empowered to lay out a route for an underground rail link and to negotiate with landowners for possession of parcels situated on the projected route. The commission was not, however, empowered to build or operate the system, whose rights were to be offered for sale to the highest public bidder. After more than a year of protracted negotiations with some reluctant Harlem landowners, who were the last holdouts against the urbanization of their once bucolic area, the commission proposed, late in 1892, two subway lines, one of which would run from the Battery up the West Side along Broadway on to Kingsbridge Road in the West Bronx and the other up the East Side along Madison Avenue across the Harlem River into the East Bronx. The rights to build this rapid transit system were subsequently offered at public sale. But when no responsible bidder appeared, the "permanent" commission was temporarily disbanded and plans for the subway were tabled.[16]

Harlem real estate and business people continued to push for rapid transit. The *Harlem Local Reporter*, which played a central role in articulating uptown sentiments, spearheaded the struggle, coining the oft-repeated slogan "Fifteen Minutes to Harlem." Reprising an argument that was made a generation earlier when the Els were contemplated, boasters proclaimed that "a rapid transit system which will bring 125th Street within fifteen minutes of the City Hall will be the greatest boon New York City can ever have."[17]

Municipal leaders finally responded positively to uptown needs in 1894 when they passed a new rapid transit act that provided for public construction of a subway system, conditional on public approval of a referendum on mass transit to be held in the upcoming city election. One of the complaints that had to be overcome—so reminiscent of objections leveled back in the 1870s—was the concern of downtown property owners that "the digging of a subway would undermine the foundations of their big buildings and obstruct street and pedestrian traffic." However, these objections did not carry the day at the polls and when the referendum was overwhelmingly approved in November 1894, Harlem's long struggle for the most up-to-date rapid transit links seemed to have ended in victory.[18]

Anticipating the construction of the newly approved subway system, Harlem realtors and builders rushed to invest heavily in previously unimproved Harlem lands. For example, a local trade journal estimated that enough "cheap semi-urban homes" were built between 1895 and 1900 on Madison, Fifth, and Lenox Avenues to accommodate approximately thirty thousand new settlers. The blocks located along 110th—120th Streets between Madison and Fifth Avenues showed the most pronounced growth during this time period. Within the ten square blocks situated in this area, six had a building concentration of upwards of 90 percent of available land utilized. The four other square blocks were 50 to 90 percent built up. [19]

The construction boom in the late 1890s was also stimulated by the desire of real estate developers to complete their jobs before new building regulations went into effect in 1900. Although the New York City Building Code failed to satisfy even the most minimal desires of tenement house reformers, this legislation concerned builders and speculators as a potential source of increased construction costs and lower profits. Poorly constructed buildings were thus rushed to completion. These tenements augmented the ready supply of houses available to different classes of prospective tenants. In other words, residences for both the poor and the successful were now again on Harlem's market.[20]

But the expected great demand for Harlem housing did not immediately materialize. Even when the go-ahead was given, it took close to a decade—up to 1904—for the subway construction to be completed. The project ran afoul of numerous unforeseen legal and financial problems. Even the geography and topography of Manhattan got in the way. The island was largely covered with "Manhattan schist," a type of rock that was difficult to cut through. For the 7,700 pick and shovel workers who at the peak of construction worked daily, it was an arduous task to build the subway in an era when there were few steam shovels and bulldozers. With the commutation dilemma still in play in the city, the newly developed sections of Harlem remained inaccessible and attracted relatively few new settlers. Soon, even before the end of this pre-1900 building boom, some thoughtful realtors realized that they had overspeculated in Harlem lands. Indeed, as early as 1898, complaints were heard from builders about a "tenant dominated" real estate market.[21]

The competition among realtors to fill up their partially rented buildings was so keen that by 1900 a rent war was underway. The problem reached such critical proportions that in April 1900 forty-seven worried realtors formed the Protective Association of Harlem Property Owners to create "an extensive union of uptown real estate operators to do away with some of the evils which have made Harlem real estate unprofitable." The new association pledged to crack down on those realtors who promised to maintain minimal base rents and then quietly offered tenants several months' free rent.[22]

During this period of renewed large-scale construction and relatively low rents, thousands of east European Jewish families moved uptown. The pages of the real estate presses were filled with discussions of the migration of the "prosperous and Americanized" who were ready and able to escape downtown and were taking advantage of the temporary glut in the real estate market. Reports told of those who gravitated to accommodations superior to and often cheaper than the better grade of apartments available on the Lower East Side. These bargain hunters who decided to move uptown were in search of houses with "greater privacy, larger quarters" and the possibility for some of "becoming a landlord." Apparently for these families, the calculus that led them to put down a deposit on a Harlem apartment was that breadwinners would put up with the difficulties of the Els for the sake of the family, Of course, the commutation dilemma would be mitigated if the worker or entrepreneur was able to find a job or set up a shop or even establish a real estate office in the neighborhood.[23]

One of the target audiences for these cut-rate yet upscale apartments was young people—especially newly married couples and young families—who had the wherewithal and desire to start their adult lives away from their parents' downtown neighborhood. One advertisement indicative of the pitch to these consumers that appeared in the Yiddish press in 1896 opened with "The Voice of Joy, the Voice of Gladness, The Voice of the Bridegroom, the Voice of the Bride"; the lead was a verse borrowed from the traditional Jewish wedding ceremony. "Young couples and growing families can receive a practical, decorated three-room apartment for $8.50–$9.50 in the great new Steinway Apartment House [at 1883 Third Avenue between 97th–98th Streets]. Do you want an elegant place for cheap rent?"[24]

For Jewish construction workers, young and old, economically diverse Jewish Harlem in the 1890s was not primarily a residential haven. Rather, it was a locus for sustained employment opportunities. When their workday was done, painters, paperhangers, carpenters, and bricklayers would live in the tenements along Third and Second Avenues. Their presence caused tensions with the Irish who predominated in these skilled occupations. By offering themselves to "lumpers" (building subcontractors) at rates considerably less than other laborers', Jews gained a firm foothold in these industries. Their efforts earned them the enmity of the Irish-dominated construction trade unions. In 1896, for example, John F. Chalmers, secretary of the Amalgamated Society of Carpenters and Joiners No. 5, complained to the New York State Bureau of Labor Statistics that his men had been "knocked out of the work of fitting up flats in the Harlem district" by, among others, "Polish Jewish" scabs who were willing to work "for $1.50–$2.50 a day," leaving union men to find employment in other construction fields.[25]

Chalmers's colleague, David Callanan, president of the Amalgamated Painters and Decorators of New York, charged similarly that "Polish Jews, Hebrew Workmen" had taken "all the work done east of Third Avenue, from the Battery to the Harlem River." These workers, he remonstrated, "work for wages that no respecting mechanic would think of accepting for his labor, some as low as 80 cents a day," making it "impossible for us to compete with them, their habits and methods of living being foreign to us." Callanan also argued that property owners, in their overwhelming desire to hire workers at the lowest possible wages, had overlooked the crucial fact that the Jewish scabs' labor "is inferior and they perform much less daily than a first-rate mechanic." Not incidentally, at this point, the unionists did not consider the option of mitigating the problem of Jewish laborers undercutting them by opening up their Irish-exclusive workers' brotherhoods.[26]

Less publicized, but no less important than job opportunities and the glut in the neighborhood's real estate market in bringing east European Jews to Harlem in the late 1890s, was the constriction of available housing for poor Jews on the Lower East Side. Thousands of downtown tenement dwellers were forced out of their homes to make way for large factories and small public parks in the immigrant hub. Ironically, much of the overcrowding and dislocations that resulted from these public and private improvements was caused inadvertently by urban progressive reformers' efforts to improve the lot of the newcomers to America.

The problem of tenement housework was a central theme in the arguments of those concerned with the plight of urban slum dwellers. Progressives struggled throughout the 1890s for passage of anti-sweatshop laws both in Congress and in numerous state legislatures. But their efforts met with only limited success. Just three highly industrialized, heavily populated states, New York, Massachusetts, and Illinois, passed any sort of health protection legislation. And enterprising bosses and wage-hungry employees easily circumvented the laws in each of these states. The Congress contented itself with an 1894 investigation of the evils of the so-called "sweating system," but no legislation was passed. The amelioration of the problem of work in the tenements still awaited adequate solutions when the new century began.[27]

Still, reformist agitation was strong enough to convince some large manufacturers to remove their sweatshops from tenements. New warehouses and factories were, thus, built all over the Lower East Side to accommodate what was called the "mercantile movement." The downtown district then experienced a very problematic loss in residential space as many tenements were torn down to make way for factories. Displaced tenants were forced to find new spaces within the already overcrowded Jewish quarter or to seek new accommodations elsewhere in the city. Confronted by this unintended consequence of well-meaning reform efforts, many immigrants who had been made homeless decided to move to Harlem.[28]

Progressive pressure for the construction of public parks for the poor had a similar troubling effect on residential space. Such bucolic respites in the midst of the city, it was argued, would help to improve the well being of young and old. These sites would also be appropriate venues for "controlled play" by youngsters, especially boys, who all too often used the streets as their unsupervised playgrounds. Games that took place amid pushcart traffic often morphed into petty crime when, for example, stickball players helped themselves to fruit from open stands as a reward for a ball well struck. For a worker at the University Settlement House, "the street was at best a rough school of experience and at worst, a free field in which the most evil and corrupting influence may work against the morals of the community." Such sentiments and agitation for "public parks and recreation piers for the people" dated from the 1880s. In 1887, Mayor Abram Hewitt secured passage of the Small Parks Act, which authorized the Board of Street Opening and Improvement to select and build small parks in New York City's poorest districts and to spend up to one million dollars a year on the project.[29]

The board failed to fulfill its mayoral mandate and spent only one-half million dollars in the eight years between 1887 and 1895. Critics, led by muckraker Jacob Riis, charged that Tammany Hall, under the pretense of public economy, neglected to use the appropriated funds properly. The case of Mulberry Bend Park—slated to be built on the southeast corner of the Jewish district nearby the East River—was cited as a prime example of the board's foot-dragging on construction. Plans for the park were filed in 1888. Six years later, the city had still not taken possession of the site.

The New York State Assembly Tenement House Committee reexamined the question of public recreation in 1894. Committee members reported that although one thirteenth of New York City's territory was used for parks, only one fortieth of park land was located south of 14th Street, where one third of the population resided. Central Park was an El ride and a walk away for visitors who lived downtown. The committee called upon the legislature to address the needs of the urban population and to establish a permanent State Commission on Public Parks. As a result of the committee's advocacy, an 1895 law provided for the compulsory expenditure of at least three million dollars for small parks. Under this mandate, the construction of Mulberry Bend Park was finally begun in 1895.[30]

In that same year, Mayor William Strong requested the Federation of East Side Workers to appoint an advisory committee to suggest locations for additional East Side parks. Former mayor Hewitt headed the resulting Advisory Committee on Small Parks of 1897. Riis was the organization's secretary. They counseled that the city acquire parts of some eleven blocks in the downtown Tenth Ward, right in the heart of the Jewish immigrant population, for use as public playgrounds. The committee's recommendations, and continued pressure from other reform circles, led to the creation as of 1902 of some seven new parks on the Lower East Side.[31]

But tenement dwellers had to make way for these public improvements. Already scarce residential space was further overtaxed. The building of the Division Street Park, for example, required the condemnation of housing holding some four thousand people. Once again, the dispossessed were faced with the choice between crowding in with friends and relatives downtown or looking elsewhere. Many choose to join the movement to Harlem, especially if they had marketable skills that could be taken with them uptown.[32]

The 1900 federal census reveals that more than seventeen thousand east European Jews made up the first wave of their invasion of Harlem. And information behind that number indicates, with some specificity, where they found housing in the neighborhood, with which other ethnic groups they mingled on Harlem's streets, and what sorts of job they found uptown, including how many of them could work locally, as opposed to having to trek back daily to the Lower East Side.[33]

Poor and working-class Jews crowded into the densely populated tenement district east of Lexington Avenue, primarily for ten blocks running from 96th to 105th Street. Few Jews settled in East Harlem's growing Italian immigrant enclave bordered roughly by the East River and Third Avenue between 105th and 120th Streets.[34] Jewish construction workers—whose presence worried and infuriated Irish union laborers who lived nearby in their own dilapidated tenements—made up a full third of the Jewish workers in that part of uptown. The good news for Jewish tobacco workers was that by 1900, some thirty-one factories that engaged more than fifty employees each, which made up 40 percent of Manhattan's total tobacco work force, relocated between 59th and 100th Streets, east of Third Avenue. Yorkville—if not their East Harlem area—was within easy daily commutation for the 20 percent of neighborhood Jewish laborers who found jobs rolling cigars and cigarettes.

And, of course, as their community customer base grew, small shopkeepers, peddlers, and dealers of all sorts, who may have operated out of uptown's so-called "Jewish Market" of 98th to 102nd Streets between Second and Third Avenues, were able to live in Harlem and serve consumer needs. Jews in the needle trades, on the other hand, still faced the daunting challenge that the absence of local industry caused, forcing them to deal with the travel-to-work issue. Thus, as of the turn of the new century, tailors and other related skilled garment workers constituted at most only one third of the Jewish skilled labor force and but 22 percent of all Jewish workers.[35]

Most of the more affluent east European Jews joined their better-off Irish and German counterparts in settling agreeably west of Lexington Avenue within brownstone flats and apartment houses (and some tenements). It seems that economic advancement mitigated tensions between ethnic groups. Most of these new uptown Jews had risen out of the working class. The most successful could be found as manufacturers or business people and even a few professionals. Among the entrepreneurs were the real estate operators and large clothing manufacturers who were the most noticed new residents of Harlem. Significantly, they faced fewer commutation dilemmas in choosing to relocate. Often, they were free to set their own schedules and could reside in Harlem while conducting their business either out of their homes, downtown, or in other parts of the city. David Cohen and his family, when they arrived uptown, fit in perfectly with these successful types.[36]

Many others in that part of uptown were at work as clerks, bookkeepers, or even as stenographers. While these people were not rich, they possessed a certain cultural cachet. They could boast of a better than average command of English verbal skills and at least some exposure to the American educational system. Similarly the agents, auctioneers, insurance sales people, and adjusters and buyers—these job designations appear time and again in the census reports of 1900—who were ambitious in attracting customers and clients from outside of their own ethnic group had to have gained facility in English and a general understanding of American attitudes and preferences.[37]

It remained for the first decade of the twentieth century for Jews—seventy-five to eighty thousand strong—to transform the section's ethnic makeup completely. Their poorer element would continue to carve out its own separate niche east of Third Avenue and south of 125th Street, supplanting the remaining Irish block by block while situating themselves directly below an expanding uptown Italian enclave. Those who were advancing economically would make the fashionable section west of Fifth Avenue, north of 110th Street, and east of Morningside Avenue their center. In so doing, they would exceed in number not only those Knickerbocker families whose history Hendrick remembered but also those central Europeans and German Jews whose presence has been previously noted. For one Yiddish newspaper reporter writing in 1907, the history of Jewish "immigration within New York City" had proceeded as follows: "Twelve years ago, Jews lived only on the East Side. Houston Street and Second Avenue was for Jews uptown. Later Jews began to move into the 'streets'"—that is, streets with numbers, like the area around 100th Street. "Later they moved uptown to the East Side of Harlem and later they captured the West Side" along with parts of the Bronx and Brooklyn.[38]

A set of forces similar to those that had first sparked mass movement out of the downtown Jewish quarter motivated this second phalanx of east European migrants uptown to seek a new neighborhood. And as in all prior Jewish settlements in Harlem, many newcomers had their moves or their resettlement forced on them. Once uptown, two classes of Jewish immigrants would be widely noted in the press of the day. For the poor who would be pushed uptown, continued slum clearance, municipal improvements, new building code regulations, and the further incursion of business establishments into residential areas all conspired to tax and ultimately destroy the absorptive capacity of the Lower East Side. For affluent Jews who sought new residences and business opportunities, the final completion of the long-awaited underground rapid transit system set off periods of rapid boom and bust in uptown neighborhood properties upon which they capitalized as home buyers and investors.

Once again, for the Jewish poor, the efforts of city planners and social activists to improve their life conditions contributed inadvertently to a residential space depletion crisis. In April 1901, after a generation of continuous prodding from such reformers as Robert De Forest and Lawrence Veiler, the New York State Legislature finally approved an effective tenement house improvement bill. The legislation prohibited the future construction of the dumbbell and rear tenements that predominated on the Lower East Side and which were present in large number in other slum areas. According to the new law, every residential building completed after January 1, 1902, had to allow for direct natural lighting of every room and conform to such minimal health and safety standards as separate toilet facilities for each apartment and safely constructed fire escapes. The law also created the New York City Tenement House Department, which was empowered to oversee future building construction and to monitor the fixing up of existing tenements. The era of cheap, unsupervised, low-rent housing in the Jewish district had officially closed.[39]

Although downtown realtors and landlords had been especially active in opposing such sweeping changes, they were ironically soon to realize the economic profitability of the new building code. They recognized the emergence of a new entrepreneurial elite within the immigrant generation and among their growing children, composed of successful merchants, dealers, and shopkeepers who desired and were able to afford the modern, more expensive type of dwelling that was to be built under this new mandate. Eager to remain downtown, near their factory or business where they could monitor goings-on constantly—even if they were not working the long hours of their employees—these newly affluent individuals wanted to reside in apartments that reflected their achieved economic status. "New Law construction," one contemporary predicted, might well transform the East Side slums into "the kindergarten for the small merchant whose name is afterward seen on Broadway"—East Broadway, that is.[40]

The creation of a higher-rent district reduced further the number of dwellings available for the poor and raised rents in the remaining so-called "Old Law" tenements. One representative of the real estate industry noted that "poor tenants were being forced into the miserable rookeries [of] the front and rear tenements" and were being made to "pay twenty dollars for four rooms, fifteen and sixteen for three miserable tenements and ten dollars for three rooms in the rear tenements."[41]

The number of spaces available for the downtown poor was reduced again when hundreds of buildings were condemned to make room for the Williamsburg and Manhattan Bridges. In 1900, parts of fourteen blocks situated along Broome, Delancey, and Norfolk Streets and the East River were demolished to create space for the Williamsburg Bridge. The owners of these structures were duly compensated for their lost real estate, but what of the tenants? This important municipal improvement would, in time, facilitate the migration of thousands of Jews over into Brooklyn, primarily to Williamsburg. From there, they could commute quickly back to the Lower East Side for work or set up their own businesses in that emerging Jewish district. But immediately some seventeen thousand of them lost their homes. Many thousands more were evicted several years later from the vicinity of Pike Street to make room for the Manhattan Bridge, which was completed in 1910.[42]

The disturbance of population arising from these bridge constructions was so pronounced that the New York City Parks Department, cognizant of the depth of the downtown housing crisis, suspended further construction of small parks downtown after 1902. Noting the municipality's changed, more thoughtful approach to urban improvement, one contemporary critic advised in an understated but piquant manner that "until there is some indubitable indication that the tenement house population has a tendency to distribute itself more than at present, it would be well not to dispossess any more people."[43]

To make the housing crisis even worse, this second contraction of residential space took place at the very moment when the tide of Jewish immigration to the United States was peaking. During the first decade of the twentieth century, some 976,000 Jews fled to America. As before, Tsarist policies undermined Jewish economic existence and the first years of the new century also witnessed spates of violence that convinced many to flee. The destination of the overwhelming majority of these new immigrants—more than six out of every ten newcomers—was the Port of New York, where they sought jobs and homes in the most congested section of the city. There they crowded in with family and friends from their old hometown or country. The Lower East Side staggered under the weight of this newest wave of immigrants. Some days, close to four hundred of those Jews wanting to be in America were processed though Ellis Island. At this critical juncture, those concerned with the future of the city or the welfare of the downtown denizens began calling for new, efficient means of "breaking up the ghetto."[44]

American Jewish relief organizations, for example, which for a generation had been striving to develop workable large-scale immigrant dispersal programs, redoubled their efforts. In 1901, the Industrial Removal Office, a branch of the Baron de Hirsch Jewish Agricultural Society, was established and charged with coordinating continent-wide initiatives to find jobs for east European Jews outside of the major Eastern centers. Their concept was that the offer of secured employment in healthier settings would induce many newcomers to leave the urban enclaves.

Though over the next decade and a half some eighty thousand Jews took the deal and settled in Midwestern and far Western towns and cities, the vast of majority were not interested in the plan. New York remained the hub. The desire of Jews to live among their own kind outweighed most economic inducements. Immigrants feared traveling to strange new places away from the ethnic atmosphere that permeated downtown—even if the air in what was called the "ghetto" was polluted. It was difficult enough for them to adjust to their relocation from eastern Europe. They were socially and psychologically unprepared for life outside the community.[45]

So disposed, far more working-class Jews who were rendered homeless, and especially those with the right employment skill sets, looked uptown for housing even if they were not trading up to the best of settings. They were joined in this largely enforced peregrination by many newly arrived immigrants who, failing to find any accommodations in the downtown hub, came directly from Europe to Harlem, where they dealt with their first American slum experiences. As one observer of the city's changing profile observed: "The taking by the city of a large amount of property for bridges and parks in recent years . . . had raised the rents and lessened the number of apartments downtown. Thus many to-day as they enter the gateway of America, Ellis Island, move at once to Harlem." Although the area in and around the Els—which had never been the best place to live—at no point equaled the Lower East Side in overcrowding intensity, by 1905 several blocks between 99th and 104th Streets between First and Second Avenues suffered from population densities of 500 persons per acre. The block between 101st and 102nd Streets bordering Second and Third Avenue had a density above 600 persons per acre, a figure that would have been judged as very high even downtown. The only other area of East Harlem more densely congested was the growing Italian section situated due north of the Jewish working class area, where population densities in excess of 700 to 800 persons per acre obtained. [46]

As more and more of the Jewish poor settled uptown, their expanding enclave inundated the Madison and Fifth Avenue section that only a few years earlier either had been undeveloped or boasted small and often elegant private dwellings. Now tenements replaced these homes and, by 1910, this once moderately inhabited section part of East Harlem was weighed down by population densities in excess of 480 and 560 persons per acre. This shift in residential patterns was clearly noted in the Yiddish press of the day. One witness to the rapid change in the Jewish neighborhood emphasized the combination of economic and social pressures that motivated those who just a few years earlier had moved in to move out of a once elegant territory. "The Best of the Jews," the writer declared, had in 1900, made "the entire area in and around Fifth Avenue the aristocratic settlement of Jews. When you asked these people where they lived, they proudly stated 'on Fifth Avenue,' as if they were close friends of 'Brother Carnegie.' But it was not long before that area became crowded and poor people who could not pay high rents on the East Side began to move in. It is now becoming crowded on the Avenue and in the Park and the 'world' is now considering moving again." Within this universe of those relocating within Harlem were "a few of the workers [who] later became real estate men and wealthy builders," surely a point of pride for former "bricklayers and carpenters." To be certain, "the poor can still not move into the same building with five-six rooms, with steam heat etc. for it costs too much for them." But nearby on side streets cheap housing was available, making the affluent uncomfortable. These all-rightniks likewise did not like the scene on "hideous Park Avenue which up to a few years ago was an Irish-German stronghold, but . . . is now lined with kosher meat markets, dinghy grocery stores etc." For this columnist, with this section of Harlem in rapid decline as "a class of Jews who want to live uptown but could not afford uptown rents" took over, the reality was that "people move to avoid other people . . . but the people and the neighborhood move after them and they move further."[47]

The destination for those Jews who demanded better surroundings was but a few blocks west in Central Harlem's new-law tenement and apartment house district that arose when the subways finally made their way uptown. A rush of construction met the underground's arrival in 1904, and by 1906 practically all the remaining vacant land north of 110th Street was built over. Speculators would have to look subsequently to Washington Heights, the Bronx, and Brooklyn for real estate investments.[48]

This Central Harlem neighborhood emerged during the first decade of the twentieth century as home to a large segment of immigrant east European Jewry's most economically advanced and socially acculturated element. Those who moved westward from an overcrowded uptown Madison and Fifth Avenue were joined and, in fact, outnumbered by "the better class of Jews," the latest arrivals from the Lower East Side. These were the Jews whom Hendrick, Steiner, and Cahan characterized as having both invested in buildings and lived in fancy apartments overlooking Central Park or situated along the wide thoroughfares of Lenox and Seventh Avenue.[49]

True, for some Jews who were doing quite well in America, the new parks and piers and, perhaps most importantly, better-built housing were a powerful inducement to stay right where they were in the old Jewish quarter. With electricity and elevators—not to mention bathrooms—readily available at the right price, "the same people who had earlier been proud of living in three rooms . . . began to be ashamed of their living conditions and they opted for these new houses." When they spoke or held forth to those around them about where and how they lived, they could boast of their wealth. And on major Jewish holidays, decked out in their best suits and hats, they would sit in the front rows of one of the larger neighborhood synagogues. They also may well have been forewarned about moving by a sentiment expressed just a few years later that "eventually with the tearing down of Lower East Side tenements," the downtown district "will become a high class neighborhood and uptown a poverty pocket." However, as a counterpoise, it was also observed that for those who chose Harlem, in addition to believing that uptown possessed excellent living comforts—as good as the best that the Lower East Side had to offer—there was a palpable point of ethnic pride to "prove that Jews enjoy and appreciate decent . . . apartments with all modern improvements and high rents and clean streets." For this local

Yiddish newspaper writer, it was evidence that "coming into the possession of these surroundings, the Jews know how to maintain them and constantly improve the standard of living. . . . There are miles and miles of streets all lined with thousands of apartment houses, containing tens of thousands of Jews." Moreover, it seems that for many families, Harlem was a fine place to raise their youngsters in "the Jewish children's own land."[50]

For one other reporter who described uptown goings-on to Jewish subscribers across the United States from a base in Cincinnati, Ohio—as Jewish Harlem now intrigued readers nationally—"this colony" bore "the mark of the second generation [that] has veiled itself with American customs and clothing." Within "this new world of Harlem they found flats to replace tenements." And as good all-rightniks, "with their first hard earned money they furnished their rooms not as necessity forced them in their narrow rooms in the tenement, but with the ampler scope of newer apartments where they lavished money and indulged newly-acquired American tastes."[51]

Predictably, Jewish socialist circles did not see any grandeur in these efforts and were quick to point out the dark side of what they perceived as capitalist machinations that made it possible for these investors to eventually luxuriate in cross-ventilated apartments, serviced by elevators on Lenox Avenue with bedroom, dining, and living rooms set off by fancy French doors. "Such a wonder and convenience" as "sinks with constant cold and hot water"—unknown to those on the rise who had once lived in cold-water flats—were standard features in the state-of-the-art uptown apartment. For Cahan, in particular, the story of the upward mobility of these self-proclaimed "aristocrats"—these all-rightniks—was rife with "boasting" and "jealousies" as "people became enemies" in their desires to be "the talk of the town" where "all that was discussed was rooms with the latest improvements." Imagine, a householder might say, "put the dishes, the laundry under the hot water and clean; even a dumbwaiter that takes down the garbage. Who knew of such things in the old tenement houses downtown?"[52]

But even as Cahan and his cohorts mocked the mores of Jews who saw themselves as "millionaires," their ire was directed most intensely at those who speculated in remodeling old-style tenements in East Harlem. As the *Forward* told it, groups of small-time investors pooled limited funds to purchase, or in some cases only lease, cheap tenements. They made the few necessary alterations to satisfy the building code and quickly raised rents to cover their expenses and to give them a fast return on their dollars. Turnover in the ownership of these properties was very brisk as speculators moved from one site to the next in search of quick returns, and rents were hiked every time a parcel changed hands.[53]

These "get-rich quick" operators were often condemned as "the greatest *schnorrers* [beggars] of the ghetto, men who save every penny, live in dirt, neglect their families, the whole year to raise sufficient capital to invest and become a landlord." Cahan was quick to declare, "Very often these men ended up in the poor house or mental institutions, but very often they became millionaires." Even more crucially, their actions fomented anti-Semitism; so much for them being touted elsewhere as exemplars of Jewish pride and achievement. "Christians in general," it was contended, "do not move as quickly as Jews. For many years Christians live in the same house without a raise in rents. Then the Jewish landlords come and raise the prices on these houses. It has gone so far that Christians are already showing their might and are once again looking to get even with the 'Sheenies.'"[54]

In the decade that followed, leading up to World War I, Jewish Harlem would continue to be home to rich and poor contingents of east European immigrant Jews and their children. As of 1917, the constantly expanding neighborhood was home to the second-largest Jewish community in the United States, standing behind only the Lower East Side's approximately 350,000 Jewish inhabitants.[55]

In 1910, a local rabbi who ministered to one of the last central European congregations in East Harlem was highly sensitive to this massive mix of Jews when he characterized uptown as "a vast conglomeration of tenements and high class apartments, more so than any other part of the city." Significantly, Samuel Greenfield of Temple Mount Zion—an uptown congregation for central European Jews whose presence dated back to 1888—recognized not only economic class differences, but "a peculiarly mixed settlement of our people here with every evidence of their habits, manners and customs of their previous habitat." For him, this "jumbling of dwelling places is typical of the religious condition as well." He spoke of "a number of downtown congregations [that] built branch synagogues uptown [having] transplanted their regime here" without the imbroglio that afflicted the Eldridge Street congregation, along with Jewish schools, "talmud torahs and *chedarim*, large and small, that were invading all available halls and thus creating a most confusing condition of affairs." He also noted, in passing, national-origin differences among these Jews, as "Harlem now boasts its Little Hungary" and "its Romanian restaurants."[56]

Rabbi Greenfield did not notice—or at least he did not note—that adding to this heterogeneous set of Jewish voices were thousands of Ladino-speaking Jews from the declining Ottoman Empire who were just beginning to be pushed and pulled from their own enclaves around Christie, Eldridge, Allen, Orchard, and Essex Streets on the Lower East Side to their ethnic spaces in Harlem from 110th to 125th Street and between Fifth and First Avenues. Given their comparable mix of economic classes they too dwelled both in tenements and apartment houses of varying sorts. Arguably, even as they confronted the same issues of adjustment to relocation as their majority Ashkenazic brethren, they lived their own separate communal and cultural experience. From what is known of their history, they did not link up with the minuscule Sephardic presence that could be found in East Harlem as early as the 1880s. Back then, a Spanish-Portuguese congregation, Moses Montefiore, moved from Yorkville to 112th Street, east of Lexington Avenue. Although in 1888, the synagogue possessed grand plans to expand its religious and religious school life according to the "Portuguese *minhag*," just five years later, their slightly remodeled tenement was sold to Chevrah Ansche Chesed. Perhaps the remaining members amalgamated with this central European congregation in the decade that followed, before most erstwhile Jews from East Harlem made their move to west of Fifth Avenue.[57]

The Jews who moved, or were pushed, to Harlem—to its tenements, brownstones, and apartments—from the end of the nineteenth century until World War I differed not only economically and ethnically. They harbored very different attitudes towards what it meant to be an immigrant Jew. Some saw themselves strongly tied still to the social, cultural, political, and/or religious life that had previously surrounded them in the immigrant hub. So disposed, they maintained close sibling connections with comrades, friends, and colleagues who resided on the Lower East Side. In many instances, the two New York Jewish communities, separated only by a subway ride, acted as one. Other newcomers separated themselves from the ideas and commitments of their prior immigrant experience and adopted, in some critical cases, new types of American Jewish identities and modes of behavior. Occasionally, these different ways of religious and political life conflicted with one another and created in their wake defining moments in the community's history during the neighborhood's Jewish heyday.

Arbeter Ring School in Harlem, 1922 (photo courtesy of the Archives of the YIVO Institute for Jewish Research).

4

Sibling Communities

Harlem and the Lower East Side

When Jewish immigrant worker H. Lang—his first name has been lost to history, but his life experience continues on—arrived in the United States and settled in Harlem in 1904, he was comforted to be around so many of his own kind from eastern Europe. He would recall many years later that residing with him in this "new quarter of New York" was "a mixed group among the Jewish immigrant masses . . . [with] Jews from Galicia, Poland, Lithuania, White Russia and Ukraine." It seems that he hailed from the "Warsaw area" and he was quite proud that even if those Polish Jews "were not numerically the most, it just seemed that way." For him, "to Harlem were brought several complete streets of Warsaw." His compatriots resided in the "then newly built tenement houses of Harlem from 97th–102nd Street from Third to First Avenue," the neighborhood's poorest section. For work, the key locale was the corner of 102nd and Second Avenue, where "Polish Jews who sought work in the building trades . . . painters, paperhangers and decorators" congregated. Notwithstanding his fears of violence from the Irish against whom they competed for jobs, Lang was gratified that "one can actually say, Jewish immigrants began to build Harlem."

Yet while the neighborhood offered housing, employment, and important connections to friends and relatives, Lang nonetheless felt an acute sense of loneliness resulting from his residence outside of the immigrant cultural hub. He badly missed the socialist and other radical voices to which he was attuned that filled the air of the renowned Jewish quarter. "Harlem seemed to us to be a forgotten spot . . . without a spiritual atmosphere which we desired." The uptown neighborhood "seemed to us remote from the East Side, downtown where there were the Jewish folk masses." Lang was lost without "downtown . . . filled with lectures and debates." Fortunately for him, and for so many others, Branch No. 2

of the Arbeter Ring (Workmen's Circle) was on the scene. It was a presence which, in his view, "simply saved the new immigrants" through its creation of a transplanted radical atmosphere in Harlem.[1]

Lang, who became an official of this socialist fraternal, mutual aid, and educational organization, was grateful to people like Joseph Anapol and Abraham Baroff who, some six years earlier, in 1898, had created this necessary "place of sanctuary, a small place where we could congregate, bring our problems together" and then—as he believed good radicals should—"ultimately build an organization which would improve the world." Once again, Harlem Jewish history repeated itself, as a group of Jews who settled uptown faced a lengthy commutation problem. What was called in those days "the poor traction facilities" distanced them from the Lower East Side. But in their case, it was not the problems of getting to and from work but rather the absence of culture and mutual aid that was the dilemma. "Harlemites," according to Anapol, "had no opportunities to attend meetings or lectures because the meetings used to be on Friday nights and would end late and since Saturday was a work day, it became difficult for the Harlem members to attend." And while many of these workers and certainly their leaders were not religious Jews, it was deemed "a great sin to miss a meeting." As important, the physicians hired by the Arbeter Ring downtown to service the health needs of members were reluctant to visit patients living in Harlem. Bereft of the social, intellectual, and tangible benefits of belonging to their movement, Harlem Workmen's Circle founders appealed to their East Side comrades for help in establishing a network of intellectual and fraternal services in their own neighborhood. The charter granted to Harlem Branch No. 2 of the Arbeter Ring early in 1898 guaranteed such assistance and would serve as a model for similar agreements reached over the next few years between the parent organization downtown and satellite groups in Williamsburg, Brownsville, and the Bronx.[2]

Sensibly, the Harlem Arbeter Ring meeting place was situated not far from where Jews who sought day labor in the building trades lined up. (Memoirists seem to be of several minds over precisely where the shape-ups took place. Some say on the corner of 101st Street and Second Avenue; others recall 102nd Street). Clubrooms were established and "on the walls were hung pictures of Marx, LaSalle and Bakunin," reflecting the multiplicity of socialist and other radical ideologies that Harlem workers harbored. Given where it was located and what the organization stood for, the Progressive Painters Club was one of the first labor groups to affiliate with the uptown fraternal association. While this workers club "was on the one hand 'local' (only painters belonged to it)" it admitted to its ranks everyone with that work skill, "not only Social Democrats but anarchists also, even Socialist Zionists." All sort of ideologues "were given a chance to lecture to the group." In keeping with its openness to heterogeneous radical thought, Branch No. 2 also created a Robert Owen Club in honor of the mid-nineteenth-century Welsh factory owner who became a social reformer and a utopian socialist. That organization maintained a small library and made copies of the socialist *Forward* and the anarchist *Frei Arbeter Stimme* available to members. When health issues arose, members could turn to a local physician who—in present-day terms—was their "doctor on call." Jewish workers who settled in Harlem embraced these multidimensional activities and the Arbeter Ring was receptive to varying strains of radical thought, even if debates over which solution to the evils of capitalism was right must have filled the neighborhood's air late into the night. For H. Lang, with that organization in place, "we young immigrants in Harlem were no longer miserable."[3]

Not long after Branch No. 2 was established with downtown radical encouragement and some monies, the uptown comrades began to return the favor to its sibling community. In 1901, Harlem-based Jews were responsible for the forming of the Zukunft Press Association. This organization helped to fund the revival of the periodical that had suspended publication in 1897 as a major socialist weekly. And then, in 1906, uptown Workmen's Circle members asserted even more significantly that their residence outside of the Lower East Side did not mean that they had broken with the culture of downtown. If anything, when the Arbeter Ring Branch No. 2 established the city's first Socialist Sunday School, they effectively said that comrades in Harlem had much to offer—and indeed to teach—brother and sister workers no matter where they might dwell.[4]

The creation of this educational program augured the beginnings of a fundamental shift in the outlook of this Jewish socialist fraternal and now educational organization. When it was begun in 1892, the Workmen's Circle's primary focus was the provision of intellectual sustenance to its members and illness and death benefits when these problems and tragedies occurred. Little thought was given to transmitting radical values to the next generation growing up in America. One longtime advocate for the organization has suggested that this lacuna "was because most of the members were then very young and had no children of school age." In any event, the Harlem Children's Educational Circle desired to meet head on what it viewed as the deleterious influence that the all-powerful public schools were having on their youngsters. These so-called Temples of Americanization were, in the view of a national leader of the Arbeter Ring, "the strongest factor in maintaining the political power [of the capitalist system]." An antidote had to be found "to weaken the influence which the public schools have on young minds." From its incipient effort in Harlem, the Workmen's Circle became, in due course, "an idealist, educational organization which also paid sick and death benefits." Starting with its model school in Harlem, during the next decade, the Arbeter Ring would sponsor ten similarly constituted schools on the Lower East Side and in Brooklyn.[5]

The curriculum of the Harlem Children's Educational Circle reflected the growth of this new mission. Pupils were exposed to "the history of civilization and . . . the rudiments of political economy, while stress was also laid on the biographies of great champions and heroes of human freedom and enlightenment." American-born teachers—some were Jews, others not—who were committed to socialism, or at least sympathetic to radical goals, were hired and instruction was conducted in English as that was deemed the most efficacious way of reaching and inspiring youngsters. By 1910, this radical school movement was enough of a presence within the city's scene that the *New York Times* warned its readers that "there are easily a thousand children" in the Harlem and other schools "who will, beyond peradventure," grow up to be "anarchistic."[6]

However, notwithstanding the *Times*' fearful hyperbole, these schools had to struggle to keep the movement's leadership fully on board. According to its Harlem educational activists, the Arbeter Ring's national officials were "concerned with a multitude of workers' problems and the problem of a Socialist Sunday School was considered a luxury." Supporters of the Children's Circle claimed that they received little or no financial backing either from the "national office" or from "the local institution." Consequently, the schools found it difficult to pay their teachers.[7]

Ultimately, however, of greater concern, both to the parents who might send their boys and girls to the Children's Circle and to the multiple voices of radicalism in the neighborhood, were the questions of what the children might be taught and in what language instruction would take place. The resulting debate that started out with that first school in East Harlem soon involved sibling organizations not only downtown, but nationally as well. The heated discussions would go a long way towards determining the future ideological direction of the Arbeter Ring and many of its loosely affiliated worker groups.

The founders of the school wished their pupils to grow up with an internationalist workers' mentality, capable of sharing Marxist ideas with other comrades from differing backgrounds. To their minds, since they were determined to integrate and inspire radicals of all extractions with revolutionary ardor, the use of Yiddish instruction was deemed an unwarranted "form of Jewish separatism." Some parents, on the other hand, wondered about and ultimately objected to a school for Jewish children that possessed no Jewish content. They wished for the rich troves of Jewish history and secular culture to be taught through their ethnic vernacular of Yiddish, a language that might link the American born with their immigrant parents. Many radical intellectuals both within and without Harlem seconded and amplified these feelings as Bundists, Socialist Zionists, and Socialist Territorialists—all of whom certainly had their soap boxes to stand on within Branch No. 2—pushed for Yiddish-language schools that would teach their people's experience through the lens of socialism.[8]

Unquestionably, Bundists—members of the General Jewish Labor Alliance of Russia, Poland, and Lithuania—spoke loudest for a Yiddish school system. This had become a critical part of the Bund's mission back in eastern Europe, although when founded in 1897, it viewed itself as a cosmopolitan internationalist socialist organization. Back then Yiddish, initially deemed an expression of Jewish nationalism, which good Marxists must reject, was used only as a propaganda device to speak the truths of revolutionary thought to the Jewish masses in the Pale of Settlement. By 1900, however, the Bund recognized that the Jewish workers whom it hoped to lead were innately nationalistic and unwilling to abandon their heritages for unrealized revolutionary promises. Facing reality, the Bund—through the articulate voices of leaders like Chaim Zhitlowsky and Vladimir Medem—adopted a uniquely *Jewish* socialist posture. It argued that the Jews were not a modern, imperialistic nation, a product of modern capitalism, and thus enemies of the working class. Rather, their identity reflected the struggle of a small minority group for cultural expression. The Bund, therefore, stood for the development of distinctive forms of Jewish identity and culture through the medium of Yiddish literature, poetry, music, theater, and art within a socialist milieu. This divergence from orthodox Marxism caused the Bund to be read out of the larger Russian Social Democratic Party. But its ideas gained much currency on east European Jewish streets.

The American phase of Bundist activity began in the wake of the failed Russian Revolution of 1905. "The reaction of the Russian government was very strong" to the attempt to overthrow the Tsarist regime, recalled a Bundist from Lodz, which "caused many revolutionaries to leave their homeland and to search for a place where the police could not reach." This Jew from Lodz would find his way to Harlem and link up "with many revolutionaries, the majority Bundists." In 1906, they established a mutual aid society and pledged to "help the cause" in the uptown neighborhood. Three years later, after recruiting twenty-five members and raising fifty dollars as an initiation fee—reportedly "it took until 1909 to raise the money"—the Lodzer lodge was "officially installed as Branch No. 324" of the Arbeter Ring. From that position and with that orientation, the Lodzers would lend their support to many others within and without the neighborhood for the Bund's robust America-based Jewish cultural program.[9]

However, the Arbeter Ring's educational initiative soon lost momentum among potential pupils' families as its national leadership, for much of the decade 1906–1916, debated the educational and linguistics values to be taught in their schools. In the meantime, other socialist and nationalist groups established their own decidedly Yiddish-language and Jewish-culture schools. During this time period, the National Jewish Workers Alliance—closely associated with the Socialist Zionists—

created their Jewish National Radical Schools, including one in Harlem, as did the Jewish Socialist Federation, which opened its doors uptown in 1915. Indeed, there seemed to have been a Jewish educational area around 104th Street and Madison Avenue as these schools competed for students with comparable curricula. These institutions were established with the assistance of local Harlem Workmen's Circle members who may have chafed at their movement's wavering on the nationality question.[10]

Finally, in 1916, the Arbeter Ring's national convention decided in a very close vote "to teach Yiddish to the children of . . . members." Under that mandate, two years later, the movement boasted of some twenty-nine schools across the country, six in New York. The Harlem Arbeter Ring School, founded in 1918, has been judged "the organization's premier Yiddish school" in the city. In the years that followed, its elementary school—and then its high school—offered the full panoply of socialist and Jewish nationalist subjects and emphases. Jewish history and literature, general cultural history, identification and glorification of the "heroes of freedom" throughout the ages, art and music, and production of plays were all parts of the school's curriculum. Its teacher training courses brought to Harlem some of downtown's leading intellectual lights as instructors and guest lecturers, as the two sibling communities complemented each other. Deemed a "model for other Yiddish schools," the Harlem Arbeter Ring School strove to fulfill its mission of producing "a new generation with higher ideals, more refined thought and a higher intelligence." By 1920, the school had close to three hundred students registered, including youngsters from families that were not exactly full-hearted Jewish radicals. School officials could not have been pleased with the estimated 30 percent of boys who dropped out of the secular Jewish school around bar mitzvah age to prepare for that Jewish religious rite of passage.[11]

These more traditional Jews—whose ideological commitment to the cause was questionable—may have been drawn into Arbeter Ring circles because for more than a generation, the radical organization had garnered significant street approval. It was an important organization to many uptown residents when it championed their pragmatic, day-to-day consumer concerns. East Harlem residents were, for example, quick to rise in support of the Women's Branch No. 2 of the Workmen's

Circle in its May 1902 campaign to reduce kosher meat prices through a boycott of Harlem meat markets. With uptown and downtown sibling communities in close communication, neighborhood protest leaders took their cues from strike developments that had begun just two days earlier on the Lower East Side. On May 16, the Ladies Anti-Beef Trust Committee called for a boycott of Harlem butchers "in the vicinity of 98th–110th Streets" in protest over what they declared to be exorbitant kosher meat prices. The precise economic precipitant was the jump in the retail prices of kosher meat from twelve to eighteen cents a pound. The committee members began their agitation by going house to house to request that their neighbors refrain from buying meat until the prices were brought down. Picket lines were thrown around the local meat markets and women who sought to defy the protest movement were stopped and pressured to recognize the merits of the boycott.[12]

One day later, the protest committee held a mass meeting at Central Hall on Third Avenue, where monies were collected and plans finalized for the expansion of the "meat struggle." Strike leaders announced proudly that "Bohemian Christian neighbors" had taken heart from the example of Jewish activists and had begun their own protest against the high prices charged in Harlem's non-kosher meat markets. Clearly, Arbeter Ring leaders were enthused that their fellow immigrant neighbors who ordinarily had little organizational contact with them were coming on board.[13]

This first attempt at consumer activism, a protest movement that often was accorded front-page coverage in the *Forward*, lasted nearly a month and was marked by several dramatic street encounters. On May 19, 1902, for example, two neighbors, Sarah Blitzstein and Tina Tass, were arrested for disturbing the peace while picketing a nearby butcher shop. According to newspaper accounts, a butcher named Wegderwitz had attempted to smuggle a chunk of meat out of his picketed store on Second Avenue in the hope of selling it downtown. His efforts were blocked by a "gang of women" who tried to grab the food away from him and drove him back into his store. This initial disturbance caused hundreds of men and women to mass outside the butcher shop. Frightened but determined to break through the blockade, Wegderwitz sent his daughter to call the police. The officers successfully drove a wedge between the protesters and led Wegderwitz, as the *Forward* reporter described it "as one leads a bridegroom to the marriage canopy," to the seeming safety of the elevated railroad. But Blitzstein and Tass did not give up their fight and were arrested when they laid down on the El tracks, blocking the butcher's escape. Esther Warfel joined Tass and Blitzstein in custody. She was taken to the station house for "ripping a chicken out of the hands of a woman" who sought to pass through the Anti-Beef Trust Committee's picket line.[14]

The meat boycott entered a new phase on June 13, when Branch No. 2 decided to open a cooperative butcher shop in Harlem. The plan was to deflate artificially the price of meat in the neighborhood through the opening of an ad hoc wholesale market that would hopefully compete successfully with the established, high-priced butchers. Any profits derived from this cooperative venture would be turned over to the women protestors. This idea was quickly put into effect and reportedly "existed for over a year."[15]

This first, limited attempt at cooperative consumerism in Harlem inspired the creation in 1903 of a neighborhood branch of the New York Industrial Cooperative Society. The downtown-based, older sibling organization had been formed in 1901 by a group of radicals who modeled their initiative on the concepts of the founders of the English Rochdale cooperative system. These cooperative pioneers of the late nineteenth century had argued that for a cooperative venture to compete successfully against capitalist enterprises, it must organize a "controlled market," wherein members of the co-op pledged to buy all the necessities of life exclusively from the cooperative stores. Under this system, once assured of a consistently reliable clientele, the cooperative store could then afford to offer its members good products at wholesale prices. Whatever profits were derived from the venture would be forwarded back to the membership in the form of dividends. Once firmly established, the movement would also attract nonmembers to its operations by offering quality articles at reasonable prices.

The keys to the success of this, or any other cooperative system, were the ability of the cooperators, in the first instance, to attract committed investors to its programs and, secondly, its success in organizing its membership for a controlled market. The New York Industrial Cooperative Society attempted to adapt the Rochdale system to the American Jewish immigrant experience by establishing a network of ten retail stores on the Lower East Side designed to serve a variety of downtown consumer needs.[16]

In 1903, in the hope of capitalizing on what was assumed to be an atmosphere conducive for consumerism created by Branch No. 2's efforts, the New York Industrial Cooperative Society funded a combined bakery and butcher shop in Harlem. Characterized as "one-quarter cooperative," it offered only "cheap meat under rabbinical supervision." In announcing the opening of this sibling venture, the society was quick to argue that its soon-to-be implemented Rochdale system marked a significant advancement over spur-of-the-moment consumerism. The new organization pledged itself to an additional goal: to make the "power of the cooperative ideal felt in Harlem."[17]

However, the uptown cooperative movement's goals of providing high-quality, low-cost consumer goods for its constituents quickly led it into conflict with the then newly established Harlem Bakers Union, which was agitating for recognition by uptown bakery owners. This labor organization was formed in June 1903 by former members of the defunct downtown Local No. 6 who had migrated uptown to find work at decent wages. Jewish bakers on the Lower East Side had faced grave difficulties in attempting to organize themselves. Bosses in the Jewish quarter had adroitly blocked most unionization efforts by hiring newly arrived immigrants who were willing to endure harsh working conditions for less than union scale. Those who moved to Harlem hoped that the owners in that neighborhood, one step up from the Lower East Side, would have less of an eager work force to choose from and would have to deal with unionists. But even as they battled the owners, the Harlem Bakers Union alleged—to their great chagrin and palpable anger—that a fellow Jewish worker group was also undermining their efforts.[18]

The union attacked the Harlem Cooperative for alleged hypocrisy in supporting the bakery owners' attempts to break the union. These uptown radicals were accused of joining with other hated capitalist retailers in selling bread from the Lower East Side and Brooklyn. This battle between siblings gained citywide attention when the

Label Agitation Committee of the United Hebrew Trades castigated the cooperative as union-busters and warned that if the co-op did not agree to use only union bread, it would initiate an action. And on the streets of Harlem, when the local staged its first strikes in 1903 and early 1904, picket lines were thrown up around local stores to prevent scab bread imported from other sections of the city from entering the neighborhood.[19]

The leadership of the Harlem Cooperative responded to these allegations by charging that the Harlem bakery strike—and the bosses' own lockout of workers—was motivated by a conspiracy of union leaders to line their own pockets and not their purported desire to improve the lot of the average worker. The Harlem Co-op announced that it would "gladly" pay the one cent per loaf increase demanded by the union to support a wage hike, if it could be assured that it would "give the poor baker a possibility to work a human work day, but it seems as if the goal of the union is to enrich the profits of its union bosses."[20]

The uptown cooperative movement survived only until April 1904. Its quick demise was due more to its inability to gain a large base of constantly committed followers than to its grief from Bakers Union leadership. The Harlem Co-op and, for that matter, all New York Jewish operations of that sort and era failed because few immigrant families on the Lower East Side, or in the working-class section of Harlem, ever accumulated sufficient assured income to invest in a cooperative venture. And even if they had the money to join the movement, most householders found it simply more convenient to purchase their necessities of life from private storekeepers who were often known to extend such important personal services as credit to steady customers during periods of acute individual financial crisis.[21]

Harlem-based radicals learned the hard lesson that mass enthusiasm for consumerism at one particular time of efflorescence was not easily translated into an enduring grassroots protest movement. There were too many half-hearted folks who had to be convinced time and again of what street activities could mean for them. The only food consumer activities undertaken in Harlem after the dissolution of its branch of the New York Industrial Cooperative were, as it turned out, those of the Bakers Union Local No. 305, which also established several temporary cooperative bakery and grocery stores during its strike periods.[22]

Meanwhile, as baker unionists endeavored through strikes and protests to assure their permanence in Harlem, one of their nagging concerns was that almost every success against the bosses caused many unorganized downtown workers to migrate uptown to reap the benefits of so-called "union conditions." Harlem bakery owners capitalized on this newly created oversupply of labor by reneging on numerous agreements. Scabs replaced union members in many shops and unemployment mounted among those committed to the local. Union membership dropped off sharply and leaders feared that conditions that had previously blocked their efforts downtown were being duplicated in Harlem.[23]

Bakers Union officials responded to this threat with a propaganda campaign about the benefits of collective action aimed at all uptown workers. More important, they lent their support to new sibling efforts on the Lower East Side. They argued logically that if "union conditions" could be achieved in the old neighborhood, it would halt, or at least mitigate, the flow of workers uptown that so threatened their hard-won gains. Harlem labor leaders thus committed themselves to work closely with comrades in several downtown initiatives in 1905 and ultimately in the successful organization efforts of 1909. Through such efforts, Harlem bakers affirmed the close interdependence of Jewish proletarian groups in every section of New York.[24]

During these same early years of the twentieth century, a similar spirit of comradeship obtained between immigrant protesters downtown and in Harlem when they took to the streets of their neighborhoods over rent increases that the poor could not handle. The *Forward* proclaimed loudly, "this strike can be as great as the meat strikes," and called upon Jewish women "to take the rent question into their hands as they did the meat question." In this "great folk struggle"—as the newspaper called the uprising—the small resident associations that were formed in Harlem in March 1904 to resist the rent-gouging practices of some uptown landlords were inspired by brother and sister downtown tenement dwellers who a few weeks earlier had initiated their own rent strike. Those who dwelled on the Lower East Side had been moved to action when real estate operators, who were castigated as "landlord czars," attempted to increase rents in the ever-diminishing stock of formerly cheap old-style tenements. Agitations to fight against high rents quickly spread over to Brownsville and from there to Harlem and even to some sections of the South Bronx.[25]

Most of the initial East Harlem committees were formed on an ad hoc basis as residents of a single building facing rent hikes joined together. Committee members solicited contributions from fellow tenants and lawyers were engaged to represent their interests. When landlords were successful in obtaining court orders directing occupants to pay their rents, strikers often responded by organizing the complete evacuation of the affected buildings. Picket lines soon appeared as efforts were made to stop owners from securing new tenants. In one incident, this maneuver led to violence between residents and real estate people in Harlem and police officers had to clear protestors from a strike-bound property.[26]

Support from every local socialist organization and some labor groups also buoyed the uptown rent strikers. With the Workmen's Circle in the lead, they pitched the specific fight as responsive to the general problem of landlord oppression of helpless workers. This assertion was among the angry sentiments expressed at a mass rally at the Harlem Terrace meeting hall in April 1904 as plans were set for the creation of a district-wide rent strike headquarters. A coalition of activist groups called upon all Harlem residents desirous of organizing against their landlords to appeal to their good offices for assistance and redress of grievances.[27]

When the Harlem rent strike ended several weeks later, socialists across the city proclaimed it a success. Like the meat protest, this agitation that again tied uptown and downtown Jews in a common cause had garnered frequent front-page coverage in the *Forward*. Cahan's newspaper linked the two events to the ongoing struggles of labor. It declared, "the meat strike was a child of the trade strikes . . . and the rent strike, in turn, comes from the same source." However, notwithstanding this temporary euphoria, the problem of rent gouging did not end. Some three and a half years later, in January 1908, Harlem tenement dwellers were back out on the streets as they joined a new wave of rent strikes that reportedly "spread like wildfire over all the poor quarters of New York." The 1908 battles over rent were far more organized than were the

1904 disturbances. Some ad hoc neighborhood tenant groups did rise on their own and conducted localized activities, such as the one that residents living at the intersection of 100th Street and Second Avenue pushed forward. But most of the Harlem-based activities were under the control and ideological influence of a coalition of five Jewish radical organizations that joined forces to form the Anti-High Rent Socialist League of Harlem. Most uptown tenement folks looked to the league for leadership to help them force landlords to reduce rentals.[28]

The district-wide umbrella organization was composed of the ever-present Branch No. 2 of the Workmen's Circle, the 26th Assembly District Socialist Party, that Lodzer lodge (which was destined to join the Arbeter Ring), the Socialist Territorialists, and the Group Charmigal—a socialist literary organization. In the few days between the start of the strike and the subsequent calling of the conference, three of the five participating organizations were deemed by the *Forward* to be "the leading spirit of the strike." But it seems that these groups were able to set aside the question of who was in charge for concentrated efforts on behalf of Harlem consumers.[29]

So disposed, the League decided at its organizational meeting of January 5, 1908, to appoint a nine-person committee to coordinate strike activities. Working from its headquarters at Madison Avenue between 104th and 105th Streets, representatives were sent throughout the neighborhood to convince the Jews of Harlem of the merits of the agitation. The organization also called for mass meetings to publicize the strike's objectives and collected money to pay whatever legal fees arose out of eviction litigation. The rent unrest lasted more than a month and affected more than forty-five different tenement houses, the majority of them located in the working-class section east of Third Avenue, south of 105th Street.[30]

Neighboring Italian tenement dwellers applauded Jewish agitation in their areas and they appealed to the League for assistance in conducting their own limited tenant protests. On January 8, 1908, a committee that represented the radical Italian newspaper *Il Momento* turned to the Jewish association, suggesting that the two immigrant groups work for common objectives against landlords. The Italian delegation was warmly received and several tenants who had been evicted from their homes received money from the Jewish socialist organization to find new accommodations. Five days later, the *Forward* reported that a "great spurt" of rent-strike activity had hit the Italian uptown quarter, where mass meetings were being held. The activities of the League also attracted the attention of non-Jewish tenement dwellers in the South Bronx. On January 11, 1908, the uptown socialist group was invited to help form an organization similar to itself in the outlying borough. The League decided to work with the Bronx German Socialist Party in organizing its neighborhood forces.[31]

For the largest contingent of Harlem's Jewish workers—namely, construction laborers with their multiple trades and skills—the control of rents where they lived was unquestionably a laudable goal. And they surely cheered the efforts of the Arbeter Ring and its comrade organizations to bring down prices. But their most pressing housing concerns had to do with finding and maintaining work in the neighborhoods' tenements and apartment houses. From almost the start of their arrival uptown in the 1890s, the ethnically exclusive Irish-dominated construction unions controlled employment opportunities in the new building area. Few Jews were ever able to secure the union card needed to secure work in that employment field. Scabbing for "lumpers"—never a profitable practice—became increasingly more difficult after 1900 as the unions grew in strength. The only major concession on membership granted to Jewish workers by the established construction unions during this early period was the admission of one thousand east European Jews to the rolls of the Amalgamated Painters' Union in 1901.[32]

Excluded from the new building arena, Jewish laborers settled for lower-paying alteration work and after a while began to agitate for better pay through their own unions. After one false start in 1907, the first Alteration Painters' Union, which included members from a variety of construction trades, was formed in Harlem in 1910. The uptown-based brotherhood quickly gained recognition from the United Hebrew Trades. The movement that started in Harlem soon extended to sibling branches in other parts of New York City and nearby towns. In 1911, the five alteration locals, representing in theory some twenty thousand workers, 75 percent of whom were Jewish, were federated as the International Painters' and Paperhangers' Union.[33]

The new International's first major effort began in June 1913 when uptown Local No. 1 joined with affiliated groups on the Lower East Side and Brooklyn in developing plans for a citywide strike of New York builders. The major goals of the proposed labor action were to be the unionization of fifteen thousand "exploited" workers and the establishment of "union conditions" in all metropolitan building projects. Just two years earlier, in 1911, the American Federation of Labor (AFL) found in studying the conditions of alteration workers that they earned on average only $3.28 a day as opposed to the $5.00 earned by new building construction workers. To address the wage-scale issue aggressively, three strike headquarters were established: at Delancey Street on the Lower East Side, Grand Street in Williamsburg, and Branch No. 2 of the Workmen's Circle in East Harlem. Once again, the fraternal and educational organization helped spearhead pressing working-class issues. The sibling centers uptown, downtown, and in Brooklyn were each charged with organizing members for a projected August general strike.[34]

The general strike was called during the second week in August and, by the end of the month, the sympathetic *Forward* triumphantly announced that two hundred bosses had already settled with the union. Two days later, the newspaper reported that so many employers had come to strike headquarters to settle with the workers that a set schedule of appointments had to be arranged for labor leaders to be able to meet with all the bosses who wished to capitulate. Less than two weeks later, it was announced that the strike had been settled and that "union shop" conditions had been achieved. All workers returning to their jobs had to—according to this report—obtain union permits to retain their employment.[35]

For union leaders, the only disquieting feature of the strike was the antagonistic attitude that the established AFL Brotherhood of Painters displayed towards their fellow workers who were on the picket lines. This federation of non-Jewish, new-building construction unions had sent out scabs to undermine the efforts of alteration workers. The Yiddish press contended that fear of competition and racial hatred had motivated their actions. Relations between the unions continued to deteriorate for over a year as each group persisted in scabbing against the other. Finally, in 1914, after years of difficulties and a short period of intense official conflict, an amalgamation was achieved linking Jewish and non-Jewish construction workers. The International became a local in the Brotherhood of Painters.[36]

This alliance did not, however, automatically reverse the course of Jewish-Irish relations in the building trades. After all, beyond these workday encounters, there was much bad blood between the two groups, particularly between neighborhood youths. The official pledges of unity and cooperation did not filter down to many of the laboring rank and file. Many Irish painters, according to published reports from Jewish sources, still felt "race hatred and economic competition . . . hurt the effectiveness of the union." In an attempt to reduce points of inter-group conflict, union leaders arranged in April 1915 for a meeting between International and Brotherhood factions "to promote understanding and unity among workers."[37]

In the realm of organizing consumer and real estate protests, uptown and downtown, activists frequently took cues from one another. In the struggle for unionization, what happened first uptown—among bakers and construction workers greatly affected Lower East Side labor developments. However, in the sphere of politics—finding ways and means to elect socialist candidates to office—it was Harlem's radical Jews who learned valuable lessons from downtown and followed their siblings' lead.

With good reasons, radical activists in the immigrant hub felt that they controlled the streets. It has been said with much authority that large, attentive audiences heard and resonated with their messages on almost a daily basis from street corner lecturers who held forth on soapboxes. Literary nights and poetry readings had many enthusiastic devotees. Far from passive observers, listeners in coffee houses, labor lyceums, and radical group clubhouses often interjected their own views about what Marxism, anarchism, and worker movements of all sorts really meant. And even more immigrant Jews imbibed socialism through the *Forward* and other provocative newspapers that critiqued unmercifully all that was wrong with the capitalist system. And then there were the myriad of journals that addressed the issues of the day. With these outlets and venues, "large numbers of people lived socialism in the streets, parks and halls of New York."[38]

Thus, with the masses seemingly under their sway, radical parties often perceived the weeks before elections in turn-of-the-century New

York as prime times for palpable optimism. Here it seemed were the moments where they would be rewarded for their advocacy of so many neighborhood causes. They would capitalize upon large-scale turnouts from people who had benefitted from the consumer and labor strikes that they had successfully championed. Cahan's lieutenant, *Forward* editor Hillel [Harry] Rogoff, would later recall "during the campaign weeks the East Side districts rocked with socialist agitation. The Socialist candidates were hailed as Messiahs. The open-air meetings were monster demonstrations of public confidence and affection. The marvels of the socialist strength would grow until the day of the elections." But then came the political moment of truth. "During the twelve hours between the opening of the polls and their closing, the strength would melt away." The electorate, to Rogoff's utter dismay, was impressed with what the radicals had to say and was grateful for what they had orchestrated on the Jewish quarter's behalf. But they did not return the favor with their ballots.[39]

These frustrating results once caused Louis Miller, editor of the *Warheit*—which competed against the *Forward* for readers—to exclaim, "Socialism seems so clear, simple and logical to us that only a dunce or a scoundrel could fail to understand it." But in fact, the movement's failures were due to several closely related and intelligible factors. First, those who actively pushed the socialist message possessed a "disciplined commitment" to the cause, which meant that they were ready "to pay dues, attend meetings, hand out literature." And most critically, they were willing to vote for candidates that stood outside of the nation's mainstream. But the overwhelming majority of downtown Jews ultimately wanted to be perceived as in lockstep with America. In other words, for so many of these new citizens, a vote for a Socialist or Socialist Labor candidate was a statement of some degree of separatism from this country's political system. And sometimes, it was deemed downright unpatriotic to step forward to support radical platforms. At the same time, the very courting of the Jewish vote by Republicans and Democrats alike was an implicit message of acceptance and a promise of integration for the new Americans.[40]

Indeed, while the Irish certainly dominated Tammany Hall—that great, overarching New York political machine—these wise and crafty leaders recognized the "Hebrew residents and their language" and when useful, they placed Jews on the ticket in the Jewish section of town. As important, even as Socialist newspapers pilloried people like Big Tim Sullivan for buying votes and corrupting elections, Jewish voters remembered how Tammany bought its constituents free turkeys at holiday time along with food baskets, not to mention the machine's street advocacy, such as stopping Irish gangs from attacking push cart peddlers. Meanwhile, Socialist candidates did not do enough nuts and bolts politicking to galvanize support come Election Day.[41]

Then there were the deep reservations Jewish immigrants had about radical candidates because the Socialist Party advocated a form of ideological orthodoxy that in one crucial area ran directly against their own personal and family interests. Socialists in America of all stripes and backgrounds always had serious problems with unrestricted immigration. In their worldview, while possessing the utmost humanitarian and fraternal concern about the fate of immigrant workers, they also saw these new Americans as ready scabs that capitalists easily coopted against labor agitations. Most Jews, on the other hand, could not support such an ideologically driven position that if ever adopted as national policy might mean that a relative or friend would be turned away from the United States. This fundamental difference of opinion also kept Jews from pulling radical candidates' levers.

Perhaps in some families, the choice among Democratic, Republican, and Socialist candidates was a complex matter as husbands and wives contemplated whether visionary radicalism or pragmatic American politics was best for them. After all, when it came to consumer protests, it was the women who occupied the streets to drive down prices and thus risked arrest, much more than did the men. If the women of the house had been given the chance, they may well have been more likely to support the cause at the ballot boxes. But suffrage was denied to them in New York State until 1917.[42]

The problems radical candidates faced in trying to win and maintain Jewish voter support was played out most dramatically from 1908 to 1914, when a series of attempts were made to unseat Henry M. Goldfogle, the Democrat from the Lower East Side's 9th Congressional District. First up, in 1908, for the Socialist Party was famous labor lawyer Morris Hillquit, who took on an incumbent whom Tammany proclaimed was "not *a* Jewish Congressman but *the* Jewish Congressman." And indeed,

Goldfogle in his three prior terms in Washington had earned his community bona fides as a champion of his people's interests, including in the ongoing battle over open immigration.[43]

Hillquit, on the other hand, ran not as a Jewish candidate but as a representative of the working class. For him, the "issues thus defined by the Socialist Party in its national platform are also the issues in this Congressional District of New York." So positioned, on the crucial question of open immigration, this "no special interests" candidate adopted the party's "straddling" position of preaching the solidarity of all workers, native and foreign born alike, while at the same time favoring immigration limits to protect the needs of American workers.

Hillquit was vilified in the Yiddish press for this unyielding stance. For example, "Where was Morris Hillquit?" was the refrain from Miller's *Warheit* as it enumerated the many times the community went to the streets in defense of Jewish interests and the candidate was nowhere to be found. Stung by such criticisms, Hillquit struggled mightily to find a way to stay loyal to his conception of the socialist leadership mission and his need to somehow court voters by addressing their Jewish needs. He tried to explain away the party's opposition to "undesirable immigration" as not applying to Jews. And he reinforced his stance that socialism's humanitarianism ensured that doors would stay open "especially for sufferers of economic exploitation, race and political attacks, refugees like the Russian Jews." He prayed that the electorate would understand that in the end socialism was their best friend since it fought valiantly against "the abuse of immigrants." However, Hillquit's apologia did not silence his critics nor swing the election his way. In 1908, Goldfogle trounced him and three other candidates, garnering more than 52 percent of the vote.

Out of the Socialist Party's bitter defeat emerged a change in stance and a new candidate in the following congressional election. Next up was another well-known labor lawyer and advocate, Meyer London. He was consistently outspoken in his opposition to any sort of immigration restriction. Additionally, to win at the polls, London said that, if elected, he would not only be the representative of the working class but of Jewish "storekeepers and businessmen," as well. One observer of this new strategy commented, "the keynote of the campaign was 'split for London.'" In other words, a strong pitch was made to voters who might back

Democratic candidates in statewide and national contests to vote for the nondoctrinaire London in the 9th Congressional District. Reportedly, as the campaign proceeded, "race prejudice was appealed to, nationality was appealed to, and, in fact, everything except the class consciousness of the voters." So positioned, in 1910, Meyer London ran well ahead of Hillquit and any prior Socialist Party congressional candidate and closed Goldfogle's gap.[44] And in 1914, in an atmosphere where Progressive politics in general were given a favorable hearing among America voters, the Jews of the Lower East Side, workers, storekeepers, and business people alike, sent London to Congress to represent them.[45]

Jewish Socialists in Harlem followed the trials and triumphs of their comrades in their electoral battles on the Lower East Side with great interest. For the longest time, they too were unable to translate neighborhood support for their consumer and labor agitations into power at the polls. From 1900 to 1914, Socialist Party candidates lagged badly behind the Democratic designees and their persistent Republican challengers. Most notably, East Harlem's 16th and its later reapportioned 20th Congressional Districts were represented during these years by Jacob Ruppert Jr., the local beer magnate, and his successor, Francis Burton Harrison, both loyal sons of Tammany Hall.[46]

The political fortunes of Harlem's Socialists began to change with the election of 1914. In that year, Republican Isaac Siegel won with but an 80-vote margin and ended Democratic control of the neighborhood's House seat. His victory, coming in a year which saw his party gain control of the New York State congressional delegation, was still quite remarkable because he beat a proven vote getter, old-time Harlem worthy Jacob Cantor, who took over Harrison's place when the congressman resigned in 1913 to become governor-general of the Philippines. Siegel's victory was fashioned through his capturing of the predominantly Jewish 24th and 26th Assembly Districts by more than 150 votes, offsetting Cantor's pluralities in the major Italian parts of East Harlem. Tammany's grip over the uptown electorate seemed to be on the wane. Of perhaps greater significance for the Jewish Socialists was the fine performance of their candidate, who received over 1,000 votes in the Jewish neighborhood. But most importantly, they paid close attention to London's triumph over Goldfogle downtown. Energized and optimistic, early in 1916 party activists met to draw up plans for duplicating London's victory in their neighborhood, touching off a spirited intra-ethnic debate over what type of Jewish representative was best qualified to serve his people in Congress.[47]

Learning from the downtown experience—where in support of London, Socialists finally did the hard work of street politicking—uptown activists strove to increase registration rolls dramatically to defeat both Siegel and the Tammany machine. Party officials established a Socialist Party Naturalization Committee mandated to make citizens out of aliens who would "have the right to take part in the elections this year." Naturalization classes were set up at the Workmen's Circle Labor Lyceum to help immigrants pass their citizenship tests.[48]

In February 1916, again taking their cues from what had worked on the Lower East Side, the Harlem Socialist Party put together a 20th Congressional District Campaign Committee. Uptown leaders directed an early effort to canvass the neighborhood to alert Socialist sympathizers to the great electoral struggle ahead. A similar district-wide canvass was taken early in July to ascertain the strength of the party's appeal.[49]

These activities were, however important, only preliminaries to the crucial question of who would be their standard-bearer. They wanted a charismatic candidate like London to spread the message to uptown audiences. In late July, the party turned to none other than Morris Hillquit. But in many ways, it was a different Morris Hillquit, one who—like his backers—had learned much from his defeat some eight years earlier. Now the candidate projected himself as the Jew best fit to represent the interests of all Jews in the House of Representatives. Careful to abandon the demonstrative character of previous campaigns, with its heavy emphasis on ideology, Hillquit's workers concentrated on the practical side of politics. They twice canvassed those who had previously voted to increase Socialist Party registration. Four major New York unions, some with branches in Harlem, did more than their share, as leaders of the International Ladies' Garment Workers Union and the cap makers', furriers', and bakers' unions along with the Jewish Socialist Federation agreed to sell twenty-five thousand stamps valued at ten to twenty-five cents each to their membership to help finance the Hillquit campaign. While his operatives worked the streets, on the stump, Hillquit vigorously attacked Siegel, especially the incumbent's voting record on the immigration question.[50]

Standing now foursquare as an opponent of restriction, Hillquit blasted Siegel's approach to the Burnett literacy test bill of 1915. Recognizing the growing strength of anti-immigrant sentiment in the Congress, Siegel and his fellow Jewish representative Adolph Sabath had drafted an amendment to this act which provided that all refugees from religious persecution be exempted from the proposed literacy test. Socialist opponents of this compromise saw the move as doing "great harm to the immigrant by easing the way for passage of the bill." The Siegel-Sabath amendment was ultimately defeated and the Burnett bill was passed without serious modification. The Jewish congressmen's efforts did, however, help convince President Wilson to fight the legislation. His veto delayed its final passage until 1917. New York's Socialist press, nevertheless, harangued the local East Harlem representative for what it saw as the insufficiency of his efforts on behalf of immigrants. Leading the chorus of critics was Morris Hillquit, who emphasized his deep sensitivity to Jewish group concerns.[51]

Democratic candidate Bernard Rosenblatt also criticized Siegel's stance on Jewish issues. Tammany Hall's designee was well known in uptown Zionist circles for his service as honorary secretary of the Federation of American Zionists. This American-born, Columbia University–educated lawyer was also president of Zion Commonwealth Inc.—a group that beginning in 1914 purchased lands in Palestine for Jewish settlement—and a member of the newly formed Executive Committee of the American Jewish Congress Organizing Committee. An intensely nationalistic Jewish leader, at a time when American Zionism was beginning to enter the consciousness of Jewish immigrants and especially their children, Rosenblatt charged that Siegel had "no definite principles in matters Jewish." And while he, Rosenblatt, supported "every humanitarian move in favor of Jews," Siegel was not "fully aware of the needs of the Jewish people." Rosenblatt further accused Siegel of taking his marching orders in Jewish affairs from "men like Louis Marshall," the German American Jewish eminence who commanded the anti-Zionist American Jewish Committee, which did "not express the needs of the Jewish masses." And while Rosenblatt did not directly criticize the incumbent's performance on the immigration question, he was nonetheless moved to comment, "Siegel's activities . . . found him lacking independent judgment."[52]

Rosenblatt's supporters were even more critical of his Socialist opponent. They characterized Hillquit as a "well-known socialist lawyer and able labor advocate who was more or less indifferent to matters Jewish, being an acknowledged representative of class issues." Hillquit's critics did not comment on his late-in-the-day conversion to activist work on the immigration question. Rosenblatt, in the opinion of those who backed him, was the only nominee "with a clear conception" of the dilemmas "facing the Jews" and possessed the "personal power to advocate them."[53]

Siegel, for his part, was not without weapons in defending himself against political attacks. He presented himself to the voters as the individual most intimately acquainted with the local needs of residents of East Harlem and as the Jewish candidate best prepared to lead their community within the country's political mainstream. His supporters depicted Siegel, who was born in New York City in 1880 and earned his law degree from New York University in 1901, as a self-made man. This son of Russian Jewish immigrants had gained his first elective office when he defeated Jacob Cantor in 1914.[54]

Siegel counterattacked by asserting that Hillquit was nothing more than a political carpetbagger imported from the Lower East Side who had little knowledge of the issues that uptown Jews faced. He further contended that the Socialist's advocacy of economic and social policies inimical to American ideals made him an ill-advised choice to represent an immigrant community in the halls of the House. Siegel's supporters argued that it was important "that Jewish voters send a Jewish representative to Congress from a Jewish quarter who is an American, a man in whom Americanization is solidly engrained with the spirit of the land." They warned that sending a man to Washington who "desires to overturn the system of society and whose chief goal is to destroy the order upon which this government is built" would certainly cast doubt upon "the patriotism of the American Jews." One critic of Hillquit suggested that the election was a fundamental struggle between the "respectable element" and the "dirt-slingers and trouble makers" within the immigrant Jewish group. With specific reference to the incumbent's performance on the immigrant-law issue, Siegel's supporters went so far as to warn that if the congressman's naturalized constituents failed to return him to this seat, it would indicate to some Americans that his immigrant district actually supported the imposition of a literacy test.[55]

Responding to Rosenblatt's attack that the congressman was not sufficiently Jewish in his outlook, Siegel's supporters repeatedly riposted that "Isaac Siegel is the only American Jewish Congressman who reads and writes Yiddish." And far from denying their candidate's close connection with Louis Marshall and other worthies of the American Jewish Committee, Siegel was depicted as the choice of "the best element in American Judaism." Indeed, he welcomed Marshall's presence at public rallies and constantly solicited his active participation in the campaign. Marshall responded with an open letter of support for Siegel's reelection that was published in several New York Jewish newspapers. Marshall was "shocked" into this particular action by his distress over Zionist contentions that Rosenblatt was "entitled to the suffrage of the Jewish electorate . . . because he is a nationalist."[56]

As this spirited campaign, described by one observer as of "a great cultural-political character," reached its conclusion, local Jewish newspapers supporting each of the contenders confidently explained why their man was certain of victory. The *Forward* pointed to the dramatic increase of 42 percent in the number of registered voters in the district as proof of Hillquit's impending triumph. Most of these new voters were deemed "workers under socialist influence." The newly established *American Jewish Chronicle* counted on Rosenblatt's nationalistic profile to insure him the win. And the politically conservative *Morning Journal* declared that Siegel was a "Republican candidate in a Republican year in a district where the younger element, which is majority Republican every year grown stronger." A week before the election, the *Forward*—which more than reporting the news, had helped run Hillquit's campaign—proclaimed optimistically that "the residents of Harlem have never been as interested in a campaign as they are today. The thought that Morris Hillquit will be their representative has raised great spirits and a new life. . . . The slumbering uptown masses have come alive with Morris Hillquit." To get its point further across, the *Forward* promoted a campaign march through the tenement district of Harlem the Saturday before Election Day. The newspaper laid out the line of the procession, with the "first division" stepping off at 84th Street and Second Avenue and the "second division" starting out at 104th Street and Second Avenue, with both contingents of backers gathering for campaign speeches at 106th Street and Second Avenue. On the day before the election the *Forward* ran a banner headline stating, "Harlem: The Whole World Is Watching," indicating that for Cahan, Rogoff, and many of their associates there was much more at stake than a single seat in the House. Rather, a victory over two major party candidates uptown—after the great downtown triumph of 1914—would be a harbinger of future Socialist Party successes throughout the United States as the two New York socialist sibling communities showed the way.[57]

When the ballots were counted, Siegel emerged as the victor by a plurality of less than 500 votes over Hillquit and 700 votes over Rosenblatt out of some 12,000 ballots cast. The incumbent retained his seat, but the Socialist Party made an impressive showing. Hillquit garnered some 3,945 votes, close to four times the number attracted to his party's line in any previous election. More importantly, he had actually outpolled his two opponents in the predominantly Jewish areas. He received 36 percent of the vote in the 24th A.D. and 45 percent in the 26th A.D., which included most of East Harlem south of 119th Street and east of Fifth Avenue. Siegel ran second in the Jewish neighborhoods and Rosenblatt trailed. In the end, Siegel was able to offset Hillquit's lead in the Jewish districts by soundly defeating his Socialist challenger in the predominantly Italian 28th A.D. Italian voters proved to be decisive, giving Siegel an 800-vote margin over Hillquit. When the votes were analyzed, it became apparent that Hillquit had won the battle for the Jewish vote but lost the electoral war.[58]

Two years later, after an unsuccessful bid in 1917 to capture the New York mayoralty, Hillquit once again went up against Siegel for his coveted congressional seat. This time both major parties, in the words of Hillquit, "quietly laid aside all pretense of rivalry" and supported the incumbent as a fusion candidate. The 1918 election was in many ways a repeat of the earlier contest as Siegel dominated the non-Jewish districts—defeating Hillquit by almost a three-to-one margin—while Hillquit held, and even increased, his strength in the Jewish areas. The two contestants met for a final time in 1920 and the now familiar pattern was once again repeated. Siegel defeated Hillquit by some 3,700 votes among Italian voters, offsetting the Socialist's lead of 700 votes in the Jewish areas.[59]

In 1922, Siegel retired from Congress and the Republicans nominated Fiorello La Guardia in his stead. La Guardia gained election after a bitterly contested fight against Democrat Henry Frank. The battled turned ugly when Frank alleged publicly that his opponent was a "pronounced anti-Semite." Offended, while at the same time understanding how it might be used to his political advantage, the Republican candidate—born of a Jewish mother and a lapsed Catholic father—called for a debate over his alleged "Jew-hatred." The battle would be conducted entirely in Yiddish. His Jewish Democratic adversary could not speak his own people's vernacular. Soon a Yiddish newspaper chimed in on behalf of the "Little Flower," characterizing the Italian American as pro-Zionist, knowledgeable of Jewish history, an enemy of anti-Semitism, and a friend who "speaks Yiddish like a true Jew." Amid this battle between major party candidates, the Socialist designee, William Karlin, ran a poor third, losing many of Hillquit's supporters in the Jewish sections of East Harlem and receiving little backing elsewhere. The momentum of Hillquit's candidacy could not be transferred to any less glamorous replacement.[60]

Meanwhile, in the mid-1910s, within their own cultural milieu in East Harlem, groups of devout Orthodox Jews, under the guidance of immigrant rabbis, attempted to create a separatist religious community for themselves and their children comparable to what had begun to emerge two decades earlier among their brethren on the Lower East Side. And, much like their religious siblings downtown, as uptown initiatives unfolded—specifically in the educational realm—Orthodox leaders proved to be of several minds over how resistant they should be to the Americanization of their youngsters.

While many radicals in the old Jewish quarter dissented vociferously from their ancestral faith, many more downtowners merely drifted away from traditional religious practices. To some extent, their deviations began while they were still in eastern Europe as, for example, working on the Sabbath to survive economically became increasingly prevalent in the Pale of Settlement. The social pressure that once obtained in the shtetls, where it was said that "if one should dare in a little town in Russia to keep his store open on the Sabbath, he would probably have to close it the rest of the week," simply no longer was the rule of life in the more open, burgeoning, and confusing urban areas of the region. In America, many more Jews went to their factories and stores on holy days not merely to survive but to advance in the new country. Of course, much of the folk traditions survived transplantation to America. Central Jewish holidays—like Rosh Hashanah, Yom Kippur, and Passover—were widely observed, as were many of the kosher laws among Jews who had yet to partake of American culinary options. However, the children born on this side showed a far greater ambivalence concerning Judaism's strictures than their parents, which caused contemporary observers to worry a great deal about the future of what was then called "the rising generation in Israel." After all, if nothing else, the public schools—those same Temples of Americanization that radicals reviled for their own reasons—inculcated disrespect for parental religious cultures. And the one-room Jewish schoolhouses did little to inspire the boys and few girls who reluctantly attended classes.[61]

Amid an era when "tradition [was] at half mast," a small coterie of deeply committed Orthodox Jews attempted to hold back the tide of disaffection, at least for themselves and their families. Their dream was to re-create on the Lower East Side major parts of the civilization that they remembered from the old side. For them, the key institution was the yeshiva, a school that would shelter young men from the ills and lures of the public schools and raise an elite of budding Torah scholars who would be models for all to emulate. In 1886, such an endeavor began with the founding of Yeshiva Etz Chaim, an elementary school for boys that exposed its pupils to extensive religious training and just the bare minimum of the "three Rs" that the State of New York mandated. Of all people, Abraham Cahan was the first teacher of general studies at the Orthodox school. He moonlighted there until it was discovered what his political views were and he was summarily discharged. In 1897, building on this foundation, an advanced program was established along the east European model under the auspices of the Yeshiva Rabbi Isaac Elchanan. In due course, by 1903, this school ordained its first rabbis, sending them out to service the immigrant generation and perhaps to inspire their children.

However, even as the school prided itself on its learned graduates, already early in the new century, voices were heard within and without the institution that criticized its mission and methodologies. Frankly, very few families, even devout ones, opted for a school that was ill equipped to prepare their charges for life in America. Not all of the graduates would choose careers in the rabbinate. Many more desired someday to be both knowledgeable Jews and skilled American businessmen or professionals. At that point, a vigorous debate began in Orthodox circles—which would last for generations—over how much of the religious and what of the secular should be offered in yeshivas to attract youngsters away from public education.[62]

It was precisely at that time, in 1907, that Harlem's yeshiva community entered the discussion, when members of two local congregations, Beth Hamidrash Ha-Godol of Harlem and Beth Knesset of Harlem opened Yeshiva Rabbi Elijah Gaon M'Vilna out of a public hall on Madison Avenue near 104th Street. Certainly most of the Beth Hamidrash people were well aware of developments downtown since they had been members of the famous Norfolk Street Synagogue and, reportedly, when some two thirds of them moved to Harlem, a branch was organized without the acrimony that plagued Kehal Adath Jeshurun of Eldridge Street. In any event, school leaders hired Rabbi Moses Sterman of Suwalk, Russo-Poland, as *rosh yeshiva* (dean) and gave him a mandate that was very reminiscent of Etz Chaim's original mission, to create a school that would show that "American boys can learn Gemara [Talmud] as well as European boys."[63]

The instructions to Rabbi Sterman were, however, quickly called into question when an insurgent group of financial backers—perhaps attuned to the downtown debate—demanded that instruction be conducted in English and that a more diversified curriculum, including biblical, Hebraic, and general studies, be offered, with Talmud remaining as a subject primarily "for appearance sake." They also went far beyond what change advocates contemplated on the Lower East Side when they insisted that girls be granted admission. Contretemps between factions within the boardroom quickly led to an institutional split with those who wanted the old ways going off and establishing Yeshiva Toras Hayim.[64]

For the first three years of its existence, Yeshiva Toras Hayim held its classes at Beth Hamidrash Ha-Godol of Harlem. An advertisement that appeared in a local Yiddish newspaper illustrates the tone of education at the school. It was looking specifically for teachers who "must be able to teach a *blat* [page] of Gemara and keep order in the classroom." In 1912, now boasting more than four hundred students, Yeshiva Toras Hayim built its own school building at 103rd Street and Lexington Avenue. The yeshiva received financial assistance from Beth Hamidrash Ha-Godol and a smaller congregation, the Bressler synagogue, evidently operated by Rabbi Noah Zeev Bressler, who also served as dean of the new school.[65]

A couple avenues to the west, Yeshiva Rabbi Elijah Gaon M'Vilna reconstituted itself as Yeshiva D'Harlem. Dropping the demand that girls be included in the student body, the school's curriculum offered a day where half of the time was used studying traditional texts and the other half was devoted to general studies. Much like in a public school, an hour was set aside for physical training. Dr. Alexander Brody, a local Jewish public school principal—one of the first of his kind of moonlighting professionals—was engaged to run the yeshiva's general studies program. His religious counterpart was Rabbi Sterman, which only suggests that he agreed with the more modern education program envisioned for the school. In the years before World War I, Yeshiva D'Harlem joined Rabbi Jacob Joseph School of Henry Street on the Lower East Side, Yeshiva Chaim Berlin of Brownsville, and Mesivta Torah Vodaath of Williamsburg as the first American yeshivas committed to dual programs of education.[66]

Meanwhile, even as the staunchly Orthodox Jews in Harlem attempted to come to grips with the question of how resistant they might be to American teachings as they attempted to raise a new generation of devout disciples, in another part of uptown—actually only a few blocks away in this crowded district where different types of Jews and their ideas constantly bumped into each other—another group of east European–born religious spokespeople tackled an equally challenging, if very different dilemma: how to engage the masses of young people who had become estranged from their parents' old-world religious and cultural values and to instill in the acculturated and American born an enduring commitment to Jewish identification. In developing their plans to harmonize American with traditional Jewish ideals, they made common cause with some of the city's, and indeed the nation's, most renowned German American leaders. This alliance between accommodating Orthodox Jews with Reform lay counterparts facilitated the building of important neighborhood educational institutions. But their joint efforts were not universally applauded. Critics within the neighborhood wondered whether these self-appointed activists who had risen out of their own streets and backgrounds truly understood and were still sensitive to their erstwhile community's values.

PREPARING FOR CHILDREN'S SABBATH SERVICE — BOYS AND GIRLS PRACTICING SYNAGOGUE MELODIES AT THE UPTOWN TALMUD TORAH

Students at the Uptown Talmud Torah, circa 1917 (*The Jewish Communal Register of New York City, 1917–1918*).

5

Partners and Protests

Isaac Siegel's reaching out to Louis Marshall for his support during his 1916 reelection campaign and the renowned Jewish community leader's ready acquiescence came as no surprise to people like David A. Cohen and his son Elias. For more than a decade, Americanized east European Jews like them had partnered with Marshall and his elite crowd of central European extraction in a variety of neighborhood efforts. Marshall's ethnicity and his beliefs and practices as a Reform Jew and the Cohens' origins and commitment to Orthodox Judaism were no barrier to their partnership in attempts both to acculturate east European Jews and to inculcate in them a more positive approach to Jewish identification. Their prime focus was the young people who were growing up in the poor tenement district of East Harlem. However, their partnership was critiqued by those who questioned the motives of those leaders whom they saw as high-handed and insensitive in their initiatives. One angry protester even went outside of the law to make a dramatic point of dissent.

Collaborative efforts marked a milestone in the maturation of east European leadership in America. Some twenty years earlier—in the 1880s—the advocates of newcomer adjustment to this country's ways came almost exclusively from the ranks of those known as the "German Jewish" elite, even if some of the activists were of Sephardic ancestry. These were the men and women who chafed at what the appearance, speech, mores, and radical political aspirations of their "benighted brethren" were doing to the reputation of American Jews among their Christian neighbors in the city and nation. Even someone like Emma Lazarus, who sympathized with the plight Jews faced in trekking to America, referred to them as "the wretched refuse of your teeming shore" in her poem later famously inscribed on the Statue of Liberty. Certain that they "would be looked upon by our gentile neighbors as the natural sponsors for these our brethren," those with time and funds to address the communal crisis of mass migration created a network of institutions to both succor and transform the lives of those whom they saw as the denizens of the "desert of degradation and despair" of the Lower East Side.

Beyond providing the newcomers with charitable assistance and medical care and creating vocational schools, settlement house work—most notably that of the Educational Alliance on East Broadway and Jefferson Street—was deemed critically important Americanization work. Organized in 1889, through the cooperative efforts of a branch of the YMHA that was dedicated explicitly to leading the newcomers, along with the Hebrew Free School Association and the Aguilar Free Library, the Educational Alliance focused on fostering the allegiance of immigrants' children to American ways. Building on what the children learned in the public schools and how they were taught to behave in those classrooms, the settlement's afternoon, evening, weekend, and summer programs emphasized good citizenship and proper speech, sought to accelerate reading and writing skills, promoted physical training to offset canards that Jews were puny, and exposed students to how Americans danced and sang; not to mention, the Alliance provided its charges with healthy environments, including shower rooms and clean lavatories. Of critical importance to its founders, it was mandated when the institution was first opened that all activities had to be conducted in English. In their least charitable moments, backers of the Alliance were apt to denigrate the Jewish vernacular as "piggish jargon . . . language only understood by Polish and Russian Jews."

These policies created a yawning gap between the institution and the immigrant generation and accentuated the growing cultural divide between the older generation and their children, who liked so much of what the Alliance offered them. First-generation mothers and fathers—if they were of the religious bent—were also unmoved, if not offended, by the goings-on at the settlement's People's Synagogue. An idiosyncratic rabbi, Dr. Adolph Radin, who had studied in the famous Volozhin yeshiva in Lithuania before acquiring secular training at university in Berlin, conducted services using German, Hebrew, and English but not Yiddish. More than a decade would elapse before any real effort was made to reach the adults of the East Side through their own language, a sign of respect for their transplanted culture. Yiddish was first countenanced at the Educational Alliance at an event in 1897 when Radin invited a popular downtown preacher, Rabbi Zvi Hirsch Masliansky, to speak in his native tongue around the time that Radin started his Russian-American Hebrew Association. He was the founder, and the only officer, of a group that aimed "to exercise a civilizing and elevating influence upon the immigrant and to Americanize them."[1]

At that turn-of-the-century moment, a small group of elite east Europeans initiated their own system of formal, organized benevolence among their brethren and began speaking of the values of Americanization both on the Lower East Side and in Harlem. In other words, it took less than a generation for some Jewish immigrants to advance economically in this country and to adopt enough of American ways of thinking to emerge as self-designated spokespeople for other east European Jews. In some cases, such as with the establishing of the Hebrew Immigrant Aid Society or the Hebrew Free Loan Association, and most certainly at Beth Israel Hospital—all before 1900—institutions were founded as alternatives to "German efforts," which were critiqued for their insensitivity to their clients' or patients' religious and cultural mores. It would be in Harlem specifically, in the first decade of the new century, that leaders of both Jewish ethnicities joined hands in Americanization efforts.[2]

The first grand move towards working together began in 1905 with the creation of the Harlem Federation settlement house on 105th Street and Second Avenue. Much like the backstory of the Educational Alliance's founding a decade and a half earlier, it was the fear of missionary triumphs among street youngsters who were drawn into Christian afterschool centers that pushed community leaders to open their hearts, wallets, and pocketbooks. In December 1903, newspaper revelations of conversionists' widespread successes in "driving stakes in Harlem . . . saving souls in a new district with the usual display of affection for the Hebrews"—specifically young boys and girls "driven to the streets by congestion and the unsanitary conditions of the tenements"—shocked the community. In this atmosphere of crisis, Anglo-Jewish newspapers pilloried Jewish leaders for failing to create suitable Jewish alternatives for those who had left the Lower East Side. One critic pointedly accused those with the ability to make a difference in the neighborhood of being so intent on studying "ghetto conditions that they are apt to lose sight of that portion of the Jewish community which has emancipated itself therefrom and migrated to a more desirable part of Manhattan. We have regarded them as healthy minded, normal individuals who need no uplift."[3]

At that point, one of the few institutions on the scene to address this challenge was the uptown branch of Radin's Russian-American Hebrew Association. When he arrived uptown in 1895 and affiliated with a small central European congregation, Tikvath Israel—commuting, as it were, between his own sibling communities—he brought with him the Alliance's untempered approach to Americanization. In 1897, for example, Harlem members heard a variety of speakers who all upheld the virtues of rapid acculturation, speaking on such pointed topics as "The Mission of the Russian Jew in America" and "The Influence of the Puritans in this Country."[4]

During the next few years, two other downtown organizations that preached the virtues of acculturation and offered themselves as models of successful integration in this country relocated to Harlem. In 1901, the Chesterfield Club, a social organization "numbering in its ranks some of the best known businessmen," moved its club house from East Broadway to Upper Madison Avenue. A year later, the S.E.I. Club of the University Settlement, a society formed by "a dozen lawyers, as many public school teachers, successful salesmen and young men in other business activities" transferred its program "of debates, declarations and readings" from the downtown hub to Harlem. However, neither of these organizations showed the imagination to deal effectively with community problems on a large-scale basis. And then came the very troubling allegation that estimated that 7,500 Jewish youths were falling prey to Christian lures.[5]

Rising first to draft plans for battle was the Hebrew Educational Union, established in January 1904 under the leadership of Rabbi Maurice H. Harris. The Council of Jewish Women and the United Hebrew Charities assisted in the Union's endeavor as both citywide organizations sent representatives to planning meetings. The treasurer of the Union was Mrs. Lillie Cowen, wife of the editor of the *American Hebrew*, which gave constant support and favorable publicity to the group's plans. Philip Cowen did his utmost as president of the Washington Irving Lodge of the B'nai B'rith to convince his brothers to join the effort. In February

1905, he went so far as to call a conference of twelve Harlem lodges—the national fraternal organization had re-established its presence uptown—to impress upon them the severity of neighborhood conditions. Although several lodges did agree to send representatives to several open organizational meetings held later that month, none showed real enthusiasm for the labors at hand. More important to the success of the Union's efforts on the streets of Harlem, Rabbi Zvi Hirsch Masliansky was among the troika of Russian-born delegates who participated in the Union's plans.[6]

Early on, as the Union moved towards establishing its settlement house, Harris and his associates evidenced that they had learned much from the problems that plagued the early Educational Alliance. The Harlem group showed greater sensitivity to the religious values and mores of neighborhood people. Thus, when in 1904 it established weekly Saturday afternoon services and religious school classes on a rotating basis at five uptown congregations, one of the participating synagogues was the Orthodox Nachlath Zvi, Harlem's first east European congregation. It may be presumed that at least at the services held within its modest locale on East 109th Street, off Fifth Avenue, prayers and instructions conformed to most traditional dicta. Although Nachlath Zvi's leaders were not articulate about their reasons for joining this combine, evidently they had no second thoughts about working hand in hand with Reform rabbis and lay people in fighting the common missionary foe. And while Union president Daniel P. Hays was comfortable defining "the underlying principles of Judaism" as only "the observance of certain moral and ethical rules" that make "a good Jew . . . necessarily a good citizen," he was amenable to having Orthodox Jews who were far more ritually observant than he as colleagues.[7]

That cooperative spirit between Jews of different backgrounds became even more evident when the Harlem Federation opened its doors in April 1905. Much like the Educational Alliance model of 1889, this multifaceted settlement house pledged to provide its constituency with the linguistic tools and social skills to enter American society and, thus, be sources of pride and not concern to the Jewish community. So disposed, its Educational Committee conducted lectures and established classes for teaching immigrants language skills "to enable them to find employment and for entering the public schools." An employment service helped clients secure work in a variety of areas. The Religion Committee conducted Hebrew classes and ran religious services on Saturdays and holidays while the Social Work Committee sponsored club and recreational activities. A library was created with a wide variety of books, newspapers, and magazines on its shelves. And a Civics Committee was created to "interest the people in good government, bring to them the knowledge of their rights and duties, [and] awaken an intelligent interest in the community wherein they live and to encourage the assumption of citizenship by those who are not yet naturalized."[8]

Where the Harlem Federation differed from its older downtown sibling was in its respect for Yiddish from the day it opened its doors. The library stocked Yiddish and Hebrew books and periodicals. Lecturers of all types held forth in the Jewish vernacular from the 105th Street rostrum. Clearly, they accepted the notion that the use of Yiddish would not necessarily retard the immigrants' progress. On the contrary, from the outset, they put their faith in the notion that the Jewish language could be the medium for teaching many basic American principles to those of the older generation and even to help mothers and fathers and their children interact more harmoniously. Unquestionably, the presence of Elias A. Cohen, scion of that important and controversial east European family, contributed to the Federation's heightened sensitivity.

Cohen joined the settlement house's leadership in 1905 as its inaugural board secretary and quickly earned his stripes as a defender of the institution when, one year later, a group called the Jewish Defense League of Harlem charged that the uptown organization had made no serious attempt to combat "the pernicious activities of missionaries on East 104th Street." Reportedly, the conversionists had opened up "individual schools" and were "bait[ing] the children with free excursions and vacations in the country." The League called for the establishment of a "Jewish center" uptown and pledged a sum of fifty dollars to get the organization rolling. This provocative group seems to have been in close cooperation with Albert Lucas, the outspoken leader of the Jewish Centres Association, which was evolving that very year downtown, to provide what we would call today "drop-in centers" for young people whom missionaries courted. Lucas was unsparing in his upbraiding of

German Jewish leaders for their unwillingness to attack Christian foes head-on through, among other techniques, street protests. Cohen, for his part, rebutted the Jewish Defense League's charge of lethargy, stating that both from its home on East 110th Street and at a new Temple Israel branch headquarters established in 1902 at East 116th Street, Harlem Federation officials were "actively working against missionaries." Unmoved by Cohen's apologia in 1907, "an auxiliary to Jewish Centre #1 which is situated at 272 East Houston Street" was "formed by the Harlem friends of the movement." Elias A. Cohen remained an active member of the Harlem settlement's board and would serve as chair of its building committee in 1913.[9]

In 1906, the Harlem Federation could boast that "after three years of hard work" it had become not only a permanent feature on the neighborhood scene, with hundreds of children attending its ongoing range of activities, but a favored institution of New York's leading philanthropist, Jacob Schiff, who donated $1,000 to its coffers. By that time, the library and recreational facilities had also been made readily available to the neighboring non-Jewish population, "justified" according to settlement house officials, "by the virtue of maintaining friendly relations with the considerable portion of Irish and Italian people living in the immediate district." The Federation received a measure of citywide recognition when Schiff's son-in-law, Felix Warburg, another of the major German Jewish benefactors of the day, joined the board and linked the Harlem institution with the Hebrew Educational Society of Brooklyn, Yorkville's YMHA, and the Educational Alliance to form a "deliberative body to devise systematic club work" for the entire New York Jewish community.[10]

Ultimately, however, the efforts of Harlem's elite east European leaders went beyond helping to make young people into good Americans and keeping them from the clutches of missionaries. After all, while for Jews every child lost to the conversionists was a terrible tragedy, at the end of the day, for all of the Christianizing efforts around Jewish neighborhoods, evangelizing yielded very few converts. In other words, while the word within the neighborhood was that some 7,500 boys and girls were falling under Christian influence, the truth was that ultimately not many of them actually apostatized. The larger problem that perplexed those concerned with the continuity of Judaism was that so many young people were simply not interested in religious identification. One observer remarked in 1904 that "the younger generation, in most cases, left the old behind. . . . American customs, institutions and the like surround them, and the Hebrews of Harlem became day by day more American." More often than not, Jews failed to remain in touch with their religious traditions. They retained only an informal connection with other Jews as they walked the streets of their Jewish neighborhood. Ever critical of their own group's institutional failings, the Cohens and those following their lead—most notably, as we will see, Harry Fischel—perceived the Jewish schools and synagogues as out of touch and incapable of reaching young people. Unquestionably, the few youngsters from devout families who might attend the yeshivas in the neighborhood had a good chance of retaining a commitment to the faith. But what of the tens of thousands of youngsters who were growing up alienated from the old ways? It was not enough to get Jewish children off the streets. New models had to be created, harmonizing contemporary mores with Jewish traditions, to hopefully "retrieve" youngsters, as out-reach work was then called, back towards Jewish identification. In proffering their initiatives, these activists reached out to Louis Marshall and Jacob Schiff and were grateful for their support. They also found backing from at least one leading transplanted east European rabbi who saw much merit in their efforts. Yet their forays into religious realms proved to be fraught with controversy.[11]

If and when most immigrant east European Jews went to services, their congregation of choice was a *landsmanshaft* synagogue. These largely storefront operations brought together Jews from the same locality, city, or shtetl who wanted to pray and, as important, interact with their own kind. Orthodox in ritual—as such was their old-world heritage—the languages of prayer and study were Hebrew and Yiddish. More than 150 operated in Harlem and many more on the Lower East Side. And when they were not serving as venues for prayer, their social functions provided newcomers to America with a sense of cultural stability as they made their difficult adjustments to America. Of course, these synagogues were an integral part of a larger *landsmanshaft* connection as immigrants from the same hometowns helped each other find housing, jobs, health and death benefits, and free loans all on an informal and comforting basis.[12]

The culture of the *landsmanshaft* had little currency with the children of immigrants. Though if they showed up in shul, the stories of the old country told during and after services may have had a captivating power, most of the ritual practices were unintelligible to them. They felt none of the nostalgia for the European past. If anything, their general education instructed them to look away from outdated ways and values. It was said that "the younger generation's . . . religious sentiments are not strengthened" in those shuls. The future of the Jewishness of those under the "influence of institutions . . . secular in nature" could not be preserved through what was useful to their parents.[13]

To make matters worse, the *landsmanshaft* synagogue made little provision for the youngsters' Jewish education. That critical role was placed in the unsteady hands of a fellow immigrant teacher—a *melamed*—who operated his *cheder* usually in his own home or a rented loft. One Harlem *melamed* used a real estate office as his schoolroom. For a few cents a week, a Jewish child—most of the pupils were boys—was taught a few prayers by rote. The functionaries who ran most *cheders*, according to one critic, "could not and did not understand their students." With the proverbial hickory stick used to discipline unruly students, most pupils were "happy to close their siddurs [prayer books], glad to free themselves from the *cheder* and their foreign, uninteresting teachers." At their worst, these schools were run by "ignorant men who spend their mornings in peddling wares and in plying some trade and who utilize their afternoons and evenings for selling the little Jewish knowledge they have to American children." Essentially, the private *cheders* were doomed to fail because of the old-world medium of their religious messages that teachers delivered so inadequately.[14]

To stem the tide of disaffection, the Cohens and their colleagues placed their faith in the building of a modern Talmud Torah system that would teach traditional religious values in a modern way. Back in eastern Europe, the Talmud Torahs bore the unfortunate reputation as schools for "the children of the poor" often located in "a ramshackle structure, situated in the poorest part of the town and was considered socially on a level with . . . the combined poor-house-lunatic asylum of the community." It was said that "no self-respecting father sent his child to the Talmud Torah. . . . The stigma of poverty was upon it." But in America, it was pledged that these schools would be different and would do much to upgrade Jewish education. And ironically, the key to their hoped-for popularity would be their teachers' reliance on methodologies and sensitivities reminiscent of the public schools that all too often-undermined second generation Jewish identification.[15]

Actually, the prototypical school that they choose as their model for excellence was better than most *cheders*. At least one of the early principals at the Uptown Talmud Torah (UTT), founded in 1892, had fine credentials as a scholar from eastern Europe. And it was seen, even in its first years of existence, as having some larger communal cachet. Most notably, in 1894, when an appeal went out for funds to save the mortgage on its building on 104th Street off Third Avenue so that "the poor children of the uptown district . . . among whom are many orphans" might receive "the moral and spiritual teachings of the Hebrew language," a seemingly unlikely patron, Rabbi Kaufmann Kohler, stepped up to help solicit funds. This leading Reform rabbi's involvement may have had something to do with the missionary threat, as the UTT was then characterized in a newspaper account as an uptown branch of the Hebrew Free School of East Broadway. That downtown institution had been founded some years earlier to combat conversionists by, among others, members of Temple Emanu-El. But despite this early assistance, the UTT was constantly plagued with financial problems. The school's first head, Rabbi Joseph Leib Sossnitz, who came to the United States in 1891 from Russia and almost immediately opened a *cheder* in his home before moving the operation to 104th Street, once even went so far as to advertise in the Yiddish press for a fundraiser.[16]

The UTT was also slow to attract to attract children to its program of Jewish study. Though it did better than the one-man schools squeezed into tenement lofts, by 1902, after a decade of existence, the Uptown Talmud Torah employed only four teachers and instructed fewer than two hundred school children. Its poorly ventilated three-story building with inadequate sanitary facilities did little to bring in pupils. Its Yiddish-speaking staff, who taught only the "Aleph-Beis (Hebrew alphabet), siddur and a bit of Chumash (Pentateuch)," did not appeal to the American-born generation.[17]

The school's financial and educational limitations undoubtedly compounded the frustrations that its second principal, Rabbi Moses Reicherson, experienced. A noted author and grammarian from Lithuania, Reicherson was sympathetically profiled by a contemporary observer of immigrant life, Hutchins Hapgood, as the emblematic "prophet without honor," the "submerged scholar." The progressive writer, a non-Jew, picked up on the tragedy of a man who, "no matter what his attainments and his value, [was] unknown and unhonored amid the crowding and material interests of the new world, submerged poor in physical estate, his moral capital unrecognized by the people among whom he lived."[18]

Reicherson, born in Vilna in 1828, was a student of the famous Russian Jewish Enlightenment figure Yehudah Leib Gordon. While a teacher in his home city, Reicherson wrote eleven books on Hebrew grammar and literature. He was also credited with translating the works of the German playwright Gotthold Ephraim Lessing and the Russian fabulist Ivan Krylov into Hebrew. He migrated to the United States in 1892 to be near his son and settled in Harlem. He soon realized that there were few employment opportunities for renowned Hebrew grammarians in New York, but nevertheless this "man of wisdom" continued to write about Hebrew grammar for a Chicago-based periodical, *Ha-Techiya*. He received no compensation for these efforts, "the editor being as poor as himself." In turn-of-the-century America, hundreds of thousands subscribed to Yiddish newspapers and journals of all sorts. Highbrow intellectual Hebrew was for the few cognoscenti. Still, Reicherson labored on "for the love of the cause, 'for universal good.'" His major means of support was his job at the Uptown Talmud Torah, which paid him a salary of five dollars a week. He lived in poverty with his wife in their "miserable little apartment on East 106th Street." His saddest moment occurred when, to cover funeral expenses for his son, he was obliged to go peddling his works door to door—"in vain." When Reicherson died in 1903 at age seventy-four, one eulogist reflected with much sorrow on the tragedy of this highly trained Hebraic scholar who ended up a "grammar *melamed* in the Uptown Talmud Torah."[19]

The fortunes of the school changed dramatically during the administration of Reicherson's successor, Hillel Malacowsky. A Russian immigrant as well, Malacowsky was one of the first of his generation to vociferously upbraid the inadequacies of the *cheder* and to offer a workable program for making Jewish schooling attractive to Jewish youth in the city. Malacowsky argued, to begin with, that the Jewish religious community had neither the money, the staff, nor the desire to create a far-reaching elite yeshiva system. Immigrant parents, he observed, were almost all committed to sending their children to the public schools to improve their prospects in this country and thus would not support educational separatism. And the *cheders* that provided supplementary education, with few exceptions, were a disaster.

Malacowsky also understood that for most Jewish young people, religious education was a part-time pursuit that was at best supplementary to their general education. For children to sit down to study about their faith, after the long public school day ended, a curriculum would have to be devised that would entertain as well as inform. He submitted that although it was impossible to "make a Hebraist" out of each Jewish pupil, every Talmud Torah student could be instructed in how to love Judaism and to follow its precepts.

Malacowsky's theories on Jewish education found practical expression in the new, modern education program at the Uptown Talmud Torah. He designed a three-level system for potential pupils. Students with no prior Jewish training entered at the first stage, where they were taught "Jewish history, morals and achievement"—all towards instilling pride in their identities—and introduced to the Hebrew alphabet. All instruction was conducted in English. Towards the conclusion of initial training, students were exposed to "Hebrew words and phrases and eventually to basic religious concepts." The second tier started with the faculty evaluating the performance and capacity of each pupil. The weaker ones would continue to be taught "the dogmas of our religion" in English, with little emphasis placed on mastering Hebrew. The stronger students would be encouraged to develop fluency in the language. Their religious classes would be conducted completely in Hebrew using the newly invented "Ivrith b'Ivrith" technique. Under this so-called "natural method," students would be "immersed" in learning Hebrew. Words would not be translated into English but rather explained "through pictures, objects and natural surroundings." They would come to feel at home with Hebrew. This style of teaching emphasized oral skills. Grammar and writing were emphasized later.[20]

The final level of educational development would be opened only to the best "five percent" desirous of entering a rabbinical school. They would receive intensive pre-seminary training, preparing them for eventual careers as the leaders and teachers of the next generation of American Jews. Malacowsky wrote of this latter group: "it is worth for this five percent to open this new school system." He described his plans as realistic and economical, recognizing both the needs and limited assets of his contemporary Jewish community. His views were first published in 1905 in the *Yiddishes Tageblatt* and then reprinted a year later in the *Hebrew Standard*, thus reaching both the Yiddish- and non-Yiddish-reading segments of the community. In Malacowsky, the UTT had found a rising star educator.[21]

Indeed, Malacowsky's modernization plans were actively supported by most members of the Talmud Torah Association, a committee headed by, once again, a real estate man, Louis Wolf, which began raising funds for the school during Reicherson's last years. In February 1904, Wolf announced that the association had begun soliciting funds to acquire an adjoining house on 104th Street for some 250 students then enrolled in the newly reconstituted school. Malacowsky joined Wolf in appealing "to the rich Jews of Harlem" who were still backing "downtown *chevrahs*" (small synagogues) to remember the Talmudic dictum that "the needs of the poor of your city"—or, in this case, neighborhood—"take precedence over those of any other place" and to transfer their allegiance and financial support to the Uptown Talmud Torah. They hoped that their "propaganda [would] help enlist thousands of members in Harlem."[22]

While Wolf and his group were attempting to raise money for a new school building, a second group of east European community activists were planning to establish their own major Jewish endeavor uptown. The Harlem Educational Institute was formed in October 1904 with the mission of building up a social educational institution "somewhat along the lines of the Educational Alliance," albeit clearly with greater sensitivity to the cause of Jewish education. David A. Cohen—who surely was prepared to transfer his allegiances from downtown to Harlem—and his son Elias headed a league to raise funds for this new organization.[23]

In February 1905, the leaders of the Talmud Torah Association and the Educational Institute, recognizing that neither organization was succeeding in accumulating sufficient funds to begin its own separate building program, decided to pool their assets and merge their plans in a new Uptown Talmud Torah Association. The conjoint organization would be both "the school where Judaism and Americanism is taught" and "the center of social and educational endeavors." Such a merger would grant the institution "a new dignity and win it a larger measure of support from neighborhood people. The social activities of the educational institute would be conducted in frank recognition that work done for Jews shall be Jewish . . . and that the spirit of Judaism should pervade all the efforts and activities." One editorialist wrote: "here will be none of that 'non-sectarianism' that mars the value of our institutions."[24]

David Cohen was elected head of the new organization, which was composed of, according to a newspaper group biography, "leading representatives of the Jewish race in Harlem." These people who worked with Cohen in Harlem were characterized as "men over fifty years of age who have been in this country twenty-five–thirty years and who from early youth trained to be intensely Orthodox, yet so thoroughly is their Americanization that they saw at once the possibility of a combination of the Hebrew school with the modern educational institute with all its accessories." In May 1908, the new Uptown Talmud Torah Association purchased a plot of land at 111th Street on the corner of Lexington Avenue and began soliciting funds for an uptown center that was promoted as "strongly Orthodox in spirit . . . [and] modern in outlook." Its backers predicted that the Uptown Talmud Torah would make the students "want to go to a Jewish school with the same desire as to public school."[25]

With this new leadership firmly in place, the UTT experienced dramatic growth over the next few years. The modern teaching methods that Malacowsky first employed and that his successor, Ephraim Ish-Kishor, strongly seconded were successful in attracting, by the end of March 1908, some seven hundred students to an expanded program of classes and social activities. Ish-Kishor, former principal of London's Garden Street Talmud Torah and founder and grandmaster of the British Zionist Order of Ancient Maccabees, became principal of the Harlem school in June 1907 when Malacowsky moved to Brooklyn. Ish-Kishor's affinity for Zionism was quickly expressed though the founding of a Zionist youth group, Jehudia, in 1908 and a Hebrew-speaking group, the Hovevei Ivirth, a year later. With the founding of another Zionist youth group, Young Judaea, in 1909, the UTT opened its doors to three of its affiliates.[26]

The Talmud Torah Association, the financial arm of the new institution, also grew stronger, speeding construction of the new uptown educational and social center. By March 1908, the association boasted of a dues-paying membership of 1,300—600 regular members, 400 in the Young Folks League, and 300 in a Ladies Auxiliary. Rabbi Henry P. Mendes of the Spanish and Portuguese Synagogue also assisted the association in February 1908. The school's fundraisers were proud of a major achievement when Jacob Schiff joined its board. Here was the beginning of another partnership between elites of two communities. Impressed by the up-to-date mission and techniques of the school, Schiff expressed a commitment to its program through a donation of $5,000.[27]

No less of a coup for the UTT in solidifying its reputation among potential naysayers who might raise their eyebrows about its modern methods was the participation of a well-respected—if unusual—member of the immigrant Orthodox rabbinate on the school's board. At first glance, Moses Zevulun Margolies, the Yiddish-speaking rabbi of Yorkville's Congregation Kehilath Jeshurun, was an unlikely supporter of a school that was so American in its outlook. After all, this native of Kroza, Russia, who had attended yeshivas in his hometown and Bialystok and Kovno before serving as a rabbi in Slabodka for twenty-two years, never received any sort of secular education. And from his arrival in the United States in 1899 to assume the post as unofficial chief rabbi of Boston through his long career of thirty-one years, 1905–1936, at one of New York's most important synagogues, he never publicly declaimed in English. Moreover, he was a member of the inaugural presidium of the Union of Orthodox Rabbis, an organization of immigrant rabbis that largely resisted acculturation efforts. The Union's ideal institutions were those small yeshivas in the city that promoted separatism and only grudgingly accepted the idea that most children of immigrants would attend *cheders* and Talmud Torahs. It ultimately and sadly had to recognize that the power and appeal of the public schools was so great that some modifications in method had to be made. Thus, in dictating how Jewish education should be provided to pupils, its constitution of 1902 asserted that in promoting "the principles of true faith and commitment [to] existing and future schools . . . the teachers are to translate" traditional texts "into Yiddish, the native tongue of the children's parents." It conceded that only "when necessary for the clarification of the topic, the teachers may also utilize English."

Although Margolies signed on to these principles—in fact, the organizational meeting that led to the creation of the Union took place in his home in Boston, in April 1902—there was another side to a leader who came to be known as "The Ramaz" (an acronym of his name). Through his actions, far more than his few words, The Ramaz averred that acculturation of immigrant Jews was inevitable and Orthodox leaders and their institutions had to accommodate reality without protest. So disposed, he worked harmoniously in his home Yorkville congregation with a young graduate of the Jewish Theological Seminary, Rabbi Mordecai M. Kaplan, who had been called to the Kehilath Jeshurun ministry before The Ramaz to help the synagogue retrieve its youngsters who were uninterested in the old ways. As significant, in 1908, at almost the same time that he joined the UTT board, The Ramaz supported student demands at the downtown Yeshiva Rabbi Isaac Elchahan that their school provide them with secular training, a diversified Jewish studies curriculum that went beyond the study of the Talmud and the Code of Jewish Law, and some exposure to the practical sides of being a rabbi in America so if they chose, upon ordination, to minister to Jews being raised in this country, they would have the capacity to communicate with, and to influence, young people. On their side, The Ramaz served as a temporary president of the yeshiva for several months in 1908 as a show of good faith from the school's board that the school would change after two crippling student strikes over mission in 1906 and early in 1908 had threatened the school's existence. One of The Ramaz's congregants at Kehilath Jeshurun, real estate magnate Harry Fischel—who would soon play a major role at the UTT—undoubtedly cheered on his rabbi when a reconciliation meeting between students, teachers, and directors of the Yeshiva Rabbi Isaac Elchanan took place in the Yorkville synagogue.

Finally, though The Ramaz was not articulate about his feelings towards the Jews of different theological leanings with whom he sat on the Harlem school board, he seemingly was comfortable sharing a table with Schiff and Marshall, notwithstanding their Reform pedigrees. Like the Cohens and Fischel, The Ramaz believed so long as the Orthodox teachings of the school would not be trammeled, assistance could come from any Jewish source.[28]

Armed with a strong board drawn out of many New York Jewish quarters, in March 1908, the UTT initiated a plan for the standardization of curricula to be used not only in Harlem but also at sibling schools elsewhere in the city. Elias A. Cohen outlined his ideas in a letter to fellow board member Louis Marshall, calling for the creation of a citywide board consisting of representatives of East Broadway's Machzike Talmud Torah, the Brownsville and Bronx Talmud Torahs, and the Hebrew school of Yorkville's YMHA, as well as from the Educational Alliance and various Jewish orphan asylums. The board would establish common grades and a unified curriculum and collect common "Jewish-English" books that would be copyrighted and sold to Jewish communities throughout the United States. The income from sales would be applied towards supporting the proposed educational system. Such a program of grades, curriculum, and books would make it possible for children moving from one part of the city to another to adjust quickly to a new Hebrew school. Harlem educators were especially concerned about students on the move without the benefit of a standardized educational program, since so many of their charges started their training downtown.

Cohen also proposed that the teaching staffs of these modern schools be composed of alumni of the Jewish Theological Seminary "into which the senior classes of the larger institutions will graduate." Certainly well seasoned teachers were needed, not only to keep order in the classroom, but also to coherently present the challenging "Ivrith b'Ivrith" style of learning to students. This endeavor would give practical citywide application to Malacowsky's early ideas and would in turn serve as one of the pedagogic models for the New York Kehillah's Bureau of Jewish Education standardization program, inaugurated just a year later. This umbrella organization constituted the most profound example of cooperation between the east European and older established communities that had become evident a half-decade earlier in the Harlem Federation and Uptown Talmud Torah.[29]

But back in Harlem, not all members of the Uptown Talmud Torah's board of directors shared Elias A. Cohen's enthusiasm for modernization. Many of the older members—especially those who had been part of Louis Wolf's original Talmud Torah Association—questioned whether the younger east European members who contently advocated new programs and curricula changes shared their dedication to strict Orthodoxy. They were especially wary of the presence of Reform Jewish lay leaders such as Marshall and Schiff in the boardroom when decisions were made. In these critics' view, such outsiders certainly could not be trusted to adhere to traditional religious dogma. Amid an Orthodox community of diverse views on the value of modern techniques in Jewish education, the position of The Ramaz on that same governing board did not allay their apprehensions. Those who opposed Cohen's pedagogic strategies made their opinions felt very sharply as they often voted as a unit and blocked efforts to expand association activities.[30]

This organized opposition was a source of great frustration for Cohen. Once, after a particularly difficult and unsuccessful attempt to "give up the Saturday afternoon Hebrew classes in Hebrew and substitute Friday night and Saturday afternoon services with an English sermon," to alter the way charity was raised for the poorest students, and to have each Harlem synagogue represented on the school's board "so that we could become a truly local movement," he angrily denounced those members who differed with him as "reactionaries" who through their "blind, unreasoned prejudice based on 400 years of ghetto life" were never able to understand "that nobody had any designs whatever upon their beloved Orthodoxy." Distressed that the opposition was "evidently concerted action, prearranged," he unburdened himself to Louis Marshall, declaring that while "I have always tried to meet the difficulties which arose, smilingly and with tact, always remembering that 'the soft answer turneth away wrath' . . . I have never been able to overcome the feeling of some that we are trying to reform their Orthodoxy."[31]

The simmering factionalism within the UTT first attracted public attention in January 1910 when members of the board of directors approached Jacob Schiff to assume a $10,000 second mortgage on the newly constructed Harlem Hebrew Institute building. Schiff acceded to their request and was willing to take over the obligation for a period of ten years, free of interest. But he had two conditions, caveats that were basic to his philanthropic point of view. First, he required that the newly created Teachers Institute of the Jewish Theological Seminary, which was then based at the UTT building, be allowed to continue to occupy classroom space. Having the school's interns on the premises would afford these young men and women a convenient way to benefit from on-the-spot student teaching. And pupils would gain much from the skill and enthusiasm of the trainees. Secondly, and along similar lines, he required that "the methods of teaching in the Harlem school meet with the approval of a committee set up by the Teachers Institute." Schiff demanded that the Uptown Talmud Torah receive annual written certification from the trustees of the Jewish Teachers' College Fund and the principal of the Teachers Institute—Mordecai Kaplan left the Kehilath Jeshurun pulpit to assume the position—affirming "that the highest educational standards were being maintained at the school." In a subsequent communiqué, Schiff was careful to state that he had no quarrel with the Orthodox content of instruction but insisted that the way instruction was delivered "conform to approved modern methods and ideas of pedagogy and hygiene and maintain at all times in your building, activities looking to the Americanization of our Jewish youth."[32]

The majority of the school's board members strongly rejected Schiff's certification demand. They feared that such a formal agreement would constitute a first step in the "subordination" of the UTT to the Jewish Theological Seminary. The negative voters also felt that such an annual report would constitute a personal humiliation to the school's leadership. There was an ongoing and robust debate within the immigrant Orthodox community over whether the Seminary—a rabbinical school with an affiliated teacher training agency, which in structure and mission was hardly a yeshiva—was ideologically in line with traditional ways of thought and action. Certainly The Ramaz trusted Jewish Theological Seminary graduates; he would share his pulpit with three of its rabbis over a more than fifteen-year period. But others feared what would become of the values taught at the UTT if it fell under the wrong types of religious influence. Schiff's and Marshall's involvement with the Seminary also raised doubts among some in the Orthodox quarters who questioned their motives.

These Jewish philanthropists supported the Jewish Theological Seminary—which interestingly enough had been founded in 1886 out of opposition to what was taught at their own Reform Hebrew Union College—because they perceived that young second-generation east European Jews, estranged from old-world practices and behaviors, were falling prey to what they saw as two frightening social pathologies. Many youngsters were casting their lot with criminality and others were coming under the influence of radical, un-American ideologists. Once again, the issue of retrieval, which the newly reconstituted UTT was trying to address, loomed large. For Schiff and Marshall, the idea that sophisticated, college-trained, English-speaking rabbis and teachers from the Seminary's Teachers Institute, with its traditional religious bent, could reach young people and close gaps between generations was worthy of their support. Yet the majority of UTT board members remained unconvinced that these Jews, who when they went to services attended Temple Emanu-El, had the best interests of traditional Judaism at heart. Isidor Hershfield, the UTT's honorary board secretary, communicated the thanks of the group to Schiff for his generous financial offer but indicated clearly that the certification conditions were unacceptable.[33]

It remained for a select committee composed of Harry Fischel, Louis Marshall, and UTT board member Max Podell to arrange a compromise between Schiff and those fearful of his hegemony. After several meetings with board members and the personal intercession of Marshall with his colleague in Jewish communal work, Schiff agreed to modify the certification condition. It was determined that it would not be necessary for the school to submit to a demeaning yearly examination. Rather, it was made a condition that the Teachers Institute—which would remain in the 111th Street building—be permitted "from time to time, not more frequently than once a year" to study the school's teaching methods. If any deficiencies were indeed found in the UTT's educational practices, it would be granted a six-month period to make any recommended changes. This compromise allayed, at least for a while, the fears of those who worried about outside domination, while Schiff's largess helped promote high standards of pedagogy at the model Harlem school.[34]

With its financial security buttressed through this compromise, the UTT experienced pronounced growth over the next few years. By 1911, the school was running thirty-eight different classes for boys and four classes for girls. It was estimated that eight thousand neighborhood people regularly used the institution's social, cultural, and athletic facilities.

In 1912, the number of boys' classes rose to forty-eight, servicing 1,707 children. That year also witnessed the organization of a children's congregation and the inauguration of a breakfast program for poor youngsters. The school received an additional major financial boost from Schiff in 1913 when he donated twenty-five thousand dollars earmarked for new classrooms and administrative offices.[35]

While the spirits of those who controlled the institution were dampened by the passing in 1911 of UTT president David A. Cohen, Harry Fischel more than adequately took his place. Fischel, according to his sympathetic biographer and son-in-law Rabbi Herbert S. Goldstein, arrived from Russia in 1885 at the age of twenty practically penniless and at times even faced starvation due to his refusal to work on the Jewish Sabbath. Armed with an abiding faith in God, he quickly and legendarily overcame his manifold difficulties to become a leading New York businessman and community figure. Fischel, according to Goldstein "was hailed in many quarters as the Russian Jacob H. Schiff."[36]

And perhaps no one cherished the partnership that had evolved between leaders of the two Jewish groups more than Fischel. He participated actively in a variety of German American institutions like the Hebrew Orphan Asylum and the Hebrew Sheltering and Guardian Society. There, among community worthies like Schiff, Adolph Lewisohn, Samuel Greenbaum, and others, he pushed strongly for these institutions to begin observing Jewish dietary laws. The Reform Jews acquiesced. His philanthropy included gifts to specifically east European institutions such as the Machzike Talmud Torah and Yeshiva Rabbi Isaac Elchanan. As a leader of the UTT, his major contribution was his financing of a Jewish school for a very different class of students at 115th Street and Lenox Avenue.[37]

Fischel believed that the Jewish community's philanthropists in their understandable zeal to aid the very visible and troubling needs of the poor and unacculturated Jews of the city had overlooked the spiritual problems of the affluent, Americanized Jews of Harlem's Lenox Avenue. He asserted that not enough attention had been devoted to convince the rich of the value of a Jewish education. Other observers joined with Fischel in noting the myopia of Jewish educational activists who were so concerned with the future of Judaism among the poor but "negligent when it comes to their own children's Jewish education." Content that their youngsters were not embarrassingly acting out in the streets or falling in with the wrong types of crowds, they permitted their boys and girls to become, in the words of one contemporary, "respectable ignoramuses."[38]

Fischel outlined his plan for a "rich man's annex" in an open letter to Harlem Jews in October 1913. "This building," he announced, would be erected "for the purpose of filling a long-felt want for a school to give proper Jewish instruction along the most modern lines to the children of the so-called 'balabatim,' that is men whom God has given sufficient means to pay for the instruction of his children. We have selected this site on 115th Street, near Lenox Avenue, because it is centrally located and within reach of all between 110th and 125th Street and because we know that that the residents of this section are well able to pay this small sum for the instruction of their children." Unquestionably aware of the demographics, economics, and psychology of that region's all-rightniks, Fischel saw the importance of a high tuition fee of three dollars per month per student as a mean of attracting those who would object to sending their children to a charity school. Under his initiative, a Jewish private supplementary school was created in the heart of Central Harlem. [39]

Under Fischel's leadership, the UTT also established and maintained close connections with the New York Kehillah's Bureau of Jewish Education. This agency, created in October 1909, was given a mandate to improve and standardize the educational methods used in all of New York's Jewish schools. Those of the Harlem school's board who had advocated for educational reforms welcomed the Bureau's citywide plans. The Uptown Talmud Torah was one of the first schools to affiliate with the Bureau, agreeing to pay the minimum salary rates it had set to duly licensed teachers and receiving, in return, financial assistance from the umbrella communal organization. Fischel himself convened a meeting in his own home of the presidents of Manhattan's five largest Talmud Torahs, in October 1911, to convince them to commit their institutions to the new Bureau. He succeeded in allaying the concerns of those in the room who were worried that the new curricula proposals "might conflict with Orthodox Jewish belief." He convinced them to pull back on their demand that each affiliated school be given veto power over all curricular changes. They ended up supporting Fischel's proposal that only a two-thirds majority be needed for approval of any reform. Fischel and his Harlem followers committed their institution further to the Bureau by allowing for the establishment on their premises of preparatory classes for girls. It was the first time Jewish young women in New York were tendered a systematized religious education. The UTT also acceded to the creation of extension school classes directed at those children and young adults who for a variety of reasons were unable to enroll in regular sessions. The Bureau seemed to be fulfilling in large measure Elias A. Cohen's 1908 dream of a unified and standardized Jewish school system.[40]

Although Fischel was successful in bringing the heads of those large Talmud Torahs into the Kehillah's orbit, he was soon to find out that members of his own board had great reservations about what outsiders wanted in Jewish schools. And criticism of modern educational techniques and the way they were fostered—or imposed—on local people was directed at Fischel personally and not at imagined interference by a Schiff or a Marshall. These Orthodox circles did not subscribe to the belief that the old-world shells of religious educational practice could be removed without endangering the essence and future of traditional faith. Board dissenters were outraged, for example, when Fischel unilaterally decided to permit the placing of a piano in the children's synagogue, even if it were certain that it would not be used during Sabbath and holiday services. And they opposed the showing of motion pictures of religious content in the school. A group of protesters—perhaps board members, maybe enraged parents, their identities are unknown—went outside the law by ripping out the wires of a newly purchased stereopticon machine, earmarked for use in teaching Jewish history to youngsters. Such a video device—the forerunner of the slide projector—in their view, violated the second of the Ten Commandments, which prohibits creating "graven images" of the Almighty. Quick to respond, Fischel had "an electrician repair it" and the lecture proceeded as scheduled.[41]

When the vandalism became public knowledge, the strictly Orthodox Yiddish daily *The Jewish Morning Journal*, rather than condemn the criminal act outright, implicitly criticized the UTT president, undoubtedly much to Fischel's chagrin. While not mentioning him by name, in an editorial called "The Root of the Trouble," it condemned "autocratic methods" used in connecting the school to the Kehillah, with its welter of "experimental methods." Reference was made derogatorily to "the official philanthropists, public providers" who did not respect the wishes of the community. Sadly, the editorial asserted, "it occurs to no one that the ordinary Jew, who sends his children to the Talmud Torah, knows what he wants and is more entitled to make his own mistakes than to stand aside and watch the more serious mistakes made by others who understand him very little and sympathize with him even less." Two weeks after it appeared, Louis Marshall was made aware that all was not well in Harlem when he received a translated version of the editorial.[42]

In fact, the controversy over community control of the Jewish school was reaching its peak at the end of February 1914, when Fischel asked for a vote of confidence from his board. When he failed to receive the support of an overwhelming majority of the members, Fischel resigned his post in dramatic fashion at the annual public meeting of the UTT.[43]

Appeals from supporters—like Schiff and Rabbi Judah Magnes, chairman of the Kehillah—failed to change Fischel's mind. He communicated his frustrations in a letter to Schiff written a week after his resignation. He offered no apologies for the use of a strong hand in leading the board, writing that "were it not for these autocratic methods, which I was compelled to use, it would have been impossible to connect our institution with the Bureau of Jewish Education and to accrue the benefits of their advice and cooperation and to accomplish so much for the thousands of children who have derived the advantages of a Jewish education." He charged that his opponents were "of the old-fashioned type" who believed "that the only way to give children a Jewish education is by teaching them in the same way as they were taught twenty-five years ago in Russia. And it is the same men who have always held back the progress of the instruction at all times. It was only by means of these 'autocratic methods' that I was able to take the institution out of chaos and to transform it to an up-to-date Talmud Torah run along the most modern and efficient system."[44]

Henry Glass replaced Fischel as president of the Uptown Talmud Torah. Glass, who was also president of the prestigious Congregation Ohab Zedek, situated on 116th Street west of Fifth Avenue—near to the Fischel annex in Central Harlem—was undoubtedly more acceptable to the dissension-ridden board. Fischel would remain active at the school, continuing to serve as a board member.[45]

Rabbi Schmarya Leib Hurwitz, founder and principal of the Rabbi Israel Salanter Talmud Torah, shared Harry Fischel's attitudes towards the modernization of Jewish education. In attempting to institute up-to-date pedagogic practices in his school, he experienced similar opposition from elements of the Harlem community. Rabbi Hurwitz migrated to the United States in 1906 and almost immediately earned a considerable reputation downtown as an able preacher who reportedly often attracted packed audiences for his Sabbath and holiday services and homiletics. In 1908, Hurwitz left the Lower East Side to assume a pulpit uptown at Harlem's Congregation B'nai Israel Salanter Anshe Sameth. Another real estate operator cum community leader, Joseph Smolensky, president of the congregation, recruited Hurwitz to the post with a lucrative contract that spared him, according to one account, "from the poverty which most rabbis find themselves in."[46]

Soon after arriving in the neighborhood, Hurwitz became engaged in the problems of Jewish education around him. He noted that those children who lived along the outer ridge of the major Harlem Jewish concentrations, north of 118th Street, were not being adequately serviced even by fine institutions like the UTT located in the heart of the uptown settlement. He perceived that thousands of Jewish children were growing up without the benefit of a Jewish education and felt that there was a critical need for a neighborhood school in the vicinity of where he lived.[47]

Rabbi Hurwitz made his feelings well known to his patron Smolensky, who agreed to establish a Talmud Torah under the congregation's auspices. Together, they prevailed upon the synagogue's board of trustees to allocate temporary classroom space within their building. In December 1909, the Rabbi Israel Salanter Talmud Torah opened its doors to the community's children.[48]

A year later, some 350 youngsters were attending twelve different (and separate) boys' and girls' classes in a newly renovated school building adjacent to the synagogue. There they were exposed to a curriculum closely resembling that of the Uptown Talmud Torah. The "Ivrith b'Ivrith" language system was used to teach everything from the basic alphabet to the most advanced Talmudic texts. Rabbi Hurwitz also organized a children's congregation to complement the pupils' classroom training. Much like Elias A. Cohen—and at almost the same time—

Rabbi Hurwitz spoke strongly of the need for a standardized curriculum for New York's constantly moving Jewish school-age population. He characterized the residential mobility that he saw around him as a "plague" against Jewish education. "You begin with a child," he complained, "and when he is about to go to a new higher subject, he is gone elsewhere." He understood that a uniform citywide curriculum would insure the continuity of the Jewish educational process. So disposed, under Hurwitz's guidance, the Salanter Talmud Torah became one of the early members of the Bureau of Jewish Education. Rabbi Hurwitz supported the Bureau's "model school" program and permitted the housing of a boys' preparatory junior high school on his school's premises.

However, Rabbi Hurwitz's advocacy of modern pedagogic techniques, and his support of the Kehillah's educational program, did not sit well with members of his congregation who feared the Bureau's tendencies even if Schiff and Marshall had no direct contact with their operation. Hurwitz was stung by criticism of his plans and programs, which he viewed as "strictly Orthodox." Realizing that the "present synagogue had the wrong atmosphere," he severed his ties with the congregation, but he did retain his close connection with Joseph Smolensky—his funding source—who agreed to assume the financial burdens of a new, independent institution. With his monetary base secured, the Talmud Torah continued to grow and by 1915 it enrolled more than eight hundred boys and girls in thirty-two different classes.

Still, as of 1917, almost ten years into the Kehillah's work and close to fifteen years since Malacowsky and then Ish-Kishor set out to address the Jewish educational needs of their Harlem community, the problem of retrieval remained unsolved. A simple head count of pupils shows that the combined enrollment at the UTT and the Salanter Talmud Torah was no more than 2,500 pupils, primarily boys. When the handful of students who attended the yeshivas in Harlem and the uncountable numbers of young people who reluctantly showed up at the *melameds'* lofts are considered, it is evident that only several thousand received any sort of training in their faith. Though the Harlem Federation did its utmost to keep its potential charges out of trouble, the streets remained a far more popular attraction for boys and girls.

Indeed, Dr. Samson Benderly, director of the Bureau of Jewish Education, who influenced much of the positive work undertaken in Harlem, had to admit that citywide—uptown, downtown, and on into Brooklyn and the Bronx—"an enormous number of Jewish boys and girls . . . grow up without any Jewish education." The little good news to report was that "some of them because of native endowment . . . grow up into fine American citizens." But "from the Jewish community many of them are certainly estranged. They are lost to the cause of Judaism." Much worse, "there is a large number of Jewish boys and girls who, as adolescents and as adults show the effect of this lack of religious and moral training. . . . Many of these constitute a disintegrating force both in the Jewish and the general community."[49]

Addressing the reality that the efforts of the modern Talmud Torahs and the settlement houses had scarcely succeeded in fostering greater Jewish identification among neighborhood youths, in 1917, Harlem Jews were offered a new type of synagogue model that promised to do even more to retrieve disinterested youngsters. Rabbi Herbert S. Goldstein's Institutional Synagogue drew upon a decade and half of "youth synagogue" initiatives and other comparable activities that had sprung up downtown, in Yorkville, and in Harlem. What ultimately developed on 116th Street not only made a good faith attempt to influence the neighborhood's young people but also served as a prototype for future developments in communities well beyond uptown.

AT WORK — GIRLS' SCHOOL No. 4 IN THE BUILDING OF THE YOUNG WOMEN'S HEBREW ASSOCIATION

Girls' school at the Young Women's Hebrew Association, circa 1917 (*The Jewish Communal Register of New York City, 1917–1918*).

6

Attractive Synagogues

Bella Unterberg was unhappy with the myopia of New York's YMHA towards the needs of young Jewish women on several counts. First, for close to its first two decades of operations, the men's movement was slow in granting females equal access to its facilities. In its first year of 1874, while still downtown, the organization voted against "a motion to admit women to full membership." A year later, ladies were permitted to join its literary circle, but not until thirteen years later was it agreed "to admit women daily except Saturday and Sunday from 10 A.M. to 2 P.M." During its brief tenure in late-nineteenth-century Harlem, the neighborhood's branch association was more forthcoming towards women. When it opened in 1879, a dramatics society for women was part of its program. And a year later, concomitant with—and perhaps due to—the Hebrew Ladies of Harlem's contribution of $300 to equip the athletic facilities, girls and young women were afforded "free use of the gymnasium and other facilities." It took the older Y eight more years before it created, in 1888, "auxiliaries" for females both in its uptown branch and in its new Lower East Side operation. Particularly in the downtown outlet, an emphasis was placed on attendees taking part in "cultural" activities and "home circle clubs" under the close supervision of Julia Richman, who had just then earned the singular distinction of becoming the first Jew appointed as a grammar school principal in New York. Unterberg, a child of east European immigrants who "received her education in the public schools," applauded Richman's Americanization efforts even if perhaps she, like many others in her community, might have questioned some of the heavy-handedness of this German Jewish matron's behavior towards her charges. It was alleged that Richman was not opposed to the dragging of youngsters who spoke Yiddish on her premises to the bathrooms to have their mouths washed out with soap. Children of other immigrant groups were disciplined similarly if they uttered their parents' foreign tongues.[1]

For Unterberg, the Y's lack of attention to the residential requirements of young, unchaperoned Jewish women was even more problematic. In the city lures of the street entrapped "Jewish working girls"—as they were then called—that transcended the juvenile delinquency to which boys gravitated. At worst, there were the notorious dancing academies, where unsuspecting young women found themselves ultimately at the tender mercies of "cadets"—a euphemism for pimps. The locations of these schools were no secret; they ran advertisements in the Yiddish press. Other white slavers enticed naïve girls with promises of marriage, actions that led innocent victims not to wedding canopies but to brothels. Clearly there was a need for safe and secure environments for female youngsters. And while on these premises, the residents could be trained in the genteel ways of American women of the time. As late as 1900, the Y movement had not addressed this troubling social and moral problem.[2]

And then, finally, there was the limited mission of the YMHAs, which in their zeal to Americanize and refine their members, did not sufficiently promote religious values and practice. In Unterberg's view, there was not enough that was "Hebrew" in the YMHAs. If anything, the existing Y's educational policies effectively undermined the Jewish identities not only of young women—Unterberg's prime concern—but young men as well.

Such was among the sentiments that were expressed in February 1902, when Bella Unterberg brought together in her home on the Upper West Side of Manhattan some eighteen women to plan for the establishment of an independent Young Women's Hebrew Association (YWHA). There it was agreed to "establish an institution akin in character to the YMHA but combining therewith features of religious and spiritualizing tendencies." Accordingly, when the YWHA opened its doors in 1903 in Harlem at Lexington Avenue and 101st Street, residential accommodations were offered to neighborhood girls. As of 1906, 18 young women were boarded on the premises. By the time the Y moved in 1917 to a location north of Central Park, 175 girls lived there. At both its original venue and later in its more commodious setting at 110th Street and Lenox Avenue, all of the recreational, social, and educational features common to a men's Y were available to the literally thousands of young women who entered its portals on an annual basis. The women's Y more than fulfilled Unterberg's original wish to give "hard working girls . . . a chance of bettering their condition and helping them, in many cases, from a condition of want and necessity to a place in the world where they can become independent and self-supporting." And as far as inculcating the values and practices of Judaism was concerned, a superintendent of the YWHA could assert in 1912 that "back of all that we do, is the thought of preserving the essential Jewishness of our people. As Jews, we want to save our Judaism. As Jews we bring these girls in here that they may find shelter and help and find, too, the God of their fathers." Creatively, the central focus in this critical area was the YWHA's building and maintenance of an attractive synagogue that the young women and also the young men of the neighborhood would want to attend.[3]

Bella Unterberg and her sisters' congregational initiative closely paralleled the growing "Young People's Synagogues" movement that emerged both on the Lower East Side and Harlem at precisely the same time. As of the turn of the century, the long-standing problem of the unattractiveness of *landsmanshaft* synagogues to young people had not been adequately addressed. The next generation of Jews stayed away in droves from services that did not speak to their identities as acculturated Jews. And to make matters worse for young women, if they showed up, they might have had great difficulties hearing the prayers as many of these storefront operations had only a single room for worship, leaving the ladies in the back room.[4]

There was, as early as the late 1880s, an alternative to the *landsmanshaft* synagogue that had some appeal to second-generation Jews. As immigrant Jews started to make their way economically in the United States, some who maintained enduring religious values, and were proud of their success in America, built commodious synagogues. There they recited the traditional Orthodox liturgy in their regularly assigned seats that often were bought at a premium price, under the leadership of a melodious cantor who was the pride of those who hired him. In fact, as early as the 1890s, a veritable "chazzan craze" was afoot downtown, as congregations competed with each other to bring over from Europe the best-trained singers whose vocal abilities would attract worshippers to their institutions. Kehal Adath Jeshurun of Eldridge Street was one of those synagogues that were deeply caught up in this performance phenomenon in the years before the struggle began with David Cohen over its institutional integrity. However, that synagogue's agenda—which interestingly enough did not include much in the way of Jewish education for its members' boys and girls—failed to engage many young people. The only noticeable greater sensitivity to women at prayer was that those who came to services sat in a comfortable balcony where they could hear the services and watch the cantor at work on the Sabbath and holidays.[5]

Harlem's Congregation Ohab Zedek likewise put its faith in the talents and reputation of its cantor to attract members and worshippers to its sanctuary on 116th Street. But wisely, it also engaged an English-preaching rabbi who it hoped could relate to younger people. This "First Hungarian Congregation" began basically as a *landsmanshaft* synagogue when in 1873 it "rented a small room on Ridge Street" in what was still Kleindeutschland and then moved on to "a small room of a frame building at Avenue A and Houston Street." In time, as finances permitted—and after an additional move downtown—the congregation in 1886 purchased a large building on Norfolk Street from Congregation Ansche Chesed, which was moving uptown, following its worshippers as part of the intra-city migration of central European Jews of that era. In 1890, Ohab Zedek was fortunate and proud enough to engage Rabbi Dr. Philip Hillel Klein as its spiritual leader. Following the path of synagogue and population movements, the congregation peacefully located to Harlem in 1906. But it did maintain a presence for "many years on Norfolk Street."[6]

However, early on in its tenure in Harlem, the congregation was stung by newspaper criticism. *The Hebrew Standard* asserted quite strongly that "a synagogue has something more to do than to engage a chazzan with a beautiful voice." And it wondered rhetorically: "Where is the rabbi? Where is the Hebrew and Religious School? What is the New Hungarian Synagogue doing for the community? Was there a need for another synagogue in Harlem for the purpose of giving concerts on Saturday and holidays? The Jewish community expects something more than that."[7]

The alleged scandal that precipitated this harsh upbraiding was a report that "a number of young men attempted to enter the synagogue when the person in charge asked for tickets." Ordinarily, many congregations, then—and now—charged for attendance at services on the High Holidays as a major fundraising device. But this request for tickets seemingly took place one Sabbath morning because the people wanted to hear the melodious recitations of Cantor Shaaye (Samuel) Meisels, who had followed the congregation uptown. "Being told that they had no tickets," the complaint continued, "they were told to go across the street to the millenary or cigar store, where tickets could be purchased." It is not known whether the coveted tickets were "scalped," but there clearly was an assertion that a desecration of the Sabbath was taking place. For future congressman Isaac Siegel—who made one of his first public Jewish communal appearances at this moment—the leaders of the congregation were "hypocrites." An editorialist agreed totally and suggested that "the menorah over the entrance of the synagogue be removed and the Sign of the Dollar over the broken tablets of the Ten Commandments be substituted."[8]

The congregation's apologia was that tickets were made available during the week at a store near 116th Street for crowd-control purposes—"to preserve order and decency during the services." And, in fact, the tickets were "the first and only experiment in this direction." The problem, as Ohab Zedek's board secretary publicly unburdened himself, was "the mob of men struggling to enter and the young dandies who came in merely to ogle the women in the balcony with their pinces nez."[9]

This public embarrassment clearly was not the sort of attention the synagogue wanted. To restore its reputation and to make Ohab Zedek a synagogue that young people might want to attend for the best of reasons, it extended an invitation to Rabbi Bernard Drachman to complement their revered incumbent religious leader, Philip Hillel Klein. The Hungarian-born Rabbi Klein was modern in many respects. But he was modern in a European way. He had received ordination from Rabbi Azriel Hildesheimer's Orthodox seminary in Germany, where he was exposed to a Jewish curriculum far more diverse than that of a traditional yeshiva. And he had earned a doctorate in philosophy from the University of Berlin. But he could not preach in English. His language of discourse was German and a "most convoluted High German" to boot. In fact, early on in his career at Ohab Zedek, a committee of congregants asked him to "simplify" his addresses because, frankly, his sermons were boring. Reportedly, when Klein rose to speak, "there was a rush to the door like from a fire." The grown men who made it outside "would gather on the street chatting and the boys would play handball until the signal emanated from inside that the sermon was over." Clearly, Klein had no cachet with young people. But hopefully the American-born Drachman would.[10]

Drachman was arguably the first modern Orthodox rabbi in twentieth-century America. A graduate of Columbia University, he went off eventually to Breslau to receive advanced rabbinical training at that city's Judische Theologische Seminar. He could also boast of a doctorate in Semitic languages from the University of Heidelberg. His problem was that when he returned to America in 1885—with all of his training, degrees, and orientation as an Orthodox rabbi—he was unable to immediately secure employment. He would later recall that "it seemed for a time that I had mistaken my vocation, that there was no room, no demand in America for an American-born, English-speaking rabbi who insisted on maintaining the laws and usages of Traditional Judaism." In his view, "Reform Judaism . . . had conquered almost the entire field of Jewish life." And while "there were a few Orthodox congregations whose members were American-born or Americanized immigrants and whose pulpits were occupied by English-speaking rabbis . . . there were no vacancies." And as far as the "eastern European, Polish and Russian . . . Jews in the East side of Ghetto districts who adhered to the Orthodox traditions of their native lands" were concerned, "they were Yiddish speaking and wanted rabbis of that type. They were strange to me and I was stranger to them." Fortunately for him, four years later, due in great measure to the financial backing he received from his father-in law, he was able to establish his own congregation, Congregation Zichron Ephraim, on 67th Street between Lexington and Third Avenues in Yorkville. His members were among the first affluent and Americanized east European Jews who very early on followed their central European brethren out of downtown. To supplement his pulpit income, Drachman taught many courses at the Jewish Theological Seminary. He would subsequently characterize his own role at the school as "a sort of rabbinic general utility man."

Twenty years later, with Jewish Harlem, in Drachman's view, on the rise and "Yorkville no longer the important center of Jewish residence that it had been," having "sunk into a position of relative unimportance," the ambitious rabbi began to look northward to extend his influence. His first foray into the neighborhood proved unsuccessful. The organizers of Congregation Shomre Emunah at 121st Street and Madison Avenue promised services conducted according to the "Orthodox ritual in an impressive, decorous manner," free of the unseeingly noise and commotion of the *landsmanshaft* synagogue. But the synagogue's momentum stalled during the economic panic of 1908. A year later, however, Drachman accepted a call to Ohab Zedek. From 1909 to 1922, he would ride an unusual circuit between two neighborhoods—commuting on the El on Friday afternoons before sundown—as he preached "on alternate Sabbaths in each synagogue." For the Harlem congregation, it had imported a man who might be able to speak to young people within and without the sermon slot on Sabbath and holidays. And if some congregational leaders had any concerns about how Rabbi Klein would react to Drachman sitting beside him at the front of the sanctuary, there was a model in Yorkville that they could hope to emulate. In the first decade of the twentieth century, The Ramaz had shared the Kehilath Jeshurun pulpit with Rabbi Mordecai Kaplan, who had been a student of Drachman's at the Jewish Theological Seminary. And from all reports, the senior and junior rabbis worked well together.[11]

However, in 1912, just three years later, the leaders of Ohab Zedek—at least in Drachman's opinion—showed that they had not divorced themselves from "the pronounced ghetto Jewishness of these Hungarian brethren" when they hired one of the greatest cantors of his day, Yossele Rosenblatt, to conduct services. Predictably, Rosenblatt, whose fame as a performer of Jewish liturgy in Muncacz, western Ukraine; Pressburg, Hungary; and Hamburg, Germany, preceded his arrival in Harlem, packed the sanctuary whenever he led the prayers. His devotees included both the devout and the dandies. One young man who sat with his father downstairs would recall that his grandmother, who was seated in the balcony, would swoon and shed copious tears when the cantor beseeched the Almighty for a "life of sustenance" as he recited the prayer for the new month, a signature piece of music. However, Drachman was not one of Rosenblatt's fans. He objected to "the exaggerated role assigned to *chazzanuth* [the art of the professional cantor] in the East European synagogues." For the rabbi, with the cantor repeating "words and whole passages . . . endlessly, the service is unduly prolonged and the entire effect is wearisome in the extreme. . . . Worse of all, this manner of rendition tends to deprive the service of its religious character." Drachman much preferred "the musical part . . . not only in accordance with the traditional Jewish methods, but also in harmony with modern Occidental taste." In his sermons, he "did not hesitate to condemn" Ohab Zedek's continuation of the chazzan craze. Yossele Rosenblatt returned the less than complimentary appreciation of his art. For him, "what attracted the multitude to the Ohab Zedek synagogue . . . was, by the admission of all, its cantor. . . . As for American-born Dr. Bernard Drachman, despite his Shakespearean diction, he was not the most effective speaker." Rabbi Klein did not render a public opinion on the abilities of his colleagues.[12]

But whether the worshippers came to hear Drachman preach in the King's English or, more likely, to listen to Rosenblatt's performance, Ohab Zedek, like the city's other large established synagogues, did not attract many who were not interested in religious life. Neither a homiletic well struck nor a chant supremely sung was meaningful to those young people who lacked an existing allegiance to their parents' synagogues. While the Drachman rabbinic model was emulated elsewhere in the neighborhood—for example, in 1910 at Congregation Ansche Chesed, the synagogue where Elias A. Cohen prayed, Jewish Theological Seminary graduate Jacob Kohn replaced German-born Gustav Hausman, who was dismissed for not "possessing the spiritual uplift which a spiritual leader and religious teacher must have"—much work needed to be done to reach out beyond congregational families.[13]

Rather than boast of its cantor or speak loudly of its preacher, the synagogue at Unterberg's women's Y attempted to attract young people to its sanctuary as a natural outgrowth of its regular nonreligious activities. The youthful residents and members were there on the premises six days a week as the institution served their social, cultural, and recreational needs. And on holy days, the young women sat decorously next to their male friends and relatives at services. There the English-language sermon had its place. But perhaps even more noteworthy and attractive was its offering of choral music.[14]

Even greater congregational participation was the hallmark of Congregation Mikveh Israel, which was founded just two years after the women's Y synagogue. There what its leadership called "the rising generation in Israel"—that frequent terminology of the day—was offered a service that emphasized the importance of congregational singing. Both Rabbis Henry S. Morais, the son of one of the founders of the Jewish Theological Seminary, and Jacob Dolgenas, a student at the seminary who had already interned in comparable forms of synagogue work on the Lower East Side, recognized that many young people were uncomfortable in synagogues where even the best of cantors droned on in solo recitations of the prayers. Thus, they instructed the men who led the services to be true "representatives of the community" through the singing of simple melodious prayers that worshippers could follow easily. Lay people were encouraged to join in singing along with the cantor, thereby making traditional forms of prayers more meaningful for all drawn to the synagogue. This style of participatory worship also helped synagogue leaders maintain decorum during services. Those actively engaged in the devotions had little time for idle gossip.[15]

Congregation Mikveh Israel was also ahead of its time in the admission of two women to its original twelve-member board of directors. Most established congregations across a wide denominational spectrum barred concerned women from synagogue office, relegating them to the leadership of a women's auxiliary or sisterhood. Though services were conducted according to Orthodox ritual—and unlike at the women's Y, the genders did not sit together during prayers—Mikveh Israel's women had an important voice in all other synagogue affairs. This was also the emerging policy within the youth synagogue movement downtown, where young women and men served on the boards and women taught Hebrew classes. Contemporary observers applauded Morais's efforts both here and as head of the Young Folks League of the Uptown Talmud Torah. One writer declared him to be the "only rabbi in Harlem who stands for principle" and his young supporters to be "Harlem's only hope for the future."[16]

Yet despite this enthusiastic endorsement, Morais and Dolgenas did not succeed in their endeavor. Persistent financial woes plagued Mikveh Israel, arising in part from the lack of economic strength of its followers, who were young and just starting out on their career paths. The 1908 economic downturn that undid Drachman's first offer in Harlem also did not help. Consequently, the synagogue was never able to raise sufficient funds to move out of its temporary rented quarters. As of the beginning of the 1910s, the uptown youth synagogue movement was represented only by the synagogue of the women's Y. Due to its well-heeled funders and panoply of activities, it not only survived but advanced. In 1912 it embarked on a major fundraising campaign that netted $200,000 for a "new dormitory and headquarters at Lenox Avenue at 110th Street." In the spirit of its multiuse facilities and agenda, the auditorium that was used for plays and recitals during the week became sacred space on Sabbath and holidays. Still, there was much room for additional efforts to reach those whom one Christian observer described "as the ones who, finding themselves unwilling to maintain the forms of Judaism and having a sort of instinctive dread of other religions are going without any religious expression or experience whatsoever."[17]

With much retrieval labors still to be undertaken, in April 1915 the founders of the Harlem Young Men's Hebrew Orthodox League identified an additional source of concern in the community about the religious values of its young people. Apparently, even the beneficiaries of a Talmud Torah education—who were projected as the leaders of the next generation—were drifting away from the faith's practices. Ten members of the Harry Fischel West Side Annex of the Uptown Talmud Torah wanted an "institution which would create an Orthodox environment and teach the great principles of Orthodoxy" to those who "upon entering academic, professional or business careers" needed "during their spare time . . . a circle that reminds him of his obligations to his faith and people." The leaders of the League were confident that they had the intellectual acumen to convince their fellow second-generation Jews "that by study Orthodox Judaism will be found to be entirely compatible with modern ideas."[18]

The League made itself known on the uptown scene in the fall of 1915 when it established a youth synagogue at the Fischel Annex emphasizing decorum and congregational singing. It quickly liaised with the Kehillah, as it was designated to be a "provisional synagogue." These religious outlets were organized throughout the city to combat the abuses of the so-called "mushroom synagogues." During the High Holiday season, private entrepreneurs rented public halls and saloons to provide a place for unaffiliated Jews to congregate. Many of those in the business of Judaism were unscrupulous individuals who hired imposters as rabbis and generally exploited the public for commercial purposes. The cry for reform of this blot on Jewish neighborhood life dated back to the turn of century, when it was observed that "the self-styled 'Holy-day Rabbi' is generally nothing more than a speculator pure and simple" whose practice "degrades Judaism in the eyes of those of our brethren who are compelled to attend the temporary places of worship." Most critically, "it estranges Jews from their religion. This is particularly true with the younger generation." The selection of the Harlem Young Men's Hebrew Orthodox League to serve the Lenox Avenue district represented an early recognition among communal authorities of its utility to the uptown community. The League promised to provide places for worship at reasonable rates under reputable leadership to serve the High Holiday overflow crowd.[19]

Now possessed of cachet within the community, the League soon inaugurated numerous social and cultural activities and put forward plans to maintain its own clubrooms, library, and gymnasium and to hold classes on Jewish topics. Among the lecturers in its early years were Jacob Dolgenas, now a Jewish Theological Seminary–trained rabbi, Bernard Drachman, who stepped outside his pulpit to encourage the young men at a neighboring institution, and perhaps the League's most important supporter, Rabbi Herbert S. Goldstein. Then an assistant rabbi at Yorkville's Kehilath Jeshurun—where he followed Kaplan and worked too in harmony with The Ramaz in the congregation—Goldstein was elected honorary president of the League in recognition of his constant backing of its activities.[20]

Indeed, Rabbi Goldstein was completely simpatico with the goals of the League and actually, two months after the group was created, offered himself as an ideal mentor to its young activists. In June 1915, he declared that the salvation of "the Judaism of the future" lay solely in the hands of the "young university-trained Orthodox rabbis" like himself. This 1913 graduate of the Jewish Theological Seminary contended that only men like him and his classmates could communicate, for example, with the "scientifically-trained, skeptical young Jew, reconcile what he learned in public school and college with the ancient doctrines of his faith." Goldstein believed that only those "reared on American soil, who have breathed the ideals of American democracy, who have been born and bred like other Americans who have received a systematic scientific education, and who are at the same time deeply saturated with a knowledge and desire of practicing the tenets of our faith" could understand the needs and desires of those eager "to break down ghetto walls . . . to live as their neighbors, their fellow citizens—the Americans." They alone "who have gone through this kind of youth" and remained true to Judaism could meet American Jewish men and women on their own level. Goldstein believed strongly in what he called "Jewish missionary work" among those "who have gone astray, to bring back to Orthodox Judaism and keep and sustain those who are in the fold."[21]

Accordingly, Goldstein was also quick to lend his backing to a comparable Harlem-based religious institution that, like the Orthodox League, was dedicated to attracting Jewish young adults back to faith and practice. The Harlem Hebrew League was created in September 1915 to "make known the ideals of Judaism" to uptown youths. League organizers established a headquarters for "Jewish men under Jewish refining influences on Lenox Avenue where social and educational programs were held every week-day evening and on the Sabbath." The organization offered its members lectures and debates in addition to dignified modern Orthodox services. Here again, Goldstein and Morais headed the list of speakers. And Drachman too stepped beyond Oheb Zedek to influence the participating youngsters as their association began to gain support in the local community.[22]

However, early on in their tenure, the two leagues absorbed some criticism—namely that, for all of their efforts, as self-designated Orthodox institutions, they served only a small minority of the neighborhood's young adults. Critics argued that there were thousands of young people who, for example, the modern Talmud Torahs had never reached "who never enter a synagogue and for them there must be some kind of training school" in Judaism. In other words, the leagues were perceived as being out only to stop those with some affinity for the faith from losing touch with their backgrounds, while so many others had no feeling at all for Judaism. Such was the vision of the founders of the new Harlem YMHA, which was organized at a meeting held at Temple Mount Zion in 1915. At that meeting and in subsequent discussions it was determined, first of all, that the YMHA at 92nd Street—the flagship of the movement, whose programs they wished to emulate—though geographically accessible, was not attracting a large share of uptown residents. The Yorkville Y's leaders, for their part, were unwilling to expand their own activities to Harlem. A special meeting of the 92nd Street organization's social, finance, membership, and neighborhood committees, also in 1915, declared it to be an exclusively Yorkville institution, even if some East Harlem boys did attend its programs. However, the established Y was willing to help its Harlem colleagues set up comparable programs at 119th Street, east of Fifth Avenue. There social, cultural, and recreational activities were emphasized, while Jewish religious classes and worship were offered on a limited, nondenominational basis. Although the Harlem men's group—like most Ys nationally, but in contrast to the Harlem women's Y—worked primarily "to provide the Jewish youth with a Jewish center of activities of such a nature that he shall find it unnecessary to go beyond the doors of [the] building for amusement [and] entertainment" rather than to provide comprehensive religious programming, Rabbis Klein and Drachman and future congressman Isaac Siegel supported the initiative.[23]

But Rabbi Herbert S. Goldstein was totally unenthusiastic about the prospects for the new Harlem Y. Sounding very much like Unterberg and her sisters at the women's Y, for him there was all too little that was Hebrew in this new branch's mission. He deemed its efforts in the Jewish social field as "partial" because "it only takes the boy off the streets and does not give him the education of a Jewish religious environment." His conclusion was that the Harlem Y's work would prove to be "negative" because it "failed to impart positive religion in the minds of the youth. It does not stand for positive religious conviction."[24]

Goldstein argued in a public letter to New York Jewry in September 1916 that beyond what he saw as the highly problematic men's Y movement, existing Jewish institutions were not up to the challenge of influencing young people towards greater observance. In reviewing what he perceived as a failed state of affairs, he began by picking up on the critique that the "Youth Synagogue" movement had been articulating for more than a decade and a half. He justly characterized the *landsmanshaft* synagogue that expressed "local European mannerism" as "unAmerican, antiquated and largely responsible for the great gap which now exists between the sons of the founders of the synagogue and the founders." Old-timers might possess some "engrained Jewish consciousness," but their children were becoming "more and more indifferent."

Needless to say, he harshly critiqued the *cheder* system as a complete failure for its inability "to impart to students the true meaning of the Jewish religion, [to] inspire in them, the proper love of their faith." For him, even the modern Talmud Torah movement, with which his father-in-law Harry Fischel and some of his own closest associates were intimately involved, suffered some important defects. First, its programs reached at most 15 percent of youngsters and these pupils more often than not were the children of "paupers." Sounding much like Fischel—though he did not acknowledge the existence of the philanthropist's Annex initiative—he noted that these schools generally did not attract families who could afford to pay tuition. And perhaps as important, the educational system's approach to Jewish youths was itself not ideal because "it is fractional in its work and divorces the child from the synagogue."[25]

Goldstein placed his faith in and directed his ambition towards creation of an Institutional Synagogue that he tendered as representing Jewry's best chance to rescue young men and women from voluntarily surrendering their Jewish identity. In his vision, "the synagogue of old was the center for prayer, study and the social life of the community all in one." He suggested that with the proper program, it could once again assume that traditional role. He envisioned a new, multifaceted synagogue that would be "a place for study for adults in the evenings and for children in the afternoons." It would be a social and recreational center for young adults where, "after plying their daily cares, they could spend a social hour in an Orthodox environment and in a truly Jewish atmosphere." This synagogue also would offer decorous modern Orthodox religious services designed specifically for an American congregation, while "keeping intact the Jewish ceremonies of our people." Goldstein was convinced that "if we desire to perpetuate the ideal Judaism of the past we must so shape Jewish spiritual activity that [it] will all find expression in one institution." He presented the Institutional Synagogue as that ideal Jewish cultural, social, and, above all, religious organization that would embrace the synagogue, the Talmud Torah, and the Y.

Finally, Goldstein submitted that he had both history and practicality on his side. From a purely financial standpoint it would be cheaper for each Jewish community to build one large institution combining all activities than to support a separate shul, school, and social center. He also reasoned that the individual Jew could, for a little higher membership fee at a multiuse operation, derive the benefits of three Jewish spaces. Implicit here was the understanding that the new organization would reach out primarily to those who could pay for membership, thus removing from the Institutional Synagogue the possible stigma of pauperism. So positioned, the three-in-one synagogue center would possess the additional advantage of making it possible for all members of a family to participate in their own age group activities within the same religious institution and thereby "bring back to family life that religious unity and enthusiasm which is sorely lacking today."[26]

It is not known how aware Goldstein was of developments at the Harlem women's Y, which resembled and, in fact, preceded albeit on a less grand scale the Institutional Synagogue initiative. As early as 1914, the 110th Street Y synagogue and auditorium had on premises a library, rooms for lectures, and a gymnasium. Although Unterberg and her colleagues never described what they had built as a synagogue center, effectively it did most of the jobs that Goldstein wanted for men and women just six blocks way on 116th Street between Lenox and Fifth Avenues. And in October 1916—seven months before the Institutional Synagogue opened its doors—the women's Y added to its panoply of activities a swimming pool. Goldstein would follow suit and included a pool in his shul.[27]

However, it is abundantly clear that Goldstein put into action and built upon ideas that Rabbi Mordecai M. Kaplan was constructing in the early 1910s. Later in both men's careers, they would become angry antagonists when Kaplan began to publicly articulate his Reconstructionist philosophies. Goldstein was among the first Orthodox leaders to oppose his heretical views. Nonetheless, while Goldstein was still a Jewish Theological Seminary student, he was caught up—as all rabbinical students were—with the professor's criticism of American Jewish life. And many of these rabbis in training were captivated by Kaplan's proposed solutions. Most notably here, Kaplan was well aware of the weaknesses of the men's Y movement as he served for a period, starting in 1913, as chair of the 92nd Street Y's Committee on Religious Work. From that position, he clamored unsuccessfully for the institution to "seek to stimulate" in its members "a positive enthusiasm for Judaism." Seemingly as always, the Y was content to make sure its young men stayed away from "worse places," like the gambling dens on Yorkville's streets. When the Harlem Y was created, Kaplan was once again sure to remonstrate that there was little that was "distinctly Jewish in the content of the movement which would set it off from non-sectarian settlement houses." In his most uncharitable statement, he characterized the Ys as "secular organizations" financed by Jewish money and called upon the national movement either to drop the name "Hebrew" from its title and openly declare itself a nonreligious organization or immediately reconstitute itself as a "distinctly Jewish organization" and commit itself wholeheartedly to the battle against "disaffection from faith and its practices."[28]

In 1915, Kaplan, the great thinker, and Goldstein, the dynamic worker, established a prototype of a multifunctional and deeply religious synagogue center as an alternative to the Y when they collaborated in the establishment of the Central Jewish Institute (CJI) next door to Congregation Kehilath Jeshurun. Kaplan had maintained personal ties with the synagogue's leaders and Goldstein had followed him into the position of English-speaking rabbi. And the Yorkville community was a fine testing ground for their approach to attracting young people to a modern synagogue. Many of Kehilath Jeshurun's senior members were drawn from among the most affluent elements in east European immigrant society. They had succeeded in less than a generation in achieving a degree of economic advancement comparable to that of Lenox Avenue's Jews. Religiously, they were depicted by one of the social work professionals who was part of the team at the CJI as "orthodox, which implies adherence to Jewish ceremonies and customs and an allegiance to Jewish life." This older generation was described as descendants of "families which were respected in the social life of the eastern European ghetto where learning was the distinguishing class mark."

But their own children's religious values were hardly in line with the faith's traditions. These young people were observed by this same professional as a "half-baked second generation who knew little of Jewish life, tending to associate it merely with the ceremonies and especially with the prohibitions observed in the home. They are generally indifferent to, if not ashamed of Jewish life." What was needed was an "agency to bridge the gap between the generations, to interpret the old traditions in terms of the new." The CJI, with Goldstein as director—Kaplan, a self-described "stationary director" was on the search committee that appointed his erstwhile student—promised to address this pressing inter-generational dilemma.[29]

Clearly, Kaplan spoke both for himself and for Goldstein when, at the CJI building's ground-breaking ceremony, he prayed that the new institution would "not merely be [an ordinary Hebrew school], but also a Jewish Social Centre, wherein there are provided a gymnasium, room for club work, kindergarten classes, and a kosher kitchen; in short a centre where the ideas of traditional Judaism will be fostered and encouraged in the minds of American youth."[30]

This first major attempt at amalgamating Jewish social, cultural, and recreational programs with a heavy dose of religious influence and education proved almost immediately to be less than the truly complete synagogue center that Kaplan envisioned and which Goldstein was eager to develop. The major defect in its multifaceted program was, ironically, the synagogue itself. Although leaders of Kehilath Jeshurun supported the endeavor, the CJI had almost no practical relationship with the congregation next door. The synagogue failed to coordinate or update its religious practices and rituals with the social and educational activities of the CJI. One critic of the Yorkville initiative claimed that it possessed all the elements of a synagogue center "but only externally so. The three departments have no close contact because the synagogue element is not bold enough. The synagogue has not developed its full capacity and its influence is small." By the spring of 1917, Goldstein was ready to move on and further uptown. In a solicitation letter to Jacob Schiff, he declared that he was "prepared to dedicate my life for . . . a revival movement everywhere in our City, beginning with Harlem." Towards that end, he was "prepared to give at least one year of services gratis for the sake of the Cause." He let Schiff know that his salary in Yorkville "for the last year was $3,000."[31]

Goldstein's proposal for "bringing the message of Jewish Religious Revival to our youth; to enlist"—as he told Schiff—"the thousands of our young men and young women who are unattached to any Synagogue work and who have drifted to Christian Science and every other kind of Science except Jewish Science" was very well received by the leaders of the still-fledgling Harlem Young Men's Hebrew Orthodox League. Its thirty-five members, taken by Goldstein's concepts, decided to reconstitute the organization and to "push with vigor its campaign for the establishment of a real Jewish center in Harlem." The League, which previously sponsored only religious and cultural activities, announced its intention to construct a gymnasium and to build a library to attract a larger segment of uptown Jewry to its organization. More impressive was the new Harlem Y's decision in April 1917 under the leadership of its new president, Isaac Siegel, to join the Harlem League in inviting

Goldstein, who had previously pilloried its work, to coordinate uptown neighborhood youth efforts. The rabbi, whom Siegel described as "fearless, staunch [and] loyal in the cause of Traditional Judaism," was called upon to lead "a revival movement to revive the faith of our Fathers in the hearts of their children." The two youth organizations were reconstituted as the Institutional Synagogue.[32]

Rabbi Goldstein accepted the call of uptown Jewry as an exciting challenge and made only two major requests of Harlem leaders: that he be granted life tenure as rabbi and that the synagogue's constitution provide that "no innovation in traditional Judaism may be inaugurated" into its rituals "if there be one dissenting vote at a meeting of the corporation." His position thus secured, Goldstein immediately made plans for creating his "Jewish revival movement in Harlem."[33]

Fittingly, the synagogue's first meetings were held at the women's Y on 110th Street. And the accommodating host, in fact, published in its bulletin that "regular Friday evening and Saturday morning services would be conducted" on its premises. Perhaps leaders of the two institutions compared notes on how those who habitually came to play could be convinced to stay and pray. Meanwhile, Goldstein made himself better known within the women's Y community by teaching a Hebrew class for the girls, a sure way also to recruit members for his organization.[34]

By June 1917, the Institutional Synagogue was able to strike out on its own into what Goldstein called the "heart of the most distressing Jewish conditions in the United States." An anonymous donor—very likely his own father-in-law, Harry Fischel—stepped up and financed the purchase of a suitable building at 116th Street between Fifth and Lenox Avenues that would house a synagogue, club and social rooms, library, pool, and gymnasium. And even as remodeling began on the new center, Goldstein, anxious to get his work going, announced plans for "monster rallies" throughout Harlem to attract thousands of young people to his movement. He proposed the leasing of local theaters on Sunday mornings for services and lectures to reach "the large mass of young men and women who cannot be reached on the Sabbath." At that time it was almost axiomatic that most immigrants and their children worked six days a week and thus would be at their jobs or shops when even the most modern of services were conducted. Sunday had to be the day where these folks could be engaged. In a closely related move,

Goldstein suggested that his congregation's leaders approach observant Jewish merchants in the neighborhood to solicit jobs for Jewish young people who themselves wished to keep the Sabbath.[35]

Goldstein's Sunday revival meetings and diversified program of youth activities quickly attracted the support of neighborhood people. By September 1917, after only several months of activity, the Institutional Synagogue brought some twelve hundred worshippers to its Rosh ha-Shanah services held at a public hall in Central Harlem. In January 1918, the synagogue reported that it had built a constituency of two thousand dues-paying members who were attending thirty-one clubs and eight religious classes conducted at the 116th Street building. A month later the Institutional Synagogue opened, in conjunction with the Jewish Sabbath Association, a Harlem branch of the association's employment bureau. And subsequently Goldstein attempted to convince all Jewish shopkeepers in Harlem to close their stores on Saturday to "arose a Jewish spirit in the neighborhood."[36]

The Institutional Synagogue's most ambitious program remained its so-called Jewish "missionary work," expressed through those frequent "monster rallies." Mount Morris Theatre, situated only one-half block away from the synagogue center, was the usual location for these gatherings, which often featured lectures by politicians and well-known local and national Jewish figures. Rabbi Goldstein explained the underlying methodology and purpose of these well-publicized events when he declared that "every community needs an occasional soul-stirring re-awakening and a revival of a religious interest from time to time. At our regular religious services we attract only those who are habitual synagogue-goers, but we must reach the wavering as well. This can only be done through revival meetings."[37]

Nonetheless, the Institutional Synagogue absorbed more than its share of criticism during its early years. The most frequently heard charge was that this Orthodox synagogue was ultimately parochial in nature and simply a recast, improved Harlem Young Men's Hebrew Orthodox League of use only to those of that particularly religious orientation. The presence of the members of the Harlem Y on the board of the 116th Street center apparently made little impression upon those who opposed Goldstein's efforts. Critics echoed the long-standing national YMHA contention that "inasmuch in a community there are young men of various religious beliefs and some of no religion at all, the problem cannot be solved by a temple or synagogue." Some dissenters were quick to observe that certain people were not inspired by synagogue activities, no matter how diversified they might be. "Shall they come under no influence at all?"[38]

Critics also noted that the Institutional Synagogue's three-in-one membership fee was proof of its elitist nature. One spokesman representing the Harlem YMHA described Goldstein's organization quite critically as "a private institution for the children coming from parents not necessarily wealthy, but those who can afford to pay for instruction." Membership rates at the Institutional Synagogue, it was contended, were prohibitive to ordinary wage earners.[39]

Finally, there were those who felt that the mass-oriented revival movement was not within the true spirit of Judaism, preferring rabbis who played a less activist—certainly less histrionic—role in community life. Opponents deplored Goldstein's decision to "resign as a minister of an established congregation to donate his entire time and energy to Billy Sundayism." Goldstein was advised to "concentrate on religious education" and leave "sensationalism" to Christian ministers. Billy Sunday was a widely popular fire-and-brimstone evangelist who in 1917—the same year that Goldstein came to Harlem—staged a ten-week campaign in the city that attracted some hundred thousand people to his sermons.[40]

Goldstein responded by asserting that his movement was essentially traditional, dedicated towards bringing the unaffiliated into the synagogue and leading those ignorant of the faith towards the house of study. He also argued that there was nothing novel or radical about the concept of "Jewish revivalism." In his view, the prophets of antiquity and the itinerant preachers of the Old World as well as those who preached about returning the masses to religiosity in the downtown east European settlement were all "revivalists" and all operated within the confines of Jewish tradition. Goldstein asserted that he had both Jewish history and modern ministerial techniques on his side.[41]

Of all the efforts of Jewish activists during Harlem's east European heyday between 1900 and the end of World War I to recapture wavering or disengaged youths back towards Jewish identification, it was the Institutional Synagogue that most strongly influenced later communal developments, both near and far. To begin with, in 1918, one year after

Goldstein brought his initiative to his neighborhood, Kaplan concretized his vision of an all-embracing synagogue on the West Side of Manhattan. The Jewish Center on 86th Street between Columbus and Amsterdam Avenue had all the elements of the Institutional Synagogue. Goldstein got his head start with the encouragement of Harry Fischel. Kaplan was assisted by a few well-heeled former members of Kehilath Jeshurun in building a home that "would bring Jews together . . . for social, cultural and recreational purposes in addition to worship." In the inter-war period, the models that Goldstein and Kaplan created were emulated and duplicated both in new Jewish neighborhoods in New York and indeed in communities all over the country. However, the "magic"—as Kaplan disciple Rabbi Israel Levinthal once described the process—whereby those who came to play eventually stayed to pray very frequently did not work. One of the many critics of the initiative that began in Harlem and spread to West Side Manhattan contended that a member has "only a certain amount of energy at his command and when, during the week, one attends a card party"—or for that matter the gymnasium or pool—"one feels that one's duty towards the Congregation is fully performed and the Friday night and Saturday morning services are of necessity neglected." As important, while rabbis like Goldstein, Kaplan, and Levinthal were indeed pulpit eminences, those who interacted with the young people in the clubs, art rooms, libraries, and gyms often did not direct their charges to the sanctuary. Brooklyn Rabbi Harry Weiss argued, for example, that he had "yet to hear an athletic director say we have enjoyed the gymnasium of the Synagogue for so long. We have served the cause of play, now come boys, next Friday night let us all turn out and hear something about our ancient Faith and about the ideals of our people."[42]

These communities—and ones to this day, as well—ultimately had to come to grips with the same challenges that had long concerned Jews in Harlem. Back in 1904, it was observed that "the younger generation, in most cases, left the old behind. . . . American customs, institutions and the like surround them and the Hebrews of Harlem became day by day more American." More often than not, Jews remained in touch not so much with their religious traditions but with one another, the rich and the poor, the devout and the secular, as together they walked on a daily basis the streets of uptown during Harlem's Jewish heyday.

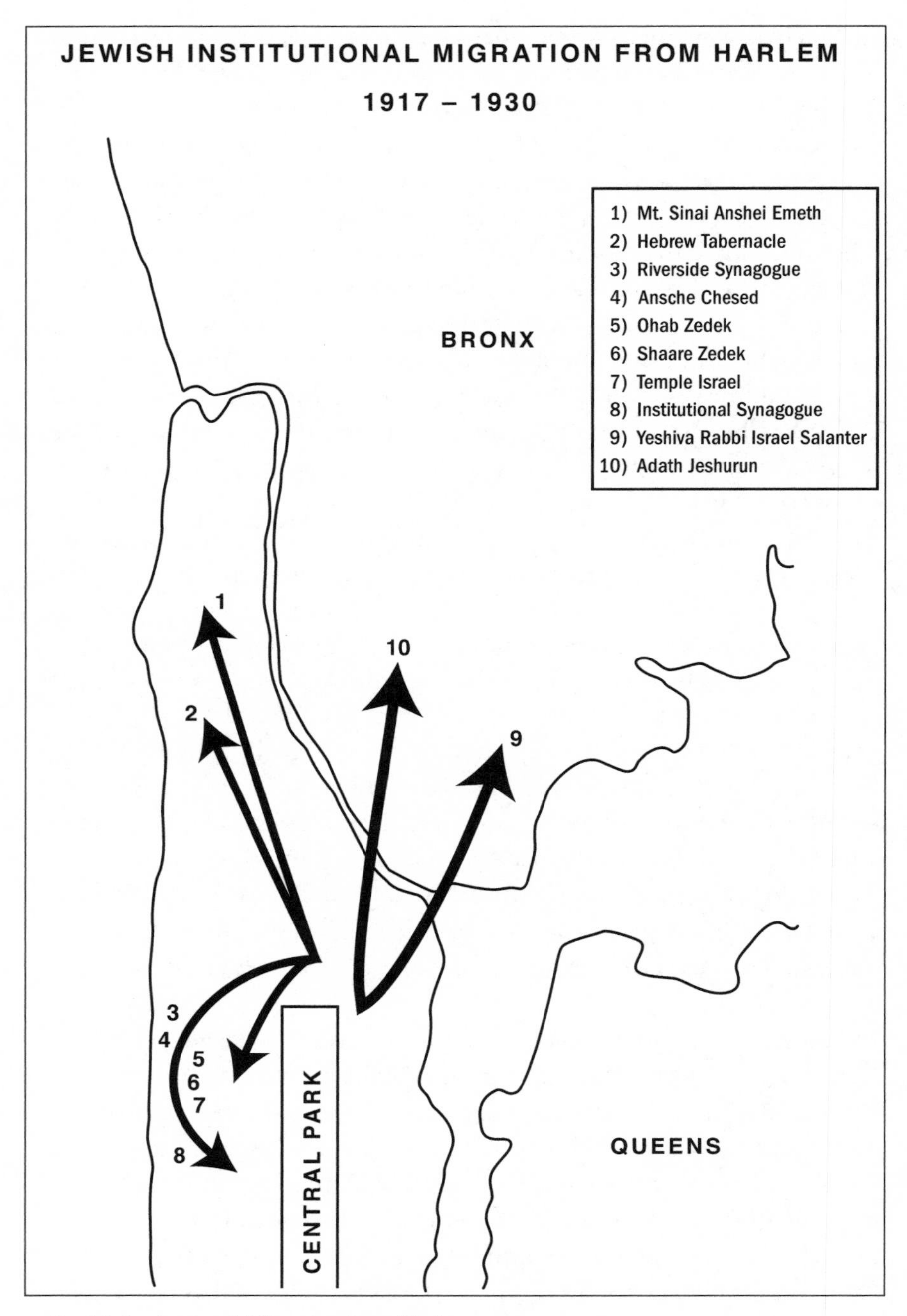

Jewish Institutional Migration from Harlem, 1917–1930.

7

The Scattering of the Harlem Jewish Community, 1917–1930

In 1929, N. Davidoff, chairman of Branch No. 2 of the Arbeter Ring—his first name also has been lost to history, but what he had to say about Jewish Harlem remains important—reflected with satisfaction and a degree of pride on his organization's past and present-day status and location. Expressing no sadness over the decision of the workers' group to leave what was now their old uptown neighborhood, Davidoff declared, "Branch No. 2 was born in Harlem and we have lived there and grown. When the time came and the majority of the members moved away to the Bronx, it was natural that the branch goes where the greatest numbers of members were. Therefore we can see that although we are growing old, we are keeping up with the times."

Several years later, an anonymous Yiddish writer put to work during the Great Depression by the Federal Writers' Project offered a terse understanding of where members of Harlem's hundreds of *landsmanshaften* had gone and why they had left the neighborhood. The migration was "not due to economic need. The removal is voluntary and the reason is not gloomy. Jews on the road to bettering themselves and making life more convenient for them moved from Harlem up to the Bronx."[1]

Israel Stone did not leave a personal account of his family's peregrinations. But census and building records tell us that, as of 1915, this onetime clothier who became a real estate operator was living quite well in his large apartment in a seven-story elevator building that boasted of a "highly-decorative brick and stone façade" at 92 Morningside Avenue, across the street from bucolic Morningside Park. There he resided with his wife, his widowed daughter, Martha, who had become a stenographer—a good occupation for a second-generation American Jewish woman—and her son, Herbert, who seemingly helped out in the business as a real estate collector. This middle-class Jewish family continued to employ a gentile servant in their home, another sign of their affluence in their comfortable section of Harlem. Eight years later, when Israel passed away at age seventy-three, the family still lived on Morningside Avenue, although his death certificate now characterized his dwelling as a tenement. But by 1930, Martha had relocated by herself to 69th Street off Central Park West, where she rented an apartment in a classy multifamily house. As of 1925, a recently married Herbert, who earned his living as an importer, had settled with his bride, Florence, in a newly built low-rise apartment building, west of the Grand Concourse. But they did not stay long in this emerging and soon to be renowned Jewish neighborhood in the Bronx. By 1930, in an unusual move for a young Jewish couple of that inter-war era, they had bought a single-family home in Floral Park, a suburb in western Nassau County. At that point, Herbert was the proprietor of a dress trimming shop. In 1931, Herbert and Florence welcomed the arrival of a daughter, Marilyn. They would live in Floral Park until the start of World War II.[2]

As these memoirs and vignettes begin to suggest, as of the end of the 1920s, Jewish Harlem's heyday was over. For the third time in its Jewish history, changes in the status of uptown housing stock, along with the growth of new neighborhood options combined with expansions and improvements in the city's rapid transit system, largely determined whether immigrants and their children would choose to reside within the uptown district. Only now, this crucial set of circumstances led masses of Jews to leave Harlem for other metropolitan areas where they would find homes and jobs. The turning point that led to Jews being pulled away from a community that was once so attractive to the affluent and struggling alike was America's entry into World War I.

As of 1917, the metropolis was home to seven neighborhoods with extraordinarily large Jewish populations, all in excess of 100,000 people. At that point, though the Lower East Side was still bursting with its approximately 350,000 Jewish immigrants and their children, more Jews had found their way out or were pushed to successor communities. These areas were either in touch with, or disconnected from, downtown Manhattan. East Harlem, starting at 96th Street, was home to an estimated 113,000 Jews, while Central Harlem north of 110th Street welcomed some 61,000 residents. Over in Brooklyn, Williamsburg, which was the first outer-borough area to attract large numbers of Jews, boasted

107,000 Jewish residents, almost as many as East Harlem. But by then, an equal number of intra-city migrants had moved to East New York and Brownsville. Up in the Bronx, the Jewish presence was divided almost equally between those who settled north and south of 168th Street. Meanwhile, Queens awaited its own era of large-scale Jewish settlement; at the time only 23,000 Jews lived in the borough, much of which was almost suburban in character. And the 5,000 Jews who were spread out in Staten Island were as remote from the heart of the city as Harlem had been some fifty years earlier. The borough of Richmond would not have a substantial Jewish community for another seventy-five years. While each of these metropolitan Jewish enclaves, until the Great War, intermittently gained and lost people as new rapid transit lines and bridge links encouraged intra-city migration, and immigrant Jews were always leaving downtown, there was a certain degree of stability to neighborhood life.[3]

For example, the starting point for the Jewish Bronx began in the mid-1880s when a spur of the Third Avenue El was extended across an iron drawbridge into the southernmost part of the borough, with its terminus at 132nd Street. Over the next decade and a half, elevated connections would be extended as far north as Fordham Road. And in 1905, the subways made their way beyond Manhattan, ultimately ending up as far north as 242nd Street and White Plains Road. Business and shopping districts began to form around stops on the line, most notably at the so-called "Hub" at 149th Street and Third Avenue, where the subway entered the borough. Not surprisingly, after 1905, north New York experienced its own real estate boom with the now familiar come-on of "easy and cheap transportation" that attracted former tenement dwellers to both "high class houses," and to four- and five-story walk-ups. Meanwhile, the Williamsburg Bridge, which had contributed mightily to the pushing of poor Jews out of the Lower East Side, ultimately served its purpose of developing that Brooklyn neighborhood as an attractive venue for Jewish immigrants and their children. The bridge—which one New York newspaper called "the Jews' Highway"—initially ran trolley lines across the East River and later subways made it highly convenient for those who might work on Delancey Street and return home to Brooklyn's Grand Street or Bedford Avenue. And in Brownsville and neighboring East New York, the tradition that Elias Kaplan started in the 1890s continued as that section of Brooklyn attracted needle trades factories and their garment workers.[4]

However, notwithstanding all of these Jewish population shifts, there was a palpable calmness throughout the metropolis about the city's ability to absorb and distribute its denizens within its existing neighborhoods. Most pre-war observers of the New York real estate scene harbored the expectation that the slow but ongoing development of new areas would offset at least partially any further large increase in population. Tenement House Department officials prophesized that Gotham's poor and working-class elements would continue to disperse until Manhattan ceased being the residential hub of an emerging multicentric metropolis. This equanimity would end once America entered World War I in 1917.[5]

Wartime governmental restrictions on all but essential construction brought apartment house and tenement building almost to a standstill. New housing starts were also severely curtailed by what one New York City official described as "the exceedingly high price of materials, the delay in obtaining them and the scarcity of skilled laborers." He further observed that "extremely abnormal conditions resulting from the great European conflict rendered building almost prohibitive."[6]

The cessation in construction occurred at the very moment when the city, due to a mass influx of population, needed new housing construction more than ever. The war industries established in, and around, the major urban centers were attracting hundreds of thousands of workers, many of them African Americans, from rural areas. Gotham received more than its share of the migrants. Between 1916 and 1920, the city's population rose by more than 600,000. Overcrowded Manhattan, which since 1910 had been slowly losing residents, quickly acquired 145,000 settlers. These newcomers, like millions before them, competed with the existing population for the limited housing available. The relatively few new apartments constructed before the war were swiftly occupied. New York's pre-war residential equilibrium was soon shattered and tenement and apartment house dwellers throughout the city were confronted with seriously overcrowded conditions.[7]

The city's Tenement House Department found, for example, that in 1917, apartments in new-law buildings were "unobtainable." It reported, "rents in such buildings were rising and families were 'doubling up.'

(Families that formerly occupied separate apartments are now living together.)" Other governmental agencies observed two years later that "over twenty thousand of the houses erected before the new law, which were not in use in 1916, were serving as dwellings in 1919. There are practically no unoccupied apartments that are fit for human habitation."[8]

The attempts of city landlords to capitalize on the increased demand for scarce housing exacerbated this home-front crisis. Armed with the knowledge that most tenants had little option but to pay whatever rents were demanded, landlords hiked prices to what a State Housing Commission described as "unreasonable and oppressive" levels. Having little need to do anything to attract tenants, landlords also permitted tenement properties to deteriorate. Another state examination of post-war housing conditions determined that, as of 1919, "families were crowded together in dark ill-smelling apartments, and were unable to find better quarters. In every block were found ill-kept apartments, in fact, certain of them were not kept at all. One tenant said that her shoes had been worn out looking for another apartment."[9]

This study also observed that the housing shortage was causing problems for all classes of city dwellers, noting that the "raising of rents resulting from the shortage of houses has affected not only the poor, but a large part of the population even among the moderately well-to-do." The study concluded, "New York's housing capacity is very elastic, but the time is near where there will actually be no more room even in the indecently rotten old-law homes."[10]

Harlem was among the most affected sections of the city. Once a safety valve for excess East Side population and a desired neighborhood for those on the rise in America, it now had to grapple with intensive overcrowding. Central Harlem, for example, experienced a net increase of some 11,000 people between 1915 and 1920, a growth in population of 15 percent over the pre-war period. Uptown housing did not keep pace, as only twenty-four more houses were available for residential use in 1920 than were ten years earlier. Harlem's most affluent district was confronted for the first time with a serious housing dilemma.[11]

Central Harlem also faced the exploitation of money-hungry landlords. Charles Marks, attorney for several tenant groups, including the West Harlem Tenants Association, testified before a Gubernatorial Commission on Housing that, in one building, twenty tenants were being forced to pay a "rental increase from $36–55." Marks reported, "in this case no repairs of any kind or nature have been made of any perceptible kind, excepting absolutely necessary sanitary repairs."[12]

In East Harlem, the era of rent profiteering only accelerated the deterioration of an already densely populated neighborhood. As early as 1913, the Charity Organization Society declared that the "problems of poverty, need and congestion" in East Harlem were comparable to those which were commonly associated only with the Lower East Side. All tenements in the area, the group said, were "narrow and thickly populated with a poor class of people." Three years later, a study conducted by the Eastern Council of Reform Rabbis determined that "there are worse congested districts in the North East Side than the East Side; only members of the Eastern Council do not see the evils that are right next door to them. Harlem notably, the West Side, Washington Heights and Brooklyn need very careful looking after."[13]

East Harlem was severely distressed by the housing shortage and by landlord neglect during the war years. A post-war study of a typical East Harlem block revealed a "great number of buildings of the old type that only demolition and reconstruction can make habitable." By that time, those in Harlem with the financial means to escape the overcrowding were well prepared to abandon the old neighborhood and were among those pressing for the revival of suitable accommodations. The housing crisis was pushing the city to a brink.[14]

In 1921, the Board of Estimate relieved palpable urban tensions when it passed a far-reaching tax exemption ordinance that galvanized new safety-valve construction. Legislators at City Hall were very worried that their metropolis might suffer the calamitous fate of twenty-five other American cities that had suffered through the so-called "Red Summer" of 1919. In places close to New York like Philadelphia and Syracuse—not to mention Chicago and the nation's capital—tensions had boiled over into race riots. Living cheek to jowl on broiling streets in overcrowded neighborhoods and coming into close contact at crowded beaches and other public accommodations, whites and blacks violently confronted each other.[15] With an eye on what had happened elsewhere, the law—which was extended several times during the 1920s—basically freed "all new buildings planned for dwelling purposes" from ten years of real estate taxes. Attractive neighborhoods would soon rise in Manhattan and the outer boroughs. This far-reaching solution to New York's most pressing dilemma profoundly affected how its citizenry lived, worked, and in many cases prospered during the next two decades.[16]

Energized by this mandate, local builders and real estate operators immediately sprang into action. In Brooklyn alone, during the first nine months of 1921, plans were filed for 6,303 new multiple-family dwellings with 22,338 apartments. Many of the buildings differed little from pre-war four- and five-story walk-ups even if promoters said that they were "up-to date . . . with spacious interior courts for light and air." But in the Bronx in 1922, the first "million dollar apartment house" signaled a new era of housing. This nine-story edifice on Kingsbridge Road and the Grand Concourse boasted "modern, fire proof apartments arranged so that each living unit occup[ied] an entire wing of the structure, equipped with high speed elevators, intercommunication system [and] a steam laundry in the building." Such construction set a pattern for new developments in the city for the entire decade until the Great Depression. In Queens new residents flowed into neighborhoods such as Long Island City, Astoria, and Jackson Heights. While Manhattan, in the 1920s, lagged behind in the number of new housing starts, its relatively few new luxury apartment houses were usually more expensive than those built elsewhere in the city. Riverside Drive, Central Park West, Park Avenue below 96th Street and, to a lesser degree, Washington Heights saw the construction of many elegant residences.[17]

Prospective tenants appreciated the opportunity to live in one of the "subway suburbs." As Gotham's history once again repeated itself, the notion that a merchant, manufacturer, or even a worker could relocate the family to a more wholesome setting and commute quickly and cheaply back to Manhattan offices, factories, construction sites, or stores represented a promise renewed. That is, if they possessed the economic wherewithal to make a move. And in the good-times decade of the 1920s, "labor was never as prosperous as it is today," reported one tenement house official. He continued: "the American worker has always been desirous of bringing up his family in the best possible surroundings. He has tried to get away from the sordidness and the present prosperity has afforded him an opportunity of which he has taken full advantage."[18] But the ability to commute every workday easily and inexpensively from home to job, seemingly as always, was critical. The extension of the subways as far north as Bronx Park, White Plains Road, Jerome Avenue, and Pelham Bay Park made these areas readily accessible. In the late 1910s and early 1920s, subway lines were constructed over and under the East River, bringing Brooklyn and some Queens neighborhoods into close contact with Manhattan. As "long as dwellings are within the 5 cent zone, such as new rapid transit routes afford," a real estate journal observed early on in 1921, "tenants are willing to go to the [outer] boroughs."[19]

First- and second-generation New York Jews were major players in this transformation of the metropolis. Their real estate people invested heavily in the new properties. Much like turn-of-the-century speculators, aggressive Jewish entrepreneurs once again, it was said, "ran lustily when they heard the bell of opportunity tolling its promise." A contemporary observer of this renewed business dynamism further reported that "aflame with schemes, plans and ambitions for bigger things," they have "grown rich, prosperous, financially independent . . . strutting in front of their skyscrapers and breathing freely with their chests out."[20] And just like before, Jewish skilled construction workers built many of the buildings. Once a building was ready to rent, the entrepreneurs who owned and operated the apartment houses got the message out to fellow Jews—either through word of mouth or local advertising—that some of the most commodious housing going up in the city was available. And as had been the case with the evolution of Harlem's Jewish districts a generation earlier, different classes of Jews were on the move and settled in distinctive communities. For an advancing class of Jews who had risen out of factory work to owning small businesses, an apartment on the Grand Concourse in the Bronx or on Eastern Parkway in Brooklyn or on the Upper West Side of Manhattan signaled success in America. Economic and social calculi called for them to invest heavily in their shop or industry while setting aside enough money to rent an appropriate home. Once word got back to friends and relatives in older neighborhoods, a chain migration began. Their destinations included the Bronx and newer parts of Brooklyn, like Boro Park, Flatbush, and Bensonhurst; some even migrated across the Hudson to sections of northeastern New Jersey.[21]

During this decade of extensive relocations that ended abruptly with the Great Depression, working-class Jews moved to their own substantial, if less elegant, venues in the city. What was different in this era, as opposed to the beginning of the twentieth century, is that such people of limited means were pulled far more than they were pushed out of their erstwhile neighborhoods to new locales. In the Bronx particularly, Jewish labor unions and radical organizations built cooperative apartment complexes for their members. In the case of the Amalgamated housing development, home by 1931 to some seven hundred families in the Van Cortlandt section of the northwest Bronx, workers benefited from another important piece of state legislation. The Limited Dividend Housing Companies law of 1926 granted tax breaks to builders who limited dividends to 6 percent, established moderate rents, and opened their doors to tenants with low incomes. Everyone enjoyed the "landscaped gardens" around the buildings and took full advantage of the "new subway and elevated lines [that] provided a quick and easy commute to jobs in Manhattan's garment district." Elsewhere in the Bronx, other Jews of limited means relied not upon union or political group initiatives but on pooled family incomes to pay rents that were only slightly higher than those charged by Manhattan tenement landlords. For example, while the Grand Concourse was economically beyond working-class Jews, for just a bit more money than they presently were paying, they could relocate to the new housing in the Morrisania or Hunts Point sections of the Bronx, where there was already a Jewish presence.[22]

Consequently, the Jewish neighborhood-by-neighborhood population profile changed dramatically in the 1920s. The Lower East Side lost two thirds of its immigrant and second-generation inhabitants and by 1930 was home to fewer than 100,000 Jews. Many of the downtown Jews who had spilled over into working-class areas of pre-war Williamsburg set their sights on the new Brooklyn enclaves. By 1930, its 800,000 Jews constituted a full one third of that borough's population. There was also a new presence of Jews in sections of Queens, like Jamaica, Astoria, Whitestone, Woodhaven, and Laurelton. There, newly successful residents came from older sections of Brooklyn, such as the poorer areas of Brownsville and East New York. Meanwhile in the Bronx, by the end of the 1920s, the northernmost borough housed some 585,000 Jews in middle- and working-class neighborhoods, up from the some 200,000 who lived there in 1917.[23]

During intra-city relocations of the 1920s, Jewish Harlem lost more of its population than any place else in Gotham. A community that crested at approximately 175,000 at the height of the housing crisis began to lose members as soon as new construction began in the city in 1921. By 1923, Jewish Harlem had dropped to an estimated 160,000 residents and communal observers were already talking about a neighborhood in decline. The Jewish Welfare Board, for example, declared that "the outlook for a steady reduction of Harlem's Jewish population due to the restrictions on immigration"—quotas that limited east European Jews coming to the United States had just taken effect—"the desire to better oneself socially as the economic status improves, [and] the influx of negroes [*sic*], Italians and Spanish-speaking groups." This report noted, however, that the Jewish migration from Harlem was "only at the rate of 1.4 percent annually." In other words, a long good-bye was predicted.[24]

But the prognostication greatly underestimated the rate of dispersion from uptown—just two years later, in 1925, another independent communal survey found that only 123,000 Jews remained in Harlem. The settlement had suffered a population decline of more than 25 percent over the preceding two years, far more than the 1.4 percent per annum predicted in 1923.[25]

The flow of Jews out of the neighborhood increased even more dramatically in the second half of the decade. By 1927, Harlem Jewry numbered only 88,000, nearly a third fewer than in 1925. Three years later, the exodus was almost complete. The highest contemporary estimate of population fixed the Jewish number at 25,000. A much later retrospective study estimated the neighborhood cohort in 1930 at 5,500. Although several thousand Jews would continue to live there through succeeding decades, Harlem's era as a landmark on the Jewish communal map of Gotham was over as of 1930.[26]

Although Jewish Harlem declined far more rapidly than other prewar neighborhoods, economic mobility and better housing opportunities pulled its residents away more than the arrival of large numbers of African Americans into the deteriorating neighborhood pushed them out. What transpired in the neighborhood between Jews and African Americans after World War I ultimately bespeaks their differing financial fates and social statuses within the life of the metropolis. A federal study concluded in 1931 may have capsulized the divergence best when it observed that while the children of immigrants possessed the "possibility of escape, with improvement of economic status to more desirable sections of the city" among "Negroes . . . certain definite racial attitudes favorable to segregation interpose difficulties to . . . breaking physical restrictions in residential areas."[27]

Actually, blacks and Jews first encountered each other uptown in the first decade of the twentieth century when African Americans were also pushed and pulled to new housing north of Central Park. In their case, frightening street violence that predominately Irish American mobs perpetrated against blacks shoved them out of the so-called Tenderloin district, that part of Manhattan that runs roughly from 23rd Street to 42nd Street between Fifth and Seventh Avenue. The most infamous riot in that part of town took place over three hot days in August 1900, when white mobs enraged by the killing of a white policeman by a black (he claimed that the cop was harassing his girlfriend) took to the streets and attacked any and all blacks that they could find. With police complicity, blacks, it was reported, were "beaten, jumped upon and the sent flying" as, in the language of the day, a "nigger chase" was on. Though cooler heads eventually prevailed—with the help of a rainstorm—the sense within the African American community was that this often-inhospitable Irish neighborhood had become intolerable. At that point, those with the means to move looked uptown.[28]

The pull of Harlem was the availability of housing far superior to anything that members of their race had experienced in any metropolitan area. As was the story with Jewish Harlem, an enterprising group of black real estate speculators capitalized upon the fluctuations that the construction of the subways brought to building values in the neighborhood. In 1905 the Afro-American Realty Company (AARC) bought up many unoccupied and semi-filled apartment houses, as the original builders had overestimated the numbers of whites who wanted to live in Harlem, and made them available to their own people. Some white realtors also filled their apartments with blacks, charging them far above market rates for the privilege of settlement. Former Tenderloin residents along with those who lived in Manhattan's other black enclave, San Juan Hill—a depressed and crime-infested area that extended from 59th Street to the mid-60s between Amsterdam Avenue and West End Avenue—made every effort to find a place in Harlem. To pay their rents, some settlers took in lodgers as many were forced to allocate up to a third of their incomes to live in what one African American observer described as "one of the choice sections of Harlem, conveniently and beautifully located, with broad asphalt avenues and streets, modern apartments . . . and admirable transportation to the city."[29]

Some Jewish firms played a role in black real estate entrepreneurship. One controversial connection came to light amid what was deemed a "real estate war" in Harlem late in 1905. Reportedly, the AARC "dispossessed" a group of "white folks . . . working men of small incomes" from three "tenement houses on 135th Street" that it had acquired to make way for black residents. The *New York Times* was quick to comment that those whom it saw as victimized "were experiencing the fate visited upon a set of negro [*sic*] tenants a year earlier." Indeed, it was the pushing out of these blacks by the Hudson Realty Company that inspired "a few well-to do negroes," further characterized as "decent, hardworking negroes," to organize the AARC. The Jewish connection was that the "real estate concern" of Kassel and Cohen, and not the so-called Hudson group, was the actual owner of the property that first evicted blacks and then conveyed the holding to the AARC.[30]

On other occasions, Jewish real estate people joined with their white Christian counterparts in sustained efforts to "protect themselves" through creating restrictive covenants against what was called "The Negro Invasion."[31] One such protective organization, the West Side Improvement Association, which the city's leading black newspaper, the *New York Age*, characterized as "composed in the main by Jews," tried to evict African Americans from the West 90th–110th Street area, encompassing parts of the Upper West Side and Harlem. Reportedly, the rationale for such behavior was not "prejudice against the race," but apprehension that "their presence in a neighborhood would cause the value of property to deteriorate."[32]

These discriminatory actions did not sit well with journalists from the *American Hebrew*. It decried the hypocrisy of those individuals who called upon blacks to improve their lives and then denied them a decent place to reside. "How are they to become thrifty and independent and give their children the best education possible," wrote one editorialist, "if they are not allowed to acquire homes suitable for persons of refinement?"[33]

The downtown voices of both the Orthodox *Yiddishes Tageblatt* and the Socialist *Forward* were even more concerned about the violence that blacks faced first in the Tenderloin district and later even in Harlem itself from those who did not to wish to live beside them. For the *Tageblatt*, the reality that in September 1900—just a month after the highly publicized Tenderloin race riot—Irish mobs attacked Jews in the streets of East Harlem may have well heightened the Yiddish daily's sensitivity towards the fears that blacks harbored. Many years later, an Arbeter Ring memoirist would recall that "the streets of Harlem to us immigrants were foreign. In the streets around us lived many Irish and we were often attacked by them." Apparently, if a Jew landed up "on the wrong side of the tracks"—that is, of the New York Central Railroad line—just a "stone's throw away [from] a thoroughly Jewish community," he—or perhaps even she—might be victimized by a gang of Irish toughs. Such was a young Jewish Socialist's "first awareness of anti-Semitism." He recounted that his first day in East Harlem, after his family relocated from the Lower East Side, he and his father were accosted and his father's hat was thrown into the gutter. "As I bent down to pick up my father's hat," he continued, "I was struck with a heavy stick across the face and almost immediately was covered with blood." In any event, the September 1900 disturbance prompted the *Tageblatt* to send what it described as a "bitter" protest letter to the local police chief. For this organ as well as for the *Forward*, street attacks against blacks were similarly nothing less than a "pogrom" against a minority. Such an emotionally laden term had to give Jewish readers pause, especially when the *Tageblatt* opined that violence against African Americans was "a terrible sign for Jews. It shows that the New York people can manifest a great hatred for a strange race. For the persecuted Jew to hearten the persecutors of the Negro is indeed despicable."[34]

There is little evidence that Jews participated in street battles against blacks in Harlem. For example, when in the summer of 1907 reportedly over one thousand whites and blacks fought it out with "razors and bats" over "a baseball wager" that left two dead in the streets, the *New York Times* report that identified perpetrators and victims by name, race, and ethnicity, did not mentioned any Jews as complicit.[35] Still, in other arenas, Jews in the neighborhood showed that they harbored many of the American prejudices of the day. In 1911, for example, the New York chapter of the NAACP took Harry K. Levy, the manager of the Lyric Theater, to court for his discriminatory policy of seating blacks only in the balcony. To test the proprietor's right to customarily keep "colored persons [out of] the orchestra," Joel E. Spingarn, a Jewish founder of the NAACP, bought two tickets for a performance at the Lyric and simply informed the cashier that his companion downstairs would be a black. When the management refused, Spingarn had a basis for a discrimination case, which the NAACP won. However, the victory was a pyrrhic one as Levy was fined fifty dollars; for the defendant, the financial punishment was the cost of doing business in a racist society. Several other times in the decade that followed, comparable legal ritual dances over racist seating patterns in Harlem were performed with Jewish owners as defendants and with similarly negligible outcomes.[36]

In the early and mid-1910s, Jews, along with other "white agents," habitually charged "prohibitive" high rents to blacks aspiring to open shops and stores in the parts of Harlem where they predominated, stifling "business undertakings." Such were the *New York Age*'s investigative findings in 1911 when it reported, for example, that the rent on a "small store property on the east side of 135th Street and Lenox Avenue, controlled by Jews and white agents, was not only 65 percent higher than such property on the west side but that there is a disposition not to rent store property to Negroes even when they are the most numerous of the population on a given block. We infer that this condition is general." And five years later, in 1916, the newspaper found out that Jews as well as a mix of other races and nationalities, including "Chinese, Germans, Greeks, Italians, Irish" were each "syndicat[ing] their interests and were securing leasehold on desirable property and these leases were given only to members of a particular race." At this juncture, the *New York Age* remonstrated that its people had great difficulty finding work in these stores.[37]

Yet at the same time that Jews were publicly identified as among those whites who tried to undermine the development of an African American community uptown, other Harlem Jews evidenced that they had no problem with residing in a racially mixed neighborhood. Quietly and without public notice, these Jews settled in the predominantly black section that emerged—despite the high cost of living there and opposition to their presence—north of 130th Street and west of Park Avenue. More than two thirds of Harlem's approximately twenty-two thousand blacks resided in this part of uptown. Reportedly, the several thousand

Jews who made the black enclave their home included merchants who liked "the conveniences it affords them in conducting trade." Other residents included those who continued to own and maintain the few private homes in the area and those who it was said "had no aversion to Negroes."[38]

These Jews remained a comfortably situated minority on many blocks north of 130th Street throughout the 1910s, whereas census figures indicate that other white groups largely vacated the area, which by 1920 had become overwhelmingly African American. Indeed, the total Jewish presence in the northwestern part of the neighborhood declined only slightly during the years before American entry into World War I. On some blocks, the number of Jews actually rose and on some streets they constituted the entire white presence.[39] When these Jews did decide to vacate the physically declining area for those new and better-built apartments elsewhere in Gotham in the 1920s, it was not because they showed any special aversion towards living in a black neighborhood.

The massive influx of blacks from the south to New York during the era of World War I fundamentally altered Harlem's residential and racial balances. Coming to Gotham in search of work in war industries and fleeing the institutionalized racism of Dixie, most of these migrants settled in Harlem's black neighborhood. By 1920, 70 percent of Manhattan's 109,000 African Americans resided between 118th and 144th Streets between the Hudson and Harlem Rivers. As rents soared during the wartime and early-post-war housing shortage uptown, thousands of black newcomer families "doubled up" and took in lodgers. Soon, however, the existing African American area was unable to absorb any more arrivals. As migration peaked during the 1920s, Harlem's black enclave inevitably expanded.[40]

Rooms in buildings within other parts of Central Harlem became readily available—though many were in structures in dire need of repair—when widespread construction resumed in the city in 1921. As Jews and other white groups began to depart the deteriorating neighborhood for newer and better sections of Manhattan and the outer boroughs, an ever-mounting wave of black migrants took their places. The numbers tell all that is necessary to know about the racial transformation of uptown. An additional 175,000 blacks, making up a net population increase of 115 percent, entered the metropolis during the 1920s.

Pulled to settle among their own kind but, even more critically, pushed away by poverty and restrictionist covenants from finding places elsewhere, most of the newcomers crowded into Harlem. There they joined thousands of the area's earlier black residents who were also stopped by convention from moving to other residential neighborhoods. By 1930, some 165,000 of New York City's 328,000 African Americans resided in Harlem.[41]

It is here that the fates of the Jews who had made Harlem their homes and the aspiring African Americans who once lived nearby them diverged fundamentally. In the inter-war period, there were only a few sections of Gotham where Jews who could pay rents or buy homes were not welcomed. Queen's Forest Hills estate area and part of Jackson Heights were especially notorious for their residential anti-Semitism. But many neighborhoods kept blacks out. And sometimes, Jews were again complicit in supporting racial discrimination. Such was the case in the 1920s in Washington Heights—destined a decade later to be home to Jewish refugees from Germany—where Jews who once lived in Harlem could settle but a Neighborhood Protective Association pressured landlords, many of them Jews, to sign racially restrictive agreements. Blacks, in almost all instances, regardless of class, were jammed together in Harlem.[42]

One of the only safety valves for middle-class African Americans within Harlem itself was the ill-fated Paul Laurence Dunbar Apartments, a six-building cooperative housing project just for blacks that rose from 1926 to 1928 at 149th to 150th Street between Seventh and Eighth Avenue. Arguably, here blacks who possessed the financial wherewithal to live elsewhere but who were kept out of white neighborhoods could still live in the most up-to-date fashion. Industrialist and philanthropist John D. Rockefeller Jr. sponsored this experiment in better housing for blacks through the construction of an enclave that boasted parks, playgrounds, and gardens and what we would call today a day-care center for working mothers. Residents invested in their own apartments and there even was a Dunbar National Bank on the premises. In many ways, the Dunbar was similar to the Jewish Amalgamated Houses in the Bronx. However, the initiative foundered at the beginning of the Great Depression, an era in Gotham's history when many groups suffered financially. For example, Jewish "cooperators" in the Amalgamated surely had trouble paying their bills. But blacks suffered most grievously, and many of the handpicked tenants in the Dunbar apartments lost their jobs and were otherwise unable to carry the cost of housing. In the 1930s, this "noble experiment" in "the adventure of community building" ended.[43]

Meanwhile, the massive influx of new poor black settlers that began in the 1920s, which offset the whites who left Harlem, afforded the landlords of older buildings the opportunity to maintain the housing status quo. Harlem realtors were not at all reluctant to open their creaking doors to blacks. These residents with few options had always paid high rents for their accommodations, very often well beyond market values. And the now greatly increased demand for scarce housing freed property owners from any real financial imperative to improve the living conditions of their tenants. Those landlords who remained opposed to black tenancy also capitalized upon the situation. They were able to use once again the old saw of the threat of a "Negro invasion" to extort higher rents from those remaining whites who were either unwilling or unable to exit Harlem but desirous, however, of continuing to live in largely segregated surroundings.[44]

As Harlem's housing crisis with its artificially inflated rental costs persisted throughout the 1920s, the vast majority of the neighborhood's Jews chose to move elsewhere. And as each Jewish family exited, one or more African American families replaced them, which furthered the predominance of black families, which promoted in turn the further departure of Jewish families. By 1930, the era of Jewish residential life in Harlem was well-nigh over.

The forces that led to Central Harlem declining, for most intents and purposes, into a black ghetto also fundamentally affected the fate of Jewish residents of East Harlem. For generations, the area around the Els had never been prime real estate. If anything, it was a place that the poor, who were often pushed there, hoped to escape from once their economic conditions improved. The wartime housing shortage only exacerbated already depressed conditions and furthered the resolve of those desirous of escaping the tenements. The resumption of citywide building activity in the early 1920s and the quick exodus of affluent residents from Central Harlem would have—under normal economic circumstances—depressed the value of rentals in the area north of Central Park, enabling less affluent people from East Harlem to follow a familiar pattern of migration to the better neighborhood, east of Fifth Avenue. Realtors in Central Harlem would also have had to improve conditions in their properties if they hoped to attract new tenants from the neighboring area. And the curtailment of European immigration due to the national origins quotas laws passed in the early 1920s coupled with the expansion of housing facilities in newer neighborhoods would have reduced the demand for existing housing, producing a new buyers' market in Harlem real estate.

The new, mass incursion of blacks eliminated all of these possibilities. Landlords in Central Harlem never had to lower rents or improve conditions to attract or to hold the newly arrived African American tenants. Out-migrating people from East Harlem quickly realized that they would, paradoxically, have to scrape together more money to move west to overcrowded, deteriorating Central Harlem than to resettle in working-class sections of the South Bronx. Most Jews took this logical course of action and settled in the Bronx. Such a dollars-and-cents reality may have been on the mind of that Federal Writers' Project observer who wrote that "Jews on the road to bettering themselves and making life more convenient for them moved from Harlem up to the Bronx." A new group of immigrants to New York, Puerto Ricans, soon occupied their vacated tenements, as El Barrio came into existence in the late 1920s.[45]

Amid this era of the long-standing Jewish community's exit from Harlem, several new and very different groups of Jews settled uptown. During the late 1910s through the early 1930s, at least four groups of Black Jews established congregations in the neighborhood. The largest and most enduring synagogue was the Commandment Keepers Congregation of the Living God, located as of 1930 at 128th Street and Lenox Avenue. In 1962, the synagogue moved to 1 West 123rd Street, across the street from Mount Morris Park. Under Rabbi Wentworth Arthur Matthew, who led his followers for half a century, the Commandment Keepers not only created a religious home uptown, they pursued "a strategy of communal economic uplift," which translated into ownership of "fifty-odd business establishments that include[d] cigar and stationery store, tailor shops, laundries, a gas-range repair shop and restaurants serving kosher dishes." Their belief in the authenticity of their Jewishness was predicated upon their genealogical assertion that there existed a "natural link between people of African descent and Judaism which . . . extended from Abraham through King Solomon and Queen Sheba of Ethiopia and a line of kings that ruled that African territory." Effectively, they claimed that the "original Jews" were, in fact, blacks. Their religious practices, from observance of kosher laws to keeping the Sabbath and holidays in traditional manners, were akin to those of the white Orthodox Jews. But this "self-contained community" lived a separate existence from their Ashkenazic and Sephardic brethren.[46]

White Jews both within and without the old uptown neighborhood were of several minds about who these people were and what their presence on the American scene represented. Black Jews were a source of "incredulity or amusement." Yiddish newspapers of the time of both socialist and religious bents were "fascinated" and "numerous feature-length articles discussed the black Jews and the kind of Judaism they practiced" even if many observers openly questioned whether these black people were "authentically" Jewish. One outraged critic declared in 1931 that "the negro synagogues are based on a mixture of superstition and ignorance that has nothing to do with Judaism." In a similar jaundiced vein, a Jewish social worker concluded that "there is no anthropological verity in their claims" to Jewishness and that the group's set of needs "resolves itself into a Negro one and therefore, outside of the realm of Jewish social service except from the broader humanitarian and internationalistic viewpoint." Very possibly, the refusal of the New York Board of Rabbis to admit Rabbi Matthew as a member was rooted in the religious sensibility that while these Commandment Keepers might behave like normative Jews, neither they nor their ancestors, whether they were of African or Caribbean origins, had converted according to the strictures of Jewish law.[47]

In addition, and arguably more important than these religious concerns, was the possible danger that the very existence of folks called "Black Jews" posed to white Jewish integration within American society. In the 1920s and 1930s, the question was still very much alive within nativist and racist circles about whether Jewish immigrants and their children were racially the same as the white Anglo-Saxon Protestants whom it was said built America. To be projected as part of the dominant white race, many Jews felt it was important to separate themselves from African Americans, who clearly were at the bottom of the country's social hierarchy. But what if Black Jews were their racial cousins? Accordingly, dismissing Matthew's and his followers' claim to authentic Jewishness blunted any "perceived potential challenge of being associated with black people in a society that embraced white supremacy." Given these fears and realities, the Commandment Keepers would live on the margins of both the ever-decreasing white Jewish presence in Harlem and the overwhelming African American Christian community and the small and yet vocal and activist Muslim groups that made Harlem their home after World War I.[48]

The central European, east European, and Sephardic Jews who scattered away from Harlem during the 1920s left no forwarding addresses for historians. Thus it is impossible to calculate with any precision what proportion of the community's Jews migrated to which new section of the city during the 1920s. But some of the directions of their dispersal may be discerned through an identification of the neighborhoods that became the new homes of former Harlem institutions. The organizations that survived and moved on were, in most cases, the larger synagogues along Fifth and Lenox Avenues that sold off their properties to churches and with the sale equity reconstituted themselves on the West Side, Washington Heights, and several parts of the Bronx. But not all such landmark congregations were so fortunate, and meanwhile, almost all of the several hundred *landsmanshaft* synagogues, clubs, and societies that dotted East Harlem simply disintegrated. In some cases, when their members set root in the Bronx or Brooklyn, their organizations consolidated with existing outer-borough groups and surrendered their Harlem identities.

The first institutions to successfully relocate from the uptown neighborhood were those situated on the periphery of the major Jewish Central Harlem settlement, north of 130th Street. Congregation Anshei Emeth of 131st Street and Seventh Avenue led the way in 1917, when it merged with a new congregation, Mount Sinai of 181st Street and St. Nicholas Avenue. This group was followed to the emerging Jewish enclave of Washington Heights three years later by the Hebrew Tabernacle, which moved from 130th Street to temporary quarters on upper Broadway.[49]

The Hebrew Tabernacle had led a tenuous existence in the northern part of Harlem from the day it was founded in 1905. Its history reflects the difficulties faced by many small synagogues that were situated away from the major loci of Jewish life. The congregation always had difficulty attracting and holding on to members and worshippers. Organizational life was burdened by the fact that most of its people had chosen to reside in a predominantly non-Jewish section of uptown. As early as 1908, for example, the congregation was obliged to hire paid worshippers to maintain morning and evening services. Despite these challenges, Hebrew Tabernacle grew slowly and was eventually able to build a synagogue building. At one point in its history, it even succeeded in enrolling some four hundred pupils in its Sunday School.[50]

By 1918, however, synagogue leaders determined that the Hebrew Tabernacle could no longer survive in Harlem. In April of that year, trustees reported that the daily minyan could not be maintained without a substantial increase in the wages paid to daily hired worshippers. Several months later, they noted that religious school enrollment had dropped off precipitously. Finally, in January 1919, recognizing that "the expenses of conducting services are largely in excess of [the synagogue's] income," the congregation authorized its trustees to "dispose of our quarters on terms which they deem proper, if opportunities present themselves."[51]

Although the majority of the members agreed that the institution had to move, there was no consensus about where the new synagogue should be located. One faction, led by Rev. Edward Lissman, who was described in congregational documents as "founder, Rabbi, life-member and former treasurer" of the Hebrew Tabernacle, was determined to relocate the congregation along Riverside Drive, south of 120th Street, in Morningside Heights. Another faction, which board of trustees member Louis Austern led, wanted Washington Heights as the future home of the congregation.

The next year was marred by congregational intrigues as Lissman and Austern fought over the synagogue's future. Austern, for example, undertook to negotiate several merger agreements with small Washington Heights Jewish groups, while Lissman tried to prevail upon the board to purchase a new site at 83rd Street and Riverside Drive. But neither combatant succeeded in gaining majority support for his program.[52]

Finally, late in 1919, the Austern group won out, the Hebrew Tabernacle was sold, and the congregation relocated to temporary quarters at 158th Street and Broadway. Two years later, Washington Heights' newest congregation was firmly reestablished in a newly altered building at 161st Street off Fort Washington Avenue. Soon the congregation could once again boast of a religious school enrollment of more than 350 students.[53]

Lissman did not follow the majority of his congregants further uptown. Instead, he resigned his pulpit and his lifetime membership and established a new congregation, the Riverside Synagogue at 108th Street and Broadway. Bitter over Austern's victory, he called upon his supporters to nullify the trustees' decision by leaving the Hebrew Tabernacle and to help him serve "a needed requirement in the immediate vicinity of Broadway between 105–120th Street."[54]

Several of Harlem's oldest congregations joined Lissman's Riverside Synagogue in the 1920s in serving the growing Jewish community on Manhattan's Upper West Side. Temple Israel, for example, sold its synagogue at Lenox Avenue and 120th Street to a group of Seventh-Day Adventists in 1920. After one temporary stop along the way, it moved to 91st Street between Amsterdam Avenue and Broadway. The congregation followed, as longtime Rabbi Harris put it, "the westward drift of our congregants."[55]

Congregations Shaare Zedek, Ohab Zedek, and Ansche Chesed continued their traditions of following their most affluent members to newer sections of Manhattan and also erected large synagogues during the 1920s on the West Side. And by 1929, Rabbi Herbert S. Goldstein followed suit when he moved to establish a branch of the Institutional Synagogue in the emerging Jewish neighborhood on the Upper West Side. Services under his auspices were first held in a rented hall at Broadway and 83rd Street in 1927. Two years later, a synagogue center was created at 85th Street between Amsterdam Avenue and Broadway.[56]

Despite its ever dwindling number of members, its apparently nonexistent dues base during the Depression, and Rabbi Goldstein's own migration out of Harlem in 1932, the Harlem Institutional Synagogue continued to operate until 1943. This achievement was due not so much to any great commitment of its remaining supporters to keep the organization functioning, as it was to its favorable rental agreement with the New York City Board of Education. In March 1933, the Institutional Synagogue contracted with the Board to rent its schoolroom space for use by a junior high school, at a rate of $10,000 per annum. When, in 1943, a new school was built in the neighborhood, the Harlem Institutional Synagogue lost its final major source of income and the building was sold.[57]

The Rabbi Israel Salanter Talmud Torah was the first major East Harlem religious institution to follow its constituency to the Bronx. In 1923, it moved from upper Madison Avenue to Washington Avenue in the South Bronx, where its mission changed. It became the Yeshiva Rabbi Israel Salanter, the first Jewish day school in the borough. In 1940, the Salanter Yeshiva moved to Webster Avenue in the Tremont section of the Bronx, where it would remain for another generation. Its older and larger sibling school in East Harlem, the Uptown Talmud Torah, did not survive beyond its thirty-year history in the neighborhood. When the children of east European Jews moved out of the neighborhood, the school sold its building to the Archdiocese of New York. In time it became an annex of St. Cecilia's Parish, servicing the Latino population of the area.[58]

On November 15, 1930, Kehal Adath Jeshurun of Harlem, the controversial congregation that David A. Cohen once led, was sold to the Sharon Baptist Church. Some of its members moved on to the Bronx, and the synagogue merged with an indigenous Bronx congregation, Agudath Jeshurun, on Gerard Avenue and 165th Street, west of the Grand Concourse. The conjoined synagogue took on the name Adath Jeshurun. The Eldridge Street Synagogue survived downtown, albeit increasingly in disrepair, for another forty years, until the 1980s when it became part of the Eldridge Street Project and was revitalized as a shul with a museum.[59]

Meanwhile, by the 1920s, East Harlem's Sephardic Jewish leaders also viewed their surroundings, as one spokesman put it, to be no longer "a little Jerusalem." Some of its better-known institutions relocated to the Bronx. Most notably, in 1925, after only a seven-year run in the uptown neighborhood, the Filo Center, which had been created in 1918 to "develop and exchange ideas, promote cultural and philanthropic causes and foster friendly and social relations," sold its headquarters on 118th Street, reportedly "because the majority of its members had moved to the Bronx, with others settling in Brooklyn and Long Island."[60]

Still, notwithstanding these institutional relocations, it is entirely conceivable that Brooklyn, which during the 1920s experienced the most prolific Jewish population growth, ultimately attracted more first- and second-generation Ashkenazim and Sephardim from Harlem. All that can be said with certainty is that in some instances—as with the Stone family—census reports have permitted us to follow the movements of an individual family emblematic of others within and then without the neighborhood over two generations. And the memoir of N. Davidoff, the Arbeter Ring leader, points to the Bronx as a new center for him and his comrades.

Finally, the north-bound relocation that Davidoff described coheres with the saga of another Harlem family that ended up in the 1930s in a multiroom apartment on 1750 Davidson Avenue, some four blocks west of the fashionable Grand Concourse, near 174th Street. In this case, an immigrant couple with five children in tow fled Gomel in 1905, two years after a pogrom hit the city in White Russia. Arriving in America, they found that there was no room for them downtown and Harlem became their place of first settlement. There the husband and wife, both tailors, opened a shop and were in time able to secure a contract to produce bloomers for girls at a local public school physical training program. Two more children were born in the neighborhood and eventually all nine of them crowded into a tenement on 100th Street and Park Avenue, with four of the boys sharing a bed. There were six brothers and one sister in the family, and Sadie basically raised her two American-born siblings, while her parents labored long hours. If and when the family went to pray, they attended the Homler synagogue, a typical *landsmanshaft* congregation of the era. Tragedy struck the family in 1926 when the paterfamilias, the prime bread winner, died of what was then called euphemistically "the miseries"—cancer. He and his descendants were buried in Lodi, New Jersey, within that part of the cemetery that the Homler Young Men's Society purchased for its members.

Early in the 1930s, with the four older boys now earning a living, these loyal children were able to each contribute money to move the family out of Harlem. Sadie and her shoe salesman husband, Sam, lived with her mother in the Bronx, and helped out with the rent. There, Sadie raised her two children, who listened in attentively as their uncles gathered weekly on Sundays to loudly debate the personal and world issues of the day. One of the young men became a lawyer and an ally of Tammany Hall and late in his life was appointed a New York State Supreme Court special referee. A second brother found work in a bank and in time rose to become an executive in that field. But back in the 1920s, it was another sibling who had the most disposable income. He was a bootlegger and ran with Waxy Gordon's gang before fleeing for a while to Canada to avoid incarceration. In the generations that followed, the score or more cousins and their spouses and their own youngsters would live all over the United States and one spent much of her life in Europe. But this family would eventually have one final Harlem connection. Some fifty years after they exited the neighborhood, the son of one of the two boys who was born in America would study not only the family's history but also place it in the context of the times within which all Harlem Jews and their neighbors lived. The family name is Gurock.[61]

Fanny Brice and "Ballin' the Jack" sheet music, 1913 (document courtesy of John Reddick).

8

Jews in African American Harlem by Day and by Night, 1920–1945

To grow up as a Jew in Harlem in the 1930s was "to be a vilified Jewish minority within a mortified black minority." Borrowing a phrase from Booker T. Washington, that was how renowned sociologist Irving Louis Horowitz characterized his experience as a youngster in a neighborhood that no longer housed a Jewish community. His memory of his family as nothing less than "rare stray cats from the Ukrainian pale" is supported by population estimates of that time and place. As of 1930, there were approximately 2,900 Jews in East Harlem living amid a growing Puerto Rican immigrant enclave. Ten years later, the numbers there had dipped to about 500. Over in Central Harlem, when the Great Depression began, only approximately 2,500 Jews resided in what had become the black mecca. Ten years later, some 900 Jews lived between 110th and 155th Streets between Fifth Avenue and Morningside Avenue. And in neither section of Harlem was there much, if any, Jewish communal life of which to speak. If anything, Horowitz believed that "their brethren [who] fled to greener parts of New York City" viewed his "extended family" as "dregs—social scourges and economic failures—simply by virtue of the fact that they remained" in a black stronghold.[1]

The Horowitz family kept body and soul together through the small hardware store that Irving's father ran where "he made keys and window shades to order, repaired locks, and made and repaired frames." In opening his business in Harlem, this bare-bones Jewish entrepreneur reasoned that this "poorest area of New York with one of the highest crimes rates" could use his "tinkering . . . skills" because "locks were constantly picked there and windows constantly broken." Nearby the Horowitzs' store on 123rd Street and Eight Avenue, the Grumbergers had their haberdashery shop and the Cushmans their bakery, and these families, too, for another generation, attempted to eke out their living.[2]

Joining the Jews who resided and worked in Central Harlem were those who lived "on the edges, the peripheries of Harlem, where their synagogues and social institutions were located." These business people came in by day and left at sundown. There was also a visible small-time Jewish economic presence in East Harlem. In this area, some Sephardic Jews perceived that they had a leg up over competitors in courting customers and clients because they spoke the community's Spanish language. A Sephardic Jew who hailed from Puerto Rico has been credited with opening La Luz, "the first Latino restaurant" in the neighborhood, before World War I. In another noteworthy case, a family from Salonika moved to Harlem from downtown before the war because the head of the family "felt more comfortable with Spanish-speaking people." Two of his sons would work in El Barrio by day as physicians and surgeons to a "primarily Cuban and Puerto Rican clientele."[3]

The Altchek brothers did quite well in their medical practices and there is evidence that they garnered widespread approbation in the neighborhood. But generally, the Jews who worked in businesses and serviced communities in a Harlem that was no longer their own "shared impoverishment"—to borrow Horowitz's characterization—with the minorities around them. Yet he sensed that those who came into his father's store and others whom he passed on the street believed that "even Jews without money had money. And there was an underlying concern that such money had a . . . source of power." Horowitz did not recall in his detailed memoir any instances of overt anti-Semitism directed at him or his family. Still, he felt a latent hostility born of the reality that "as visible enemies" he was part of "a vilified culture fearfully sharing the capital of the black race."[4]

Far greater opprobrium was openly heaped on Jewish women—"matrons" from the new and fashionable Bronx—for their ill treatment of "Negro girls," as they were called back then, whom they hired on a day-to-day basis to clean their apartments. In 1938, a sympathetic observer of the plight of these domestics reported on how many of them gathered at offices like the ABC Employment Agency on West 135th Street, waiting for hours on end in the hope of securing work for "pennies a day." Although often only "one in twenty" found a good job and typically had to kick back a significant amount to the agent, "at least they could revel in the fact that their disappointment came in warm dry, surroundings." Many others "fared much worse in these times" because they were subjected to the greater indignity of the so-called "slave markets," one of which was located at West 167th Street and Gerard Avenue in the Bronx. In that lineup spot, "a dejected gathering of black women of various ages and descriptions ranging from youths of seventeen to elderly women of maybe seventy," who had to travel up from Harlem with no guarantee that they would work that day, sat "on crates and boxes" and on blustery mornings tried to shield themselves from the wind and the cold as they awaited the arrival of the Jewish "madam." The selections had to remind these folks of how their ancestors were bought and sold at slave lineups in the antebellum South. One domestic would recall that Jewish women used to come to the "auction block" and, almost as in slavery days, feel their muscles, "looking at their knees to see if they had crust on their knees." Apparently these employers of domestics believed that crust on a potential hire's knees meant that a worker "would get on their knees to wax" their apartment floors. "And the muscles, they had to have good muscles, to change those mattresses all the time," said one unhappy employee. "You see, the Jewish people change their mattresses all the time, and they wanted strong women." Not only that, but the competition for fifteen- to fifty-cent per hour jobs during a ten-hour workday was so keen that often fights broke out when one woman tried to undercut another. The concept that they might unite and "say yes at once or no together" to oppressive employers was foreign to those who struggled to merely survive.[5]

By the mid-1930s, this abusive behavior was so notorious—even the well-known journalist Damon Runyon wrote a biting exposé in a New York tabloid—that the new Domestic Workers Union, a local of the American Federation of Labor, gained some traction in its demands to assist these exploited workers. Specifically, it sent out "suggestions to the rabbis of the various synagogues and white clergymen" imploring them to tell their congregants to "stop hiring the girls from the slave market at starvation wages." There was even talk that "a minimum wage law be agreed to by arbitration . . . to help do away with the slave market." And to ministers of black churches an appeal was directed imploring them to reach out to these women in economic crisis and "to impress upon [them] the direct harm they do to themselves and others by going to these slave markets and accepting the low wages that these heartless employers offer them."[6]

In time, some Jewish groups got the message and called upon their community to think through what the slave market was doing to their reputation, not to mention how the exploitation was afflicting the unfortunates whom they were employing. In 1939, after a meeting of black and Jewish newspaper editors, publishers, and politicians who were concerned about inter-group relations, the Yiddish newspaper *The Day* forcefully compared the slave market to "the horrible days of Uncle Tom's Cabin." And it editorialized that "to our shame, be it said, that the Jewish women too come to buy the labor of black slaves." Subsequently in the Bronx neighborhoods, Rabbi Jerome Rosenbloom organized a committee to "remove a condition which is certainly no credit to our people." His colleague Rabbi Simon Kramer wrote to his worshippers that while "we cannot conceive of any Jewish housewife being guilty of such practices," nonetheless, "I am asking you to be very careful in your treatment of these part-time colored houseworkers." He implored congregants to consider carefully "the reputation of the Jewish community and the right of human beings to fair and honorable treatment."[7]

For African Americans in Harlem during the 1930s, the hiring practices at some of the large local department stores that Jews owned were no less galling. Most notably, Blumstein's, on 125th Street, constantly courted black customers but did not employ black workers except for the most menial jobs. In 1934, a boycott movement was organized that focused on this store, the largest local retail establishment. The Citizen's League for Fair Play, which united black churches and women's organizations like the Harlem Housewives League, along with community social, fraternal, and political clubs, energized by street corner orators, impressed upon its economically oppressed rank and file that it was critical not to patronize stores where their people could not work. An "honor roll" of picketers, more than a hundred on some days, soon forced Jacob Blumstein to employ fifteen African American saleswomen and to promise to hire twenty more the following fall. However, this street victory did not endure. In 1935, the League reported ruefully that Blumstein had not hired the promised additional employees and, in fact, seven of those hired the previous year had been laid off.[8]

Black protestors were more successful with Morris Weinstein, who in 1932 took over Koch's Department Store, also on 125th Street. The prior owner, H.C.F. Koch, a central European Jew and a member of Temple

Israel, had for decades refused to sell to African Americans. In 1930, he closed his store rather than serve the growing minority community. The proactive Weinstein, believing that courting the neighborhood market would increase his sales totals and anxious to head off boycotts, pledged and seemingly followed through on his vow to hire blacks as one third of his clerical force.[9]

Concerns and conflicts such as these provided ammunition for neighborhood anti-Semites, who magnified the tensions. Demagogues like street-corner Muslim preacher Sufi Abdul Hamid and hate organizations like the Harlem Labor Union shouted about Jewish economic control over Harlem, asserting that "Jews are the exploiters of the colored people" and that "Jews and leprosy are synonymous." Hamid and the Union also made rousing capital out of the slave market abuse. It was alleged that Hamid had proudly proclaimed that he was the "Black Hitler" and that he was the "only one fit to carry on the war against the Jews." Interrogated by black writer Claude McKay about his sounding like a Nazi, Hamid retorted that he had made himself aware of *Mein Kampf* to better comprehend the nature of anti-Semitism and that the allegations against him came from those same Harlem Jewish storeowners who "did not want to face the issue of giving" his people "a square deal." McKay was taken with Hamid's response and argued that "there was never anti-Semitism in Harlem and there still is none, in spite of the stupid and vicious propaganda which endeavored to create an anti-Semitic issue out of the legitimate movement of Negroes to improve their social condition." However, predictably, the Harlem Merchants' Association, made up of Jewish business owners, refused to accept Hamid's apologia. Its public denigration of the rabble-rouser was seconded by the *The Day*, which warned its Jewish readers that Hamid had called for "an open bloody war against the Jews who are much worse [to blacks] than all other whites." Concomitantly, a black organization, the Negro Labor Committee, averred that the Harlem Labor Union, its own long-time enemy, was instigating a "terroristic attack in Harlem against Jews" as well as against whites and the legitimate trade union movement. Two eminent Black newspapers, the *Amsterdam News* and the *New York Age*, supported the allegations against Hamid.[10]

Fortunately, harsh rhetoric and street demonstrations did not degenerate into inter-group violence. The voices of responsible black journalists and sensible community organizers helped militate against physical neighborhood confrontations. It is also conceivable that Jews as a group gained a degree of street credibility from the activities of Communists of Jewish ancestry in Harlem even if these universalist radicals rejected their ancestral ties and often did their utmost to hide their ethnic heritages. Activists with Jewish sounding names—many of whom came down from CCNY, situated on the bluff of Harlem Heights to be part of consumer and employment protests—"contravened . . . rather than reinforced" the image that haters promoted of Jews as "neighborhood exploiters." Those who put themselves on the line, especially when they stood among their fellow black comrades, "did not make convincing exploiters, since they appeared to gain very little from their participation." Similarly, founders and members of the Teachers Union, "radical teachers, overwhelmingly Jewish, who were assigned to teach in Harlem" were known,—at least by "black teachers in almost every school" in the neighborhood—for their advocacy for "physical improvements, free lunches and better conditions," towards securing "for the children of Harlem educational opportunities equal to the very best available to the most privileged child in New York City."[11]

In any event, when African American rioting that threatened local white businesses, including many that Jews owned, rocked Harlem in 1935 and 1943, explicit anti-Semitic sentiments did not fuel the core frustrations that sparked the violence. The 1935 outburst against rumored police brutality was "directed at property and not at people" and was devoid "of clashes between racial groups," though two million dollars worth of damages were incurred. As far as Jewish storekeepers were concerned, the *Amsterdam News* was quick to report that although "Jewish merchants in the Harlem community naturally came in for their share of attacks upon the stores, there does not seem to be any foundation for the report circulated at first that these attacks were directly at them." It seemed to the newspaper that as the amount of street violence escalated, "the personality or racial identity of the owners of the stores faded out and the property itself became the object of . . . fury." Indeed, "stores owned by Negroes were not always spared if they happened to be in the path of these roving crowds bent upon destruction." Similarly, after the 1943 outburst, the Anti-Defamation League of B'nai B'rith (ADL), a Jewish defense organization that closely monitored Jew-hatred, averred that in its opinion "no anti-Semitic angle" could be found. The League did, however, declare that "there is no doubt whatsoever, that there is a definite feeling amongst the negroes [*sic*] of Harlem . . . that they are oppressed by whites."[12]

For a generation after World War II, Jewish-black tensions in Harlem of these sorts abated due in significant part to the decline in neighborhood economic interaction. Many Jewish businesses relocated elsewhere, reflecting post-war economic upward mobility. But Louis Blumstein stayed on 125th Street and his store's persistence was, in fact, praised in at least one corner of the black community. In 1949 the *Amsterdam News* lauded him as one of the Jewish storeowners who remained uptown, calling him one of Harlem's "top ten" leaders, the only white so honored.[13]

Anti-Semitic rhetoric and the identification of Jews as major sources of black misery also did not play a major role in disputes over employment practices at some of Harlem's theaters that Jews owned and managed. In fact, neighborhood people were of several minds over whether Leo Brecher and especially Frank Schiffman, who ran the renowned Lafayette Theatre at 132nd Street and Seventh Avenue and later the world-famous Apollo Theater on 125th Street, were their friends or exploiters. Friends of the duo—the entrepreneurial Brecher, who hailed from Austria, and his partner, who after graduating CCNY was initially a school teacher on the Lower East Side—credit the men with opening up orchestra seats to blacks at the Lafayette. Until they took over in 1925, blacks could sit only in the balcony in what was derogatorily called "nigger heaven." Previously, there and elsewhere in what had become a predominantly African American neighborhood, public entertainment venues had made black patrons "walk up the back stairs" or told them that the show was "sold out." As manager, Schiffman in particular—with the assent of Brecher—would have none of this. Instead, he saw blacks as a ready and anxious clientele who would pay what they could to see movies and, more importantly, to witness live shows from the best seats they could afford. Contemporaries were not beyond praising him as no less than "a self-ordained great white father of Harlem" for his integrationist efforts. Renowned African American novelist Wallace Thurman has one of his characters praise "the Lafayette [as] the Jew's gift of entertainment to Harlem colored folk. Each week the management . . . presents a new musical revue of the three day variety with motion pictures . . . sandwiched in between."[14]

Schiffman was known to boast that he was "the largest employer of colored theatrical help in the country." Local legend has it that his valuing blacks as customers, and making a point of his feelings, did much to get African Americans accommodated at local restaurants all up and down 125th Street. A black woman who lived and worked on the thoroughfare recalled that whether it was Frank's Lunchroom or Child's Restaurant or Loft's Candy Shop or Fabian's Seafood Shop, African Americans "couldn't get served there. All the bars and everything else was the same way." That is, until Schiffman personally desegregated Frank's Lunchroom when he demanded that a friend, black film producer Oscar Micheaux, be served at his table. One historical account depicts Schiffman as "God—a five foot nine inch, white Jewish, balding, bespectacled deity."[15]

However, other voices back then within the African American community, as well as later commentators, saw the Lafayette Theatre's owners in a very different light—as essentially self-serving. Critics have described them as "white men using black talent for their own gains" with "uptown Negroes . . . doubly used because they were the audience as well as the performers . . . as white promoters made money . . . [through] a commercial exploitation of Harlem." And as far as desegregating eateries were concerned, while they employed neighborhood people and served them respectfully as customers, almost exclusively white ownership long prevailed on 125th Street.[16]

Criticism over the Lafayette's own employment policies surfaced in 1926 not long after Brecher and Schiffman took control of the business. At issue were the low wages paid to black film projectors, salaries far below those of white counterparts. Initially, neighborhood protests were focused against those many other establishments that did not hire blacks at all. The protesters' arguments, similar to the complaints against department stores, was that businesses should hire folks from among the people who patronized their theaters. The *Amsterdam News* spoke for many when it editorialized that Harlem residents "are almost the sole support of those places showing pictures to thousands each week."[17]

The workers' struggle against the theaters turned against Brecher, Schiffman, and the Lafayette on Labor Day 1926, when black employees "failed to show up" in the morning and later that day threw up a picket line calling out the owners to pay "the same scales of wages as the same owners in question have been paying white operators in another one of their houses." Spokesmen for the Motion Pictures Operators Union, Local 306 of the American Federation of Labor, which only recently had admitted black projectionists to its ranks, joined the fight with the allegation that Brecher threatened to "close the Lafayette Theatre rather than accede to the union in their demand for full and equal rights for the operators of color." The union had agreed to integrate its ranks in order to hold on to its "craft exclusivity," to keep blacks from organizing a competitive labor force. In response, Brecher and Schiffman alleged that the problem of wages lay not with them but with the union, which "gives the jobs of chief operator to the white members while colored operators are given the relief jobs and not all the colored men are working." In other words, they recalled, for all who might listen, their fair treatment of black employees before the union came along and grabbed the good spots for its white brethren.[18]

In the days that followed, the union, ostensibly in support of the Lafayette's employees, enlisted black musicians at that theater and white musicians at other movie and musical venues that Brecher owned to join in the boycott. The president of the local, Sam Kaplan, told Brecher that "every angle that can be lawfully brought to bear will be called into play" to make the owners submit to union demands. In response, Brecher filed injunctions both against the picketing operators and against the Musicians' Union, Local 820, prohibiting it from joining the boycott. Brecher and Schiffman also signed up replacement black operators to highlight their policy of hiring local people. Amid the strife, Schiffman complained bitterly that the "five years of my labor in Harlem" was being undermined. He contended that the Lafayette "is an institution. . . . We must not forget that the present management has improved and dignified the Lafayette Theatre and that it brings to the colored people of Harlem motion picture and musical comedy entertainment which is not equaled elsewhere in the city." In the following months, charges and counter-charges of racism and disingenuousness came from all quarters, until June 1927, when Brecher and the Local reached an agreement whereby the black projectionists went back to their jobs under that year's union wage scale.[19]

Throughout all of these disputations, missing from the rhetoric of protesters who shouted loudly about the Lafayette management "sharing their profits" was any statement—either implicitly or explicitly anti-Semitic—that the alleged exploiters were Jewish. For example, when social critic Edgar M. Grey of the *Amsterdam News* harshly upbraided "those owners of the playhouses which employed Mr. Schiffman to manage them . . . [whose] first act is to discredit all of the social and educational instruments among us which refuse to do their will," no mention was made of their ethnic backgrounds.[20] Nor, for that matter, were the leaders of the union—Kaplan and his vice president, named Eichorn—identified as anything other than white. Typically the battle lines that the black press drew were between "the Negro motion picture operators and the Leo Brecher interests ably defended by Mr. Frank Schiffman." If anything, to the great chagrin of protest leaders—including neighborhood Communist spokespeople who desired to make capital out of what they deemed a clear case of class conflict—Schiffman and Brecher had earned much community support from among their patrons. Early on in his tenure as owner of the Lafayette, an *Amsterdam News* columnist described Brecher as "a most personable gentleman" and one who would gladly "break the bonds," presumably of racial segregation.[21] And it is noteworthy that during the labor struggle, reportedly "not a single vaudeville or musical comedy show failed to play to full houses . . . the show went on." It has been suggested that mass nonresponsiveness to the strikers "reflected their mistrust of the labor movement"—which typically pushed white workers' interests ahead of those of the black laboring class—and "their desire to control their own leisure time and their *loyalty* [emphasis mine] to the Lafayette," which was owned and operated by two entrepreneurial Jews.[22]

With that labor imbroglio behind them, Brecher and Schiffman set their sights on a grander theatrical venue. In 1935, they acquired the stately Apollo Theater on 125th Street. The neoclassical building had gone through several programmatic incarnations since it opened in 1914. During its earliest stage in the 1910s, it had welcomed Yiddish shows. Soon thereafter, as Hurtig's and Seamon's Music Hall, it was basically a whites-only dinner club where patrons imbibed orange bitters for fifteen cents and a "Tom Collins for thirty." With the coming of Prohibition, it became a burlesque theater that featured performers like George

Jessel and Fanny Brice, not to mention the many exotic dancers who stripped down to "white or flesh-colored stockings." Downstairs there was a separate music club called Joe Wood's Coconut Grove, where "it's said Louis Armstrong made his first New York appearance" to, again, a whites-only audience.

When Fiorello La Guardia became the city's mayor on January 1, 1934, Hurtig's and Seamon's New Burlesque Theater ran afoul of the new incumbent's campaign pledge to close down infamous strip joints. The hard-pressed building owners, Sidney Cohen and Morris Sussman, taking a page out of Brecher and Schiffman's book, attempted to make a go out of a renamed Apollo Theater, which they now boasted was "The finest theatre in Harlem." Offering "variety revues," they "redirected their marketing attention to the growing African-American community in Harlem." On its new opening night of January 26, 1934, the showstoppers include such black talent as Aida Ward, Benny Carter, the three Rhythm Kings, and Sixteen Gorgeous Hot Steppers, playing to an integrated audience.

Challenged for supremacy in the neighborhood's market, Brecher and Schiffman closed their 132nd Street entertainment property and bought the Harlem Opera House on the same block as the Apollo. A neighborhood landmark since Oscar Hammerstein I opened its doors in 1889, the opera house had gone through multiple ownerships as each proprietor sought to attract patrons from within and without the neighborhood with either high- or low-class cultural offerings. A battle royale for customers ensued, with the competing venue owners bidding for the top stars and cutting prices to fill their orchestra and balcony seats. Both sides even went to war over the radio airwaves as the Apollo's shows were broadcast live on WMCA and the opera house offerings were featured on WNEW. However, when Cohen died suddenly, Brecher and Schiffman quickly convinced Sussman to merge his interests with theirs. The duo took charge of the Apollo while Sussman showed movies (and perhaps had to deal with projectionists' wage issues) at the Opera House.[23]

Once under Schiffman's control, the Apollo earned a deserved reputation not only as a prime-time spot for the best black performers but as "uptown's showbiz incubator" even as over the generations popular music styles changed from vaudeville to jazz and then to rock and roll. The great jazz musician and actor Lionel Hampton asserted in the 1940s that "if you were a black entertainer of any kind—musician, singer or comedian—being a headliner at the Apollo was your proudest achievement." Meanwhile, the testing ground for rising talent was the theater's renowned amateur nights. Record producers and talent scouts joined raucous audiences in evaluating the abilities of those on the stage. "The audiences were very kind if you were good," one backstage employee recalled. "But they could be very, very cruel if you were bad." In fact, an announcer who asserted that "you have the power" egged on the audience to boo or cheer the performers. And if an amateur failed in the opinion of experienced listeners, who flocked week in and out to 125th Street, an "executioner" rudely escorted him or her off the stage. It was widely believed that if "an act could survive the Apollo, they could play anywhere in the world." Meanwhile, the hundreds of judges in the crowd left the theater with a sense of "audience proprietorship."[24]

However, the true proprietor was Frank Schiffman, who ran the Apollo for forty years. The management style of this entertainment magnate has received mixed reviews. Critics of Schiffman have portrayed him as "ruthless with artists, particularly when he had no competitors." It has been said, "the price for a gig was to be nice to Mr. Schiffman and accep[t] his salary offers." One disgruntled performer characterized the boss as not so different from "a plantation owner." Others, however, have noted how he kept the prices of tickets at reasonable rates to fill up his auditorium and deemed him a "genius who understood . . . black show business." His only run-in with explicit anti-Semitism took place late in his life when, in 1962, picketers marched outside the Apollo protesting his plan to start a "low-cost restaurant with prices that potentially would threaten the business of a more expensive black-owned eatery." He was denounced as "a Shylock who wanted to extract a pound of flesh from the black community." To his defense rushed the iconic baseball star Jackie Robinson, who utilized his "syndicated newspaper column to condemn the protestors' blatant use of anti-Semitism." Following Robinson's unequivocal lead, other black leaders echoed his reprimand. Soon thereafter, the picketing ended. All told, though never "to be named Mr. Congeniality," Schiffman preserved his reputation for integrationist moves and "by and large he co-existed well with the community, which defined the theater as a proud centerpiece of 125th Street."[25]

But the history of the uptown neighborhood's music halls and other entertainment emporia of the 1920s–1930s is more than just the story of

Jewish owners and operators—with their multiple intentions—and their black employees and the talented artists who brought out appreciative and critical audiences. Right along with these economic and social intergroup encounters is their interface on the cultural scene, which engaged Jews and blacks in developing, presenting, and promoting the music that was heard not only in neighborhood theaters but also in some of the clubs that were often off-limits to African American patrons. And the sounds that emanated from these places, which started out in Harlem, like so many other aspects of uptown life, did not stay there. Rather they became part of America's musical cultural heritage. If anything, the two groups' dealings with each other in the uptown entertainment world during this era involved a complicated relationship, one that, for some observers, was far from equally beneficial. It had its roots in prior decades, in which Jewish performers appeared on stages in blackface in minstrel shows and appropriated a style of entertainment that had both demeaned and served African American musicians and other black show business people.

From the very start of the twentieth century, white audiences had flocked to Harlem to enjoy what they liked to believe were authentic black sounds and behaviors. The word on the street was that such nocturnal visitors liked to "slum," to take in the sights and sounds of a different world, albeit in entertainment spots where often the only blacks to be seen were either on the stage or serving their tables.[26]

Patrons particularly liked minstrel-type shows, or "specialty acts"—uninhibited mélanges of "purportedly Negro jokes, tall tales, sing and dance routines and spoofs of elite art and contemporary manners." Certainly, in the racist environment of the time, these shows stayed completely clear of "open correctives to white distortions of black character," as the "coons" or "darkies," as they were called, played coyly to the prejudices and expectations of those in the theaters and clubs. And for the longest time, there were shows that featured whites with their heads hands, and necks smeared with black greasepaint. It has been sugges that "playing black gave white comedians a freedom" to express selves in ways that "they would not otherwise have enjoyed." An audiences, the ribald ambience of "ridicule and caricature," measure of libido and sexuality, "gave license . . . to puri audiences "who would otherwise have stayed home." T uptown and midtown streets was that "to call yourself a New Yorker, you must have been to Harlem at least once." Night clubs "are the shrines to which white sophisticates, Greenwich Village artists, Broadway revelers and provincial commuters make eager pilgrimages." With the coming of Prohibition in the early 1920s, many of the evening and after-hours clubs served an additional purpose. They doubled as speakeasies, owned and operated by organized crime figures. In these outside-the-lines establishments, "the crowd [was] more select, the liquor more fierce [and] the atmosphere more intimate." When all was said and done, with performers "singing and dancing on the periphery" of the American world of entertainment, customers could see "blacks imitating and fooling whites, whites imitating and stealing from blacks, blacks reapportioning and transforming what has been stolen, whites making yet another foray on black styles and on and on."[27]

Among the white performers who cagily wore blackface or had the greasepaint pushed on them, Jews from the late nineteenth century into the 1920s were the most prominent. And many of them started their show business careers in Harlem. In 1906, for example, Sophie Tucker, née Sophia Kalish, and later to carry with pride the moniker of "Last of the Red Hot Mamas," first had blackface foisted on her when she showed up for an "amateur night" at a vaudeville theater at 125th Street and Third Avenue. This was her tryout appearance, as she hoped to outdo fifty or sixty other aspirants and move beyond singing for her supper, and not much more, in the beer gardens of what she called the "German Village." Tucker had come down from her parents' home in Hartford, Connecticut, after a failed early marriage to pursue her dream as a singer. Concerned that the corpulent neophyte would be "razzed" by the crowd out front "because she was 'so big and ugly,'" the manager told his assistant "better get some cork and black her up." The combination of her vocal talents and her "look" carried the day for her. Soon she was appearing at venues like "a ten cent theatre owned by Marcus Lowe, Adolf Zucker and Nicholas Schenck at 116th Street and Lenox Avenue." Promoted as the "World Renowned Coon Shouter" or as "Sophie Tucker, Manipulator of Coon Melodies," she would recall that "all they showed was a one-reel slapstick comedy and me in blackface for the ten afternoon shows and whiteface for the ten night shows. Twenty shows a day for a salary of twenty dollars a week."[28]

Tucker was clearly far from fully comfortable in blackface, as she quickly gained a fine reputation as a singer, and was known to rip off her gloves at the end of her songs to show the crowd her white skin. And when she debuted in Boston, she broke away from blackface when fortuitously her costume trunk was lost. She appeared, so to speak, "au naturel" and then reportedly told her audience, "You-all can see that I am a white girl. Well I'll tell you something more: I'm not Southern, I'm a Jewish girl and I just learned this Southern accent doing a blackface act for two years." In time—that is, after four years of being billed as "America's most prominent coon singer"—she would be able to do without blackface completely.[29]

Though by 1914, Tucker had abandoned the coon song format in favor of ragtime tunes, still her music would continue to integrate "Negro and Jewish inflections, with her Jewish speech overlying black diction and pronunciation." Moreover, her audiences evidently equated her "robust singing style and expressive body movements" with a "freedom from civilized restraint" that was imputed to blackness as she indeed became a red hot mama. As significant, her professional connection to black music was also long maintained through her theme song "Some of These Days," which African American songwriter Shelton Brooks wrote for her back in 1910.[30]

A woman five years younger than Tucker, occasional Harlem resident Fanny Brice, who similarly would become an entertainment star, had no compunctions about appearing in blackface. In fact, this singer, whose life Barbra Streisand would portray generations later on stage and screen in *Funny Girl*, was very attuned to affecting voices and comfortable with accents of cultures that were not her own. And that included taking on a Yiddish accent if it suited her role. For though Jewish by ancestry, she was raised in a highly assimilated family—one that chose "to live far away from Jews" and had no interest in having their daughter connected to any ancestral religion or ethnicity. But after starting out at an amateur night and then being stuck in a chorus, she got her big break when fledgling songwriter Irving Berlin recruited her to sing "Sadie Salome" with a Yiddish accent that had "all the intonation of Hester Street." Brice would remember, "I put my soul into Sadie Salome," a vaudeville parody of the "Dance of the Seven Veils," and "she rewarded me." The singer had found her niche. But Brice averred that had the songwriter cast her to do "an Irish song and dance," she would have enthusiastically complied if it advanced her career. (Brice did allow, however, that she was not sure how an Irish American audience would have taken to her affecting a brogue.) Soon thereafter, "Loving Joe," written by African American songwriters Will Marion Cook and Joe Jordan, became her signature piece, which she performed in blackface. Given the tenor of the times, however, the composers of her hit tune could not "go even in Harlem into a lot of theaters where she was performing."[31]

But certainly, Al Jolson was the most famous Jewish performer to appear in blackface. His portrayal of Jakie Rabinowitz, the son of a cantor in 1927's *The Jazz Singer*, the first "talkie"—"actually a silent movie with poorly synchronized musical numbers with a few sentences of spoken words"—is undoubtedly known to every student and aficionado of American film. There he brought his "loose-limbed, uninhibited dance moves, jazz-charged rhythms and shout-it-out vocal manner" to the silver screen as the "mammy singer" par excellence. His Harlem connection began very early in his career when, as a young man, he "was fascinated by black music" and in the 1910s was reportedly "the only white man admitted to Leroy's, a black cabaret." (His admission may have had much to do with his favorable report in *Variety* of African American heavyweight Jack Johnson's victory over Jim Jeffries in 1910. In Jolson's description of the black fighter's triumph over the "Great White Hope," he asserted that notwithstanding the racism that surrounded the bout, "the majority at the ringside must say that Johnson is the greatest fighter that ever lived. Jeffries did not hit him with one good punch.") Jolson's on-the-spot learning experience at Leroy's helped him emerge as a Broadway attraction in *La Belle Paree* in 1911, where he appeared in blackface to an approving audience. Over the next few decades, he rose to stardom in plays and variety shows and in clubs all over the country as "an impudent and joyous harlequin . . . liberated" through his burned-cork makeup to "display an élan no other performer—black or white—could exhibit." And late many evenings—after regaling white audiences downtown with his growing repertoire of gestures, faces, and songs—he was off to Harlem to enjoy the company of Jewish and black entertainers with whom he felt a very strong bond. On one such occasion, at a somewhat notorious venue, Bessie Bloodgood's whore house, Jolson heard fledgling Jewish songwriter George Gershwin perform "Swanee." He was taken with the song that the Harlem-born composer and his lyricist, Irving Caesar, had created, which rhapsodizes about an ex-slave's desire to return to Dixie, where his "Mammy" awaits him. Jolson decided to integrate it into his current Broadway show, *Sinbad*. In 1920, Jolson recorded the song for Columbia Records and Gershwin had his first great hit.[32]

To some degree, Jewish actors clearly wore blackface as "shrewd opportunism" to please their audiences as they made their mark in the highly competitive world of show business. But there may have been much more socially and psychologically and even politically to this mode of appearance and presentation. Some see this pastiche as affording artists a way of acting out Jewish emotions—like separation from their past and families—through the metaphor of blackness. In a sense, "black became a mask for Jewish expressiveness with one woe speaking through the voice of another. . . . Yiddish schmaltz and blackface sentiment went well together." Effectively, that disguise gave Jews on the stage the opportunity to "reach a level of spontaneity and assertiveness in the declaration of their Jewish selves" that they would not have been able to obtain otherwise. Or to put it another way: By "moving out of their own culture, singers like Tucker or Jolson" could "sentimentalize their Mammy . . . and the past world dimly desired but long ago forgone in the push for American life and success." In Tucker's case, she eventually returned to her own background and yearnings, romanticizing her own lamented "Yiddishe Mama."[33]

Others have gone further and argued that blackface was an ironic expression of Jewish empathy for the racism and discrimination that blacks faced in the early twentieth century. For example, the *Forward* suggested that, in *The Jazz Singer*, Jolson demonstrated that he "knows how to sing the songs of the most cruelly wronged people in the world's history," namely African Americans. However, a totally different view identifies blackface as a means whereby Jews knowingly and strategically distanced themselves from blacks. When they took off their masks and gloves they showed other whites that these sons and daughters of immigrants were nothing less than full Americans. Arguably and comparably, it was the same anxiety that contributed to their distancing themselves from Black Jews in Harlem. In other words, on the stage they "learned to use their access as Jews to African-Americans and black music as evidence of their racial health—that is of their whiteness." In that estimation, blackface was a "form of racial masquerade. It passed ethnics into white Americans by distinguishing them from the African Americans for whom they spoke and who were not permitted to speak for themselves." In so doing, it has been averred that Jews "played a central role in the creation of a racialized twentieth-century mass culture." And as Jews dove into the melting pot, with their blackfaces on, they loosened the ties to their own ethnicity.[34]

Whatever their feelings and motivations regarding other Jewish performers who wore blackface, it is certain that when it came to Jolson, the African American community in Harlem of his day applauded his artistry and appreciated the affinity he had shown for their culture. Ironically, in some present-day racially charged quarters, Jolson has been characterized as a racist. But that was not the opinion of those neighborhood people who attended the premier of *The Jazz Singer* at the Lafayette Theatre. The *Amsterdam News* opined that it was "one of the greatest pictures ever produced" and "every colored performer is proud of him." The newspaper reported that during "the most dramatic moments . . . sobs [were] heard all over the theatre." The audience was clearly moved when Jolson sank to his knees and cried out musically that he would "walk a million miles" for one of his "Mammy's smiles."

But then again, Jolson had already earned respect from his efforts to oppose racism and help black performers advance on stage. Just two years before *The Jazz Singer*'s premiere, in 1925, he was instrumental in seeing that black playwright Garland Anderson's play *Appearances* made it to Broadway with an all-black cast, a first for the "Great White Way." Furthermore, this show that Jolson chose to back had a most unsettling theme—the trial of a black man falsely accused of raping a white woman. Even before his success in convincing hard-boiled producers to mount *Appearances*, Jolson was "known to cross the color line to perform in the streets with black friends" and, like Schiffman, demanded that his African American associates be served in the same restaurants as he. Jolson's reach on behalf of his fellow artists extended beyond the opening of *The Jazz Singer* when its popularity among moviegoers of all races motivated "Vitaphone and other major companies to produce musical shorts, featuring some of the top black entertainers of the time." Jolson's efforts yielded significant financial rewards for such stars as Duke Ellington, Louis Armstrong, the Nicholas Brothers, and Ethel Waters.[35]

Perhaps fittingly, even as Jolson reached out on behalf of black performers, African American sounds and rhythms were instrumental in one of his favorite composers, George Gershwin, finding his musical voice. Their inspiration helped him create not only "Swanee" but many other crucial contributions to American jazz. It was in Harlem during the 1920s and 1930s that an uncommon confluence of musical traditions came to together within the mind and ear of one of the great musical talents of his time.

Actually, Gershwin had already lived for a while in Harlem as a young boy and then as a teen. Uptown was one of the many places in the city where his peripatetic Gershowitz family—which included his brother Ira, the future lyricist—resided as his family aspired to move up economically. According to Gershwin's own often repeated recollections, it was when he was six years old, at a time when his father and uncle operated a series of restaurants in Harlem, that he first became hooked on music. As the story goes, around 1904, the boy "stood outside a penny arcade" on 125th Street—already the neighborhood's music center—and "was mesmerized by the sounds from a battered player piano" as he soaked up Aaron Rubinstein's "Melody in F" and "the particular jumps in the melody kept him rooted." Gershwin's formal music training began when the family purchased a second-hand piano, initially for his older brother to take lessons. Evidently, his family was prospering, as the acquisition of a piano for the parlor was often how Jewish immigrants first proudly signified the achievement of some modest affluence. Having a parlor was proof in its own right that the family was doing well enough to have moved beyond the crowded quarters of the old-style tenements. Initially, Gershwin was schooled as a classical musician—which certainly stood him in good stead as a composer—but early on he was "intrigued by modern music, such as jazz."[36]

At age fifteen, Gershwin dropped out of high school and entered the music industry, gaining some initial public attention as a "plugger" for a sheet music company. Selling popular music was a big-time operation in Gotham and the key to success for firms like Jerome H. Remick and Co. was to get its army of agents out into local venues to convince entertainers to sing their songs. In an era before radio made the scene, this was the way to get music better known. "Nightly . . . some eight pluggers, accompanied by song-and-dance artists . . . would sing and hoof the new tunes into the popular ear." When employees like Gershwin were not plugging their bosses' offerings, there was time to push their own creations. While with Remick, and as he was polishing his own style of composition, Gershwin benefited "from more-than-casual encounters with black music and musicians." Pianist Luckey (Charles Luckeyeth) Roberts would credit himself with teaching Gershwin "some of those terribly difficult [jazz] tricks that only a few of us could master." Gershwin used these tricks of the trade as he eventually began riding a circuit of clubs and private gatherings pushing his own songs, leading to that fateful night when Jolson adopted his and Irving Caesar's "Swanee" for use on Broadway. As he matured further in his integration of white, black, and classical styles, he often "spent time up in Harlem where he could hear jazz and listen to the masters of the stride piano." Some Jewish families frowned upon such associations with blacks, and young Jewish musicians thus tended to keep such relationships to themselves—the interactions "often took place in apartments, away from the public eye." The Gershwin family seemingly did not harbor such racial feelings. And George Gershwin came to believe—as one student of his genius would write—that black musicians "had put something together that could supply fresh melodies, harmonic and rhythmic directions through the literal and implied elements of blues, idiomatic syncopation and swing." At "the homemade academies of jam sessions and rent parties and private lessons" where he studied under black artists in Harlem, he would ultimately learn to "incorporate blues inflections, syncopation, and jazz harmony into his work in a way that appealed to black and white audiences alike." Gershwin would later reminisce to a sympathetic biographer that he wanted to put together an opera that came out of "the melting pot of New York City, which is the symbolic and actual blend of the native and immigrant strains."[37]

Gershwin's first effort in 1922 to create just this sort of grand production was a Broadway flop called *Blue Monday Blues*. Its Harlem connection was that its tale of a "tragic lovers' quarrel" was set in Mike's Tavern, a basement bar on 135th Street and Lenox Avenue. Apparently, one of the problems with the show was that its all-white cast used blackface before an audience that just "a season earlier welcomed with open arms the all-black musical hit, *Shuffle Along*." They wanted the real thing—African American performers. But out of that failure came "a crucial aesthetic realization about his Negro influenced music," namely that "what he heard in his inner ear, the fulfillment of his muse, could only be realized through the voices of African-American singers." The influence of African American music on the composer was seen dramatically two years later when the American classic *Rhapsody in Blue* was first performed. His arrangement brought together all of his many skills and backgrounds as he "bridged the gap between orchestral and popular styles." Most important, he "demonstrated that jazz, a black music, was worthy of elevation to symphonic arrangements and performance on the concert stage."

So much of what Gershwin had learned in Harlem and elsewhere about himself and his music came together in a folk opera par excellence whose setting was not New York, but Charleston, South Carolina. When *Porgy and Bess* first appeared in 1935, Gershwin, in his own words, asserted that his music reflected the "drama, the humor, the superstition, the religious fervor, the dancing and the irrepressible high spirits of the race," sounds that he had heard in spirituals in African American churches when the composer traveled down south in contemplation of composing this future masterpiece. In the end, what would make *Porgy and Bess* so effective was his combination of the rural authenticity of what he called the "Negro life in America" with the urban black sounds of "the blues scale and syncopated rhythms" that he had learned through his education within the jazz scene of Harlem.[38]

Meanwhile, even as Gershwin learned so much from his uptown black connections, Jewish musical entrepreneurship was unquestionably a vehicle for African American composers and artists to have their songs published and performed before audiences both within and without Harlem. This relationship has been described as one that ranged from collaboration to exploitation. It has been said that it is a "story of alliance, animosity, success, failure, exploitation, transcending friendships and ongoing shifts of attitude and economic position."[39]

Jews who capitalized on the industry of black music saw a niche market for their investments that was unchallenged based on their understanding of the racist times within which they and African Americans were living. In other words, since "a close association with black entertainers and artists was not a reputable way to earn a living, this business imposed few if any obstacles to entry and Jews faced little competition."

Yet in so doing, they also implicitly asserted that they were "whites who could see past the phobias of color to the creativity that a despised minority exhibited."[40]

But critics of Jewish business behavior have contended that "particularly in Harlem . . . Jews—and Jewish gangsters especially—control[led] entertainment venues." It has been said that "the only monetary returns in their own community" was "the salaries paid to the Negro musicians, ushers, janitors and door-men. The rest of the profits [were] spent and exploited outside of Harlem." And when it came specifically to the treatment of those whose abilities brought in the crowds, apparently for "every . . . Jewish club owner or artist manager who showed honest concern for an African-American performer" there was "an equally corrupt and exploitative one." In what constituted a best-case scenario, no less a notorious gang boss than Arnold Rothstein—reportedly "a good friend and supporter of Fats Waller," the famous stride style pianist, composer, and comedian—put his money behind a black show in 1927. Another commentator on this interface between racial groups has noted more simply that with their "experience as brokers and intermediaries . . . Jewish immigrants from Europe" were able to "act as mediators of black culture." And by the 1920s, "Jews were heavily involved in publishing, booking agencies and eventually independent record labels specializing in black music." As "middlemen . . . between the community that was so cruelly excluded and mainstream of American society," they were necessary for the work of black artists and entertainers to "be packaged and presented to appreciative audiences." Yet even those who are upbeat about the Jewish-black engagement in the business of music have noted that "disputes over money and royalties likely led to the downfall of black and Jewish musical collaborations in Harlem," which did not long survive the 1920s.[41]

Ultimately, the era of "slumming" that brought white fun seekers uptown by night in search of an "emotional holiday" and to hear the music that blacks provided—with differing types of Jewish assistance—ended after the Harlem riot of 1935. Despite the absence of pronounced racial antipathies fueling this outburst, from that point on whites were increasingly reticent about an evening or after-hours venture uptown. As a consequence, for example, not long after the riot, in the face of declining white patronage, the owners of the Cotton Club hotspot moved their famous cabaret out of Harlem.[42]

Meanwhile, even as uptown nightlife declined, Jewish musical entrepreneurs were increasingly looking beyond New York—to the Midwest, West, South, and especially the West Coast—as places where they could bring their entertainment business and acumen to bear. In these new, expanding venues, the Harlem scenario was largely replicated as Jews "provided black musicians with unprecedented opportunities to record and acquire fans." Nonetheless, "Jews also almost invariably exploited black artists who were doubled vulnerable individually as musicians lacking in independent capital and collectively as members of a subordinate social caste in a still largely segregated society." Not until the rise of Motown in the 1960s, would black businesses play "a prominent role in serving the African American record market," offering sounds that all races enjoyed. Until that time, "black musicians and A&R [artist and repertoire] men were most often the Jews' employees who only occasionally managed to become their competitors."[43]

In the next period in Harlem's history, roughly from the 1950s through the 1970s, the neighborhood would become inhospitable to Jews both by day and by night. Certainly for many of the Jewish storekeepers whose businesses were among the white-owned establishments that fell victim to the Harlem riots of the bitter summer of 1964, attacks upon their property ended their long association with the neighborhood. In the years that followed, the neighborhood came to be regarded as even more off-limits by whites, as more than at any prior time, Harlem was seen as crime riddled and drug infested. Needless to say, it was African Americans who were most unhappy with the conditions, living as they did in dilapidated buildings amid a community in distress. But many blacks, who were among the poorest all New Yorkers, had no place else to go. Remarkably, during this era when day-to-day contact between Jews and blacks became ever rarer in Harlem, that iconic place name came to symbolize all that was wrong in African American–Jewish contretemps citywide and throughout the United States. Gotham's streets and airwaves resounded with charges of anti-Semitism and racism as inter-group relations reached their nadir.

"This Is a Black Store" (photo courtesy of AP/Wide World Photos).

9

Harlem's Nadir for Blacks and Jews, 1950–1980

In the decade immediately after World War II, there was a slight uptick in the Jewish population in both East and Central Harlem. It was a growth that was perceptible primarily to statisticians and city neighborhood researchers but not to greater New York's ever-expanding Jewish community. A Jewish population study committee's estimate of its group's presence as of 1940 in the black enclave west of Fifth Avenue and north of 110th Street put the figure at less than 1,000 people. Ten years later, the number was said to be to approximately 1,300, but that group was deemed less than 1 percent of the population. In 1957, some 5,500 Jews were counted as residing in the area, less than 3 percent of all those in Central Harlem. In the decades to follow, the numbers and percentages would decline again.

A similar settlement pattern reportedly obtained in East Harlem where, as of 1940, only 500 Jews lived among the predominantly Latino population. Ten years later, only 1,300 Jews were counted as dwelling in El Barrio, constituting less than 1 percent of the neighborhood. As in Central Harlem, in the mid-1950s there was an increase in Jewish numbers, up to about 8,000, even as their share of all residents was calculated as at most 5 percent. Similar to Central Harlem, here too, in the next few decades, the Jewish population would decline again.[1]

Comparable findings from a 1955 Community Council of Greater New York study indicated that Central Harlem was almost exclusively African American, except for "a small group of Puerto Ricans, most of whom lived between 110th and 116th Streets." That report estimated that native and foreign-born whites constituted less than 1 percent of the area's population. Jews were not identified as a group. Over in East Harlem, Puerto Rican migrants to Gotham were identified as the predominant group and there was an expectation that their share of the neighborhood was destined to grow as they took "the places of some persons in other cultural groups who have moved away." Reportedly, "among the 9,500, foreign-born whites, natives of Italy, the Spanish American countries, the U.S.S.R., Eire, and the Scandinavian countries" were the principal groups. Again, whatever Jewish presence existed was not analyzed in the survey.

However, no matter what the actual number of Jews in Harlem, it is clear that they—along with everyone else there—lived in some of the worst conditions in the city. The 1950 census had revealed that in Central Harlem "the buildings were old . . . the dilapidation marked . . . and that overcrowding existed." The same was true in Spanish Harlem, where the findings were that more than three quarters of the buildings, most of which were built before World War I, were falling apart. Many of the tenements lacked such basic amenities as private bathrooms. Reports on high rates of juvenile delinquency were attributed in a large part to the sad reality that "many of the children and youth are without a stable background in a home with both parents." In Central Harlem, for example, more than a third of married women did not have husbands resident in their homes.

A subsequent study of conditions in Harlem schools likewise did not contribute much hope for the future generation that was growing up in these slums. As of the mid-1960s, reportedly three quarters of the pupils in the area's overcrowded and underfunded schools were found to be reading below grade level. Those who graduated high school often earned only the general educational development (GED) certificate, which was largely useless in the coveted white-collar job market and did not qualify its holder for college admissions. Sadly, in many respects these young people were following in the faltering footsteps of their parents. In the 1950s, the median education of adults over twenty-five years of age in the neighborhood had been determined to be less than nine years of schooling.[2]

A major stumbling block to African American and Latino occupational advancement at this time was the change in Gotham's economic profile. Much like after World War I, the city attracted large numbers of African Americans from the South who were escaping the poverty and overt racism in Dixie. And Puerto Ricans likewise gravitated to the city, which had fulfilled promises for earlier immigrant groups, as they fled the island's economic distress. But they arrived at the wrong time in the history of the metropolis, for the 1950s witnessed the slow beginning of the end of New York City as a manufacturing hub, with jobs lost in both the skilled and semi-skilled sectors. Some occupations were made obsolete due to mechanical improvements. Others were ceded to sun-belt areas that—with government assistance—promised owners greater profit margins. Thus when poor newcomers to the city settled in their sections of Harlem and blacks made their way into existing African American enclaves in Brooklyn, they found that their employment opportunities had diminished. Making matters worse, segregated unions denied them equal access to the jobs that remained. In other words, existing labor groups took care of their own, denying minorities access to that all-important union card. This combination of deleterious factors meant that only the lowest-paying jobs, like "slaving" as a domestic, were left for these newcomers. In 1961, the black unemployment rate of 10 percent was twice the city average. Looking back at this unhappy early post-war era, one observer would attribute much of what was wrong in Harlem to a lethal combination of "poverty, racism, joblessness, health, education" that seemed to render "the Negro Mecca . . . beyond redemption."[3]

Not all of the blacks in Harlem were ill educated and ill equipped to prosper in Gotham. There were those within the community who—despite the racism and unequal opportunities that had long stymied the rise of those of their race—had become "civil servants, teachers, nurses" and the like. In the 1950s, these members of the black middle-class exited in appreciable numbers from the neighborhood and resettled within the better outer-borough areas, while the most fortunate found places in new suburban locales. That is, if they were approved for mortgages, which were not always forthcoming as banks designated neighborhoods by race—a practice known as "redlining"—frequently led them to deny those hoping to own their first homes. One option in the city proper was southeastern Queens, in neighborhoods like St. Albans, Laurelton, and Springfield Gardens. These areas "contained single-family houses and thus exuded the kind of suburban atmosphere that blacks were prevented from enjoying outside the city." In fact, in the case of St. Albans, prominent entertainers like Lena Horne and Count Basie had led the way out of Harlem in the 1940s. Thus, even as the hopeless inundated uptown, which was plagued additionally by criminal elements who exploited the sad state of affairs, enough of those with aspirations for their families left Harlem, yielding a net decline in population.[4]

The intensifying atmospherics of "squalid living conditions and barriers to employment . . . horrible ghetto conditions . . . the lack of good schools, the inadequate recreational facilities" all contributed mightily to the anger and ultimately to the rioting that consumed Harlem, and from there spread over to the Bedford-Stuyvesant section of Brooklyn, in the summer of 1964. The street violence by those whom the *New York Times* described as having been "condemned . . . to life on a near-animal level" was touched off by an instance of police brutality more egregious than that which had brought rioters to the streets in 1943. During that wartime conflagration, it was alleged that a police officer had fatally shot an African American soldier. Word had spread fast and property destruction ensued. Robert Bandy, in fact, survived the wounds to his back. Now, on July 18, 1964, violence began when New York City police lieutenant Thomas Gilligan killed a young African American, fifteen-year-old James Powell. After a protest at a Harlem police station, thousands of angered residents took to the streets. They reportedly "raced through the center of the neighborhood shouting at policemen and white people, pulling fire alarms, breaking windows and looting stores." This initial outburst of anger and frustration resulted in thirty arrests. Violence continued for two days in Harlem and then, on the third day, Bedford-Stuyvesant erupted. In the aftermath of the rioting, white storeowners in Harlem and the Brooklyn black community tallied up their losses as the attacks seemingly targeted "only businesses owned by white persons." In Harlem, the damages from the first night were estimated at $50,000.[5]

In the days and weeks that followed the outbreaks, both instant analyses and more detailed examinations made clear that the root cause went well beyond the police shooting. Rapacious landlords and storekeepers, "greedy white folks," and "prejudiced employers" were identified as the malefactors whom the rioters hated the most and upon whom they sought revenge. All of these enemies were routinely characterized as part of "the white power structure" intent on "keeping us [African Americans] down."[6]

However, the Harlem riot of 1964 was not a battle of blacks against Jews. For all of the raw emotions that were expressed, neither in the rhetoric of the rioters nor in the criticisms of the commentators did anyone suggest that the attacks were directed specifically against Jews, as opposed to whites, even if Jewish names abounded on the lists of local entrepreneurs whose places were looted. "No observer of any of these first series of riots to afflict great American cities [in the post-war period] recalled hearing anti-Jewish slogans," wrote a sociologist several years later. And while Nation of Islam spokesman Malcolm X, in the spirit of 1930s street-corner agitator Abdul Hamid, was frequently on the record, before and after the riots, as comparing Jewish business in Harlem to "colonists . . . intent on exploiting the black community," only his devoted followers connected with his inflammatory worldview.[7]

And for that matter, except for perhaps the storekeepers who were grievously affected, Jewish voices both near and far from the trouble zones did not detect any widespread anti-Jewish sentiment on the streets. The most that the Jewish Telegraphic Agency (JTA) would say is that some "anti-Jewish slogans [were yelled]." The Brooklyn-based *Jewish Press*, an organ hypersensitive to any manifestation of anti-Semitism, shared the JTA's appraisal. At that point, one of the weekly newspaper's editors was Rabbi Meir Kahane who, as the future founder of the Jewish Defense League, was destined to be the most outspoken, demonstrative, and habitually outraged respondent to black-Jewish confrontations. But back then, some weeks before the riot, when one of its headlines stated, "Racial Crisis in the U.S. Brings Increase in Anti-Jewish Bias," the haters identified in the piece were the KKK and the American Nazi Party. A week later it highlighted that boxer "Cassius Clay had pledged to fight with the United Arab Republic in any future war against Israel." Its July 31, 1964, edition simply reprinted the JTA release. Kahane did not comment at all on the 1964 riots. Nor did any of the *Jewish Press*'s readers care, in subsequent editions, to offer views on the etiology of the outbreak of urban violence.[8]

Arguably, the absence of a strident, or apprehensive, Jewish reaction to what had happened on those mean streets had much to do with their separation both geographically and emotionally from the uptown scene and from African Americans more than thirty years after Harlem had been Jewish. For Jews, the first two decades after World War II were an era of good times. For hundreds of thousands of them, newly constructed suburban communities on Long Island, Westchester, and over the George Washington Bridge in northern New Jersey beckoned. With their low-cost government loans in hand, thanks to the G.I. Bill of Rights, Jews settled comfortably in these salubrious settings as in most communities white gentile neighbors, also fulfilling the American dream of home ownerships, welcomed them into the new enclaves. Significantly, in these cul-de-sac locales, African Americans generally were not to be seen. Restrictive covenants—far more pervasive than those that Jews had previously faced—barred those who had the economic wherewithal, and comparable meritorious wartime credits, from making such a desirable move.

During this same era of Jews on the move, tens of thousands of New Yorkers left the snow-covered streets of Gotham and environs to find houses and jobs in emerging sun-belt communities, especially Los Angeles and Miami. Such was the case with Herbert and Florence Spitz and their by then seventeen-year-old daughter who, in 1948, departed Floral Park and relocated to Sherman Oaks, California. There Herbert became an "importer of laces and fabrics"; selling those products was one of the jobs that he had pursued during the Depression when he was not trading stocks out of his own home back in Nassau County. The family has remained in California for the past seven decades. The Harlem roots of the descendants of Israel and Emma Stone are well-nigh unknown to Marilyn Spitz Maxwell and her two Los Angeles–born children.

At the same time that "golden cities" in the West and South beckoned, many Jews who a generation earlier had left Harlem for neighborhoods in the Bronx and Brooklyn saw no reason to leave their still-hospitable urban environs. In 1960, an admiring *Fortune* magazine article spoke glowingly of the "Jewish Elan" in Gotham that still "contributed mightily to the city's dramatic character—its excitement, its originality, its stridency, its unexpectedness." The report emphasized a "condition of non-crisis" among post-war Jews, "occupying as they frequently do in a residential area or in an industry a majority position and exercising such wide influence." Neighborhood persistence was visible almost everywhere. For example, the "main Bronx artery" of the Grand Concourse—which in the 1920s had replaced Lenox Avenue as a Jewish mecca for former Harlemites—housed "a solidly middle-class society inhabiting large old-fashioned apartments in large old-fashioned buildings." Meanwhile, Queens became a desirable midpoint for Jews who wanted new housing for their families and did not want to deal with the burdens of daily suburb-city commutation. Queens Boulevard, for example, joined "the great boulevards of Brooklyn [and] the Bronx" as "essentially 'Jewish' avenues constructed by Jewish developers for a Jewish clientele." And Forest Hills Gardens, which was once off-limits to Jews, finally did away with its restrictive covenants.

Certainly, not all New York Jews experienced such favorable circumstances. Late in the 1950s, the construction of the Cross Bronx Expressway that cut through the heart of the then still-vibrant Bronx's East Tremont neighborhood decimated its working-class Jewish community. Eventually, those who were unable to move out were forced to deal with many unsavory criminal elements, including blacks who squatted in dilapidated buildings. Over in Brownsville, Brooklyn, the construction of city-financed high-rise projects augured to—and in time did—change the economic, social, and racial profile of that area of Gotham. But a more compelling fact on the ground was that black-Jewish encounters and palpable tensions were minimal because racial segregation characterized New York City. At least it was possible for most Jews to feel that way. Blacks were a small minority in the predominantly Jewish Bronx communities. Almost no African Americans lived in Brooklyn's Boro Park. Similarly, as of 1957, some 123,000 Jews lived in nearby Flatbush, with only 3,000 blacks. By contrast, in Bedford-Stuyvesant, 166,000 of its 253,000 residents (66 percent) were black, while only 6 percent of the denizens of the very poor neighborhood were Jews.

Sometimes racial issues bubbled to the surface. Such was the case late in the 1950s when the NAACP initiated a campaign against liquor stores in Harlem—most, they said, owned by Jews—that were "closed to Negro salesmen." Reportedly, local residents expected more out of Jews because "the Jewish attitude on integration [was] more liberal than [that of] Protestants and Catholics." Indeed, protestors "expressed amazement" that given what the spokesmen for the group believed to be "the closeness that has existed between Jews and the Negro community," that Jewish storeowners did not immediately accede to their requests. More significant in light of the major contretemps that would soon pit Jews against blacks, was an *Amsterdam News* report in 1958 that "denounced the Jewish principal of a Bronx school in a predominantly Jewish neighborhood for accepting five classes of Negroes from a nearby school, but isolating them on a separate floor." Still, during the 1950s and early 1960s, the two groups, living largely apart, rarely confronted or even engaged one another. In most parts of town, there were few pressure points to produce conflagrations. Thus, while most New York Jews may have felt sympathy for those whose businesses were looted in July 1964, the riots did not immeasurably change their lives in the city nor their attitudes towards the minorities who neither resided nor worked among them.[9]

In 1968, the two groups confronted one another in a widely publicized and protracted battle that not only hit home in local neighborhoods but also resonated throughout the city and beyond. Although most Jews and blacks lived in different places in Gotham, substantial and ultimately vocal elements of both communities met on an ongoing basis, as teachers, parents, and pupils, in New York City's school system. The battle royale that then ensued centered in the Ocean Hill–Brownsville section of Brooklyn over the contentious issue of community control of the metropolis's educational enterprise. It pitted the largely Jewish United Federation of Teachers (UFT) against black parents who were abetted by a radicalized leadership that came to Brooklyn from all over the city. However, there had been a dress rehearsal for this attitude-changing struggle in Harlem just a few years earlier when local parents took their youngsters out of local schools. They organized a boycott to make clear that they had had enough of a system that was dominated by white educators who, to their minds, were not properly educating their youngsters.

The flash point uptown between 1964 and 1966 was a plan to build a new school, Intermediate School 201 at the corner of Madison Avenue and 128th Street, which supposedly was to be well integrated, with white students brought in daily to Harlem. The perceived advantage of a mixed student body was that schools with white students received more attention and money from the centralized Board of Education than those that were predominantly black. However, as the plans for the institution moved towards fruition, it became clear to neighborhood observers that the advantaged white students slated to be bussed over the Triborough Bridge from Astoria and Long Island City would not be arriving. Families in the Queens neighborhoods were not taken at all with the opportunity to avail themselves of education pitched towards "successful living in a democratic, multi-cultural and multi-racial city." As frustrations built, Harlem parents began to assert that the only way they would get a fair shake would be if they had control of the schools. Collaterally, the protesters began to assert that the curricula that their children were being exposed to failed to instill in them a sense of pride in their African American identity and heritage. Civil rights activists as well as leaders of the incipient Black Power movement championed this latter complaint. By 1966, Mayor John Lindsay had acceded to their demands and sections of Harlem were designated "experimental school districts," under which neighborhood schools would be administered by community boards. This decision angered and frightened the predominantly white administrators and teachers who had long worked in the area. Effectively, all the elements that would make the 1968 Brooklyn battle so contentious and vituperative were in place except for one critical dimension. In Harlem, the white villains of the piece as the protesters portrayed them were not roundly identified as Jews. In the Brooklyn battle, the confrontations elicited strident anti-Semitic and racist sentiments from many quarters. The ideological fires set in Brooklyn involved allegations that Jews controlled the schools, which was just one part of a larger narrative of Jews undermining African Americans' survival. Those ideological fires quickly spread back to Harlem.[10]

Concisely put, the times of troubles in Brooklyn began when City Hall designated Ocean Hill–Brownsville likewise as an experimental school district and soon thereafter the new district unit supervisor, reputed to be a follower of Black Nationalist Malcolm X, moved to fill administrative vacancies with fellow African Americans who shared his sentiments. Jewish leaders of the UFT saw their positions in great jeopardy and, as important, were outraged by statements that the new school administrators, leaders of the African-American Teachers Association, made about the "death of the minds and souls of African-American children" due to "the systematic coming of age of the Jews who dominate and control the educational bureaucracy of the New York public school system." Unknown to protestors—or conveniently forgotten—was the history of the UFT's predecessor, the Teachers Union, which in the 1930s had worked with black educators against the tide of racism of that era to improve the lot of Harlem's schoolchildren. But then again, the members of the predominantly Jewish UFT were not radicals, even if some of them quite recently had demonstrated their civil rights bona fides. Most notably, union president Albert Shanker, whom protesters pilloried persistently, had marched with Dr. Martin Luther King in Selma, Alabama. On guard to protect its members' rights and positions, the union was quick to respond when nineteen teachers and administrators were summarily dismissed on the grounds that they were deemed to be "unsupportive or ineffective." All but one of those removed were Jews. Charging that the dismissals were made without due process, the UFT turned for relief to the courts, which ruled that the terminated teachers had the right to stay on. When the mayor refused to implement the decision—clearly siding with the black community—the union called out its rank and file on the first of three strikes that effectively closed down the entire city's public school operations for close to three months. Amid these labors actions, Brooklyn's air was further fouled by a letter that found its way into the mailboxes of UFT members at one district school. It declared, among other canards, that so-called "Middle East Murderers of Colored People"—meaning Jews—could not teach "African-American history and culture to our black children" for they lacked "the insight, the concern, the exposing of the truth that is a must."[11]

In 1969, even as the Brooklyn school crisis dragged on, another controversy over race further stoked the tensions and ill will between Jews and blacks. Though it did not take place in Harlem, the neighborhood was very much invoked as a metaphor. At that point, with the city in turmoil, the Metropolitan Museum of Art commissioned the mounting of an exhibition entitled "Harlem on My Mind: Cultural Capital of Black America, 1900–1968." Its director, Thomas P. F. Hoving, seemingly with the best of intentions and recognizing a growing "communications . . . gap between people and particularly between black people and white people," hoped that the show would engender "a discussion . . . a confrontation, an education" between groups. But rather than achieve an "intervention," he and his associates ended up having to cope with animosity from all sides.

First, the black community was alienated long before the exhibit opened because while it had been promised that the show would be "created with the direct participation of members of the Harlem community of all levels and all ages," in fact the planning and execution had become largely the province of Allon Schoener, noted widely as "a white and a Jew." The African American community's sentiment was "that whites (on their own) could not even begin to know the African-American experience." If anything, the choice of artistic leadership was but another example of the powerful imposing their will upon the lives of the people of Harlem, much like whites and Jews, they believed, had long controlled their employment, housing, and education of their children.

Confirming their worst fears that they were to suffer from "patronizing racial politics" was Schoener's decision not to include any paintings or sculptures by black visual artists. In other words, there was no evidence shown "that contributions had been made since 1900" by some of Harlem's foremost talented people. The work of renowned black photographer James Van Der Zee was exhibited, but his shots of Harlem lives and its great leaders were shown as "documentation" of uptown life, not as artifacts of cultural creativity. Schoener had naïvely—or effetely—determined that paintings, of any sort and by any group, had "stopped being a vehicle for valid expression." His conceit supposedly was to produce a "multi-media extravaganza." But critics swiftly noted that just two years earlier Schoener had been the curator of an exhibit on Jewish life downtown called "Portal to America: The Lower East Side, 1870–1925." And in that exhibit, in addition to his multimedia elements, Schoener found room for lithographs, paintings, drawings, and one sculpture. Moreover, to supplement "Portal," its sponsoring organization, the Jewish Museum, put out an anthology of essays that lauded the immigrant Jewish neighborhood experience. No such volume was planned or executed for "Harlem on My Mind." For black artists, the Met's Harlem exhibit was little less than "a slap in the face . . . an uncomfortably familiar scenario, corresponding to a painfully long history of close doors in the art world." The pain for them was acute, "just as the issues of discrimination, blocked opportunities and exclusion had tremendous currency for blacks generally." The museum's director and the curator would come under withering attacks for their failure to portray and extol the values of struggle and survival that were foremost in the minds of the black people of Harlem.[12]

When the exhibition was close to completion, Jews stepped up with their own searing complaints. Their palpable anger and distress was directed at the Met over the tone and content of the introductory essay that accompanied the show's catalogue. Its author was Candice Van Ellison, a black high school student and a resident of Harlem, who had initially written her piece as a term paper in a class at Theodore Roosevelt High School. Schoener—again perhaps acting quite naïvely—wanted to include her thoughts as the voice "of an ordinary citizen, a true representative of the people." But if her words really reflected the feelings of those in her neighborhood—and a subsequent public opinion poll found that by a substantial majority "the young girl's feelings were shared by most other young black people"—then her manifesto bespoke long-simmering community antipathies towards those whom they believed had brutalized them or exploited Harlem economically.

Van Ellison surely took some hard shots at the "strong Irish influence exerted on Harlem through the city's police force" and spoke graphically about "police brutality" that started back in 1900 with the "arresting of Negroes and beating them senseless inside the precinct" during the Tenderloin riot. It was that traumatic event which, ironically, had initially brought so many African Americans uptown. But she had much more to say about the Jews who, she claimed, now dominated their lives. In her recounting of Harlem's Jewish history, she asserted that as African Americans "pour[ed] into lower-income areas of the city . . . they push[ed] out the Jews. . . . [T]he Jewish shopkeepers [were] the only remaining 'survivors' in the expanding Black ghettoes. This is especially true in Harlem where almost all of the high-priced delicatessens or other small food stores are run by Jews. . . . The lack of competition in this area allows the already badly exploited black to be further exploited by Jews."[13]

Predictably, Jewish defense organizations of all stripes were outraged. The usually even-tempered ADL heatedly called the essay "something akin to the worst hatred ever spewed out by the Nazis." Its leaders were only partially placated when Mayor Lindsay called the work "racist" and requested that the catalogue not be sold. However, they were less than satisfied with the atmospherics around City Hall because Hoving—who had previously served under Lindsay as the city's parks commissioner—defended Van Ellison. They were troubled by his assertion that what she wrote "is her personal observation of life in her block. . . . It is not inflammatory. It is the truth. If the truth hurts, so be it." For the executive director of the Synagogue Council of America, Hoving's statement was "politically speaking . . . far more serious" than the words in "a confused black girl's essay," for his remark "implied that it is indeed the Jew who is the villain of the piece." It constituted "a subtle shift from the tolerance of anti-Semitic rhetoric to an acceptance of its substance." Meanwhile, Meir Kahane's Jewish Defense League rallied in front of the Met, demanding that the exhibit itself be taken down. In due course, after veiled and overt threats within and without government-funding circles, Hoving walked back his statement and Van Ellison partially retracted at least the most problematic implications of her critique of life in Harlem. In an insert that was placed inside the catalogue, the young black woman claimed "the facts were organized according to the socio-economic realities of Harlem at the time, and that any racist overtones which were inferred from the passages quoted out of context are regrettable."[14]

Most Jews remained unmoved by this weak apology and some saw even darker days ahead in inter-group relations. Statements like those from Charles Kenyatta of the Harlem Mau Mau Society that "Jewish leaders were blowing the Museum incident out of proportion and that this was itself an indication of Jewish anti-Negro feeling" did little to calm the controversy.[15] However, as in all social and political issues, Jews were not of one mind on how they were to come to grips with such tensions in Gotham. There were those who sympathized with black complaints and questioned their own group's behavior whether in Harlem and elsewhere in the metropolis. One articulate liberal voice went so far as to suggest that while "Jewish merchants [in Harlem] should not be thrown out on the street simply to satisfy legitimate black aspirations . . . tensions [could be] resolved if for instance, the large Jewish organizations [bought] out the Jewish merchants in Harlem and then turn over the stores—at a loss—to black merchants." He also thought that it was the "responsibility of the Government to subsidize this effort, because it is not the fault of the Jew that he is found as a merchant in Harlem." When all was said and analyzed, it was clear that to a great extent, attitudes towards race depended on where a Jew lived in the city. There certainly was a very hard core of the worried and disaffected—particularly those who lived in or who had moved from "changing neighborhoods"—who were frightened and appalled by black anti-Semitism, unhappy with the prospect of minorities living among them, and chagrined that City Hall seemed not to be on their side.[16]

But in the decade that followed—that is, the 1970s—while racial tensions citywide did not abate, the streets of Harlem would not see any dramatic conflicts between Jews and blacks. Daily interactions between unfriendly neighbors, and with them racially tinged misunderstandings, were minimal because the Jewish presence in the area was almost nonexistent. Although hard numbers are difficult to come by, estimates from census reports place, as of 1970, the percentage of whites, inclusive of

Jews, in the Central Harlem neighborhood at approximately 4.25 percent, fewer than seven thousand people. A decade later, a Jewish communal survey of its poor in the city estimated that in both East and Central Harlem, there were no more than one thousand Jews.[17] These numbers are exclusive of the Jewish merchants who still worked in Harlem even after the neighborhood and their stores suffered through that hot summer night of trouble when during the evening of July 13, 1977, a regionwide electrical grid failure caused the entire city to lose its lights. During the blackout, criminals roamed the streets all over town, breaking into stores and setting fires indiscriminately. If the Harlem experience entered at all into Jewish communal discussions at this point in Gotham's history, it might be referenced as a lament that that once proud enclave, now long gone, had declined so completely. When it came to Harlem, the more pressing point of concern for middle-class New Yorkers—be they Jews or other whites or blacks—was their apprehension that the neighborhood was a crime-riddled trouble spot to be avoided at all costs.

For generations, uptown had been among the poorest of New York's enclaves. But now a lethal combination of social and economic factors conspired to make many of its streets quite treacherous. First, there was dismay and worry in the neighborhood because Harlem's African American working class was continuing to suffer from the city's ongoing decline as a manufacturing center. Extending a downward spiral that had started in the 1950s, New York's garment trades and printing industries, as well as food processing plants, continued to migrate south, in many cases on the way to leaving the country entirely. Located near superhighways, these businesses had plenty of room to expand operations and goods could be easily transported to, rather than from, old city markets. And owners' profits benefitted from the labor of nonunionized employees. As the city's revenue base declined due to out-migration of businesses, short-sighted increases in municipal corporate taxes on the firms that remained and the always annoying permit and inspections fees further exasperated manufacturers. Second, Harlem's group of recently hired civil servants was hit hard by municipal job retrenchments. During a worldwide recession that began in 1973, the administration of Mayor Abraham Beame instituted a wide range of budget cuts in a failed attempt to right the city's budget. Blacks who had come on board to city agencies "as a result of pressure in recent years to provide more opportunity to minorities" were among the first to receive layoff slips. Job seniority meant that those who were the last to be employed were among the first to lose their coveted positions.[18]

The numbers computed early in the 1970s—as jobs were lost or never secured—told a grim tale as the proportion of families on welfare in Central and East Harlem was two and a half times the overall city rate, while median incomes were the lowest in the metropolis. Observers, from the police to social commentators, were also quick to note how, as one report put it, a "deepening recession especially as it affects employment for young non-whites could ignite more crime in slum areas," like Harlem. "[A]t a critical disadvantage in the job market . . . this age group is the most likely to have trouble with the police."[19]

Making matters worse, Harlem, along with the other poor neighborhoods citywide, suffered from a decline in decent, affordable housing. A 1974 study of Harlem's close to one-quarter million housing units, which included "brownstones, tenements, walk-ups, and multiple-dwelling buildings constructed" before the Great Depression, revealed that one in five was "badly deteriorated and need replacements soon." But relief was not in sight as the building of replacements was moving at about two thousand units a year while three thousand units were lost annually through "demolition, abandonment or conversion to non-residential use." The reality was that in many cases "landlords walked away from their buildings rather than pay outstanding mortgages, taxes and other outstanding expenses." The housing crisis was even worse in the South Bronx and in Brooklyn's Crown Heights, Brownsville, and East New York. There far more of the most unscrupulous of owners, on the way out of the deteriorating neighborhoods, were complicit in torching their investments to collect insurance compensations. Nefarious "finishers" found lucrative opportunities to help complete the job. Before the suspicious fires were set, these criminals stripped the buildings of salvageable parts. Still, even if Harlem did not look nearly as much like an area that "had experienced wartime air raids," its physical decline was readily apparent to a historian who had chronicled its rise as a black nexus. Gilbert Osofsky would comment mournfully, "Harlem was unique. Its name was a symbol of elegance and distinction, not derogation; its streets and avenues were broad, well-paved, clean and tree-lined, not narrow and dirty. . . . Harlem was not a slum." But now, with "some buildings, technically abandoned . . . hous[ing] squatters or becoming drug centers," the neighborhood was in existential crisis.[20]

Although the problem of drugs was not unique to Harlem, since so many other poor enclaves suffered from this manmade epidemic, not only were junkies seemingly everywhere needing money and committing crimes for a "fix," but the industry of heroin was readily apparent on uptown streets and growing both in volume and in sophistication. One frustrated city prosecutor declared late in 1975 that "it's wide open again. We've got more heroin than ever before. The quality has increased and the price has stabilized." A narcotics rehabilitation worker reported with similar angst, "I've never seen it the way it is now. Walk up Eighth Avenue and you can hear the pushers calling out brand names." Four years later, in 1979, a state senator from Harlem reported sadly that Adam Clayton Powell Boulevard (Seventh Avenue) was a "free trade zone, an open-air supermarket for drugs." Cutbacks in crucial city services, most notably law enforcement, certainly did not help matters. Left largely free to operate without police interference, African American and Latino organized crime syndicates had come to the fore. Indeed, an evil form of ethnic succession was underway in both East and Central Harlem as "black and Hispanic importers and distributors nudged the Mafia out of its dominant position." One of their headquarters was the Gold Restaurant on Seventh Avenue near 123rd Street, where the "Council of 12" met to coordinate their "game plan to avoid violence among themselves" and to root out "cowboys," independent operators who "attempt to rob or kidnap members of existing narcotics groups." Meanwhile, it was reported that "the people of 123rd Street contend that the problem has taken over their block and has made life virtually intolerable for them." For the law abiding, having to cope with "aggressive" dealers who "pursue potential heroin sales (as well as cocaine and other drugs) with many passersby," selling name-brand drugs, these streets were no place to be.[21]

A 1973 Louis Harris poll found that Harlem's hard-pressed black residents were devastated by the crime and violence all around them and "gloomy on [the] future of [their] area." Economically depressed and fearful of conditions around them, an overwhelming majority said that they lived "in Harlem because they had no other choice." Stuck where they were, interviewees enumerated "crime in the streets, drug addiction, burglarizing of apartments, youth unemployment," not to mention "dirty streets, pollution and poor housing," as key impediments. Only the most optimistic of respondents believed that while existing conditions had "reached rock bottom . . . the only way to go is up." Reacting to the study, African American intellectual Orde Coombs opined that Harlem was more than a physical entity, "it is also a state of mind and it lacks a philosophy to face the future." In his jaundiced view, "it has stopped being a showcase for chocolate dandies. It has wiped the phony grin from its face and replaced it with a scowl." In this environment, "the poor working class . . . [lived] in the ghetto, coiled against attack, while the underclass, released from hoping for the future, see[s] every person as a potential mark."[22]

Several months later, an African American member of the *New York Times* editorial board walked one evening through the streets of his old neighborhood and found that "fear" radiated up from Harlem's sidewalks. He depicted "the image of a community of some half-million people barricaded until daylight behind double and triple-locked doors." When Roger Wilkins stopped to query a local barber about the "major changes that occurred" since the journalist had left Harlem some years earlier, the "short and clear" response was, "mainly it's the fear. Up here, people don't go out at night any more unless it's urgent."[23]

Needless to emphasize, for whites during the 1970s, the era of slumming in Harlem was a distant memory. For them, Harlem was largely off-limits day and night. For example, it was an unwritten rule among the overwhelmingly white Columbia University students who studied and resided on Morningside Heights—on the bluff, running from roughly 110th to 120th Street, that overlooked the black neighborhood—that Morningside Park had to be avoided. This once bucolic preserve, which Frederick Law Olmstead and Calvert Vaux had designed in 1877, was now "a run-down park" with garbage strewn everywhere and overgrown with "weeds and underbrush" that "chok[ed] existing shrubs and trees" but provided excellent hiding places for muggers. This "raw no-man's land between a ghetto and affluence" was considered the "most dangerous place in the city." So concerned were Columbia University and "other educational, medical and institutions" around it that visitors might mistakenly take the wrong subway line uptown and "wind up in Harlem . . . east of the [Morningside] Heights" and then "cross through Morningside Park" that in 1975 they pressed the Metropolitan Transit Authority (MTA) to post signs as far south as 42nd Street to alert those "naïve, or unaccustomed to New York . . . that it is dangerous to walk through Morningside Park." A year later, a *New York Times* feature article called the "Metropolitan Baedeker" was certain to indicate at the beginning of its guide to Morningside Heights' "impressive concentration of cultural and educational institutions" that "if you are taking the subway from downtown, be sure to take the Broadway local to 110th Street–Cathedral Parkway, not the express train."[24]

The subways that generations earlier had played such a defining role in Harlem's growth and ebullience now testified to the neighborhood's nadir. In 1941, Duke Ellington had invited the world to visit uptown when his band played "Take the A Train." Now, reportedly, "spreading unemployment, declining neighborhoods and fear of crime" all contributed to a substantial drop in ridership to Harlem. The "most spectacular loss," according to the financially strapped MTA, took place at the 125th Street station, close to where Ellington once held sway before swaying audiences of all races. Between the 1950s and the 1970s, that stop lost two thirds of its riders, mostly white straphangers.[25]

Meanwhile over in East Harlem, in another sign of unhappy times, Latino storeowners and residents were "angry and frustrated" that construction on the promised Second Avenue subway that had begun in 1968 was going nowhere. This conveyance was designed to replace the Second Avenue El, so much part of Harlem's early history, which had been torn down in 1942. The source of complaints ranged from those who were injured by construction accidents to those who were robbed by "youths who hid in the underground passageways" to merchants who lost business because patrons could not park on the now narrowed avenue. With the city suffering its fiscal crisis of the mid-1970s, the projected completion date was pushed back to 1981. Some thirty-five years later, the project remained unfinished.[26]

As a Columbia University undergraduate, Steven Schleifer was certain to avoid Morningside Park. Upon graduation in the spring of 1971, he was accepted into Mt. Sinai Hospital's Physicians Program. On October 11, 1971, he and a fellow medical trainee walked north and then west from Fifth Avenue and 105th Street towards his girlfriend's apartment on Riverside Drive. Their peaceful stroll ended, however, at 110th Street and Central Park West, just one long block from Morningside Park. They were accosted by six high school and junior high school students whom the police would later say had been "responsible for four to five robberies a day in the Harlem area."

What made this encounter somewhat unusual was that Schleifer, an Orthodox Jew, had no money on his person since that day was a Jewish holiday and he adhered to his religious tradition. Denied their demand for twenty-five cents, the perpetrators shot Schleifer in the back. Fortunately for the victim, after immediate treatment at Metropolitan Hospital, the low-caliber bullet was removed and Schleifer soon recovered.[27]

For the young man, there was no real aftermath to this unfortunate encounter and he was subsequently "busy with other stuff . . . getting back to school, getting married." But back in his home neighborhood of Kew Garden Hills, Queens, there was some chatter among "some JDL types" that this was a black versus Jew confrontation and some sort of retribution was in order even if no epitaphs were mouthed. However, no one actually moved in that violent direction. Additionally, there was some talk in Orthodox Jewish circles—in light of this incident and other such occurrences on Jewish holy days—that those who passed through minority neighborhoods might be allowed to carry a limited amount of money with them, in case of a potential holdup. Such was the tenor of ongoing tension that was part of the city's fabric during a difficult era in Harlem's and Gotham's history.[28]

However, Harlem's history and its Jewish stories would not end in the cul-de-sac of the early 1980s. In the generation and more that followed, the neighborhood would take part in, and benefit from, the revival of New York City as an increasingly safe, secure, and desirable urban center. Uptown would become one of the gentrified old inner-city locales and a welcoming spot for young people of all races, religions, and nationalities, many of whom were doing quite well economically. The newcomers would reside in restored brownstones or in rehabilitated apartments or find their places in newly constructed high-rise luxury buildings. And they all liked the short subway commute to their jobs and to entertainment in midtown. In this renewed environment, suburbanite Steven Schleifer would have no compunction about walking through Morningside Park on the way to a Columbia University reunion up on the bluff. And perhaps his children, if they desired to return the family to the city from their New Jersey hometown, might rent or buy in Harlem's upscale real estate market. Presently, Harlem's Jewish history has begun to repeat itself within a dynamic and ever-changing metropolis.

Harlem Hebrew Language Academy Charter School (photo courtesy of Yeshiva University Office of Communications and Public Affairs).

10

The Beginnings of Return

Even in its most dismal decades, there were some incipient developments on the ground in Harlem that augured the possibility of a revival for the neighborhood. As early as the mid-1970s, small groups of middle-class blacks settled on the outskirts of the neighborhood—to be precise, within Harlem Heights around Convent Avenue near City College. Despite the area's reputation as "overcrowded . . . garbage filled" and plagued by "a high crime rate," they were motivated to move in by "an opportunity to live in the black community and in brownstones that can be bought at reasonable prices . . . satisfying a yearning to own property." The city's human rights commissioner, Eleanor Holmes Norton, and her attorney husband, Ed, were among those identified as the first "pioneers," along with playwright Larry Neal, theatrical producer Woodie King Jr., Courtney Callendare, director of the Studio Museum of Harlem, and a cohort of "doctors, lawyers, architects, journalists and other professionals." The objects of their attention were seventy-five- to one-hundred-year-old houses that stood in relatively poor condition but possessed reminders of some good old days like dumbwaiters and crystal chandeliers. In a classic chain migration fashion, once they were settled comfortably, they "turn[ed] on some of [their] friends . . . to the good things that are available here." In some respect, their enclave in the making was a late-twentieth-century version of "Strivers' Row"—a two-block area on 138th and 139th Streets between Seventh and Eighth Avenue—which in the early decades of the century was "the most aristocratic street in Harlem." In those days it was said that "when one lives on 'Strivers Row,' one has supposedly arrived." The major difference for affluent African Americans in the 1970s was that previously segregation had precluded affluent blacks from settling in many other places in the city.[1]

The experience of the Michel family, which late in 1973 took over a brownstone on 147th Street off of Amsterdam Avenue, evidenced how times had changed and that options were now available for well-to-do black families. Harriet Michel, executive director of the New York Foundation, "the only black woman head of a self-endowed foundation," and her accountant husband who also owns a fleet of medallion taxis left predominantly white Riverdale in the suburbanized, northwest corner of the Bronx for Harlem because they "were tired of commuting" and "there was no sense of community in Riverdale." Moreover, they wanted the financial benefits of real estate equity and were unable to find any affordable properties until they looked into Harlem. It also stuck in Harriet Michel's craw that when she and her husband were first married and living in Yorkville, she had grown "tired of walking into stores over there and hearing *schwartza*" (the Yiddish word for "black," often used derogatorily). Looking around their new neighborhood, the Michels certainly were concerned about the high crime rate. But then again they had been burglarized twice while residing in Riverdale. Their biggest concern moving forward was the poor quality of schooling in Harlem. Other potential black buyers whom they hoped to attract to the neighborhood were similarly worried about the "educational facilities . . . there is no high school in Harlem and the public schools are inadequate." The Michels' solution at that point was to send their three-year-old son, Christopher, to a private school on Park Avenue.[2]

As of the early 1980s, the word "gentrification" was already being heard around the neighborhood and there was talk in the streets about the "rebirth" of Harlem "springing" reportedly "not from the souls of poets but from the creativity of developers and the sinews of construction workers." Already on the drawing boards were plans to revitalize 125th Street, complete with "an enclosed shopping mall and a center for the arts, including theaters and space for rehearsals, workshops and classrooms." The dream was to "reestablish Harlem" as "the tourist spot that once attracted people from throughout the world." Planners hoped to recapture the "excitement and luster enjoyed during its heyday." Their prime target client base was that class of "young, middle class professionals . . . white and black suburbanites . . . hit by soaring housing costs and energy shortages" who would be willing to buy and revive the uptown area. The expectation was that as these newcomers populated Harlem, the "official neglect" about which longtime Harlemites complained would end and strengthened police protection would bring the crime rate down sharply. Withal, there was already much talk along the avenues about what would become of the poor people in Harlem who were still coping with substandard schools, closing hospitals, and "able men [who] remain jobless and children liv[ing] in freezing temperatures." These residents worried openly about whether attention would be devoted to their needs in the Harlem of the future, indeed if there would be room for them at all.[3]

A 1984 study by two Columbia University social scientists strongly suggested that the fears of the community's existing population were well founded. Richard Shaffer and Neil Smith "warned that the city's redevelopment plans for Central Harlem would almost certainly fail to achieve the stated goal of upgrading the area without displacing low-income residents." They opined that with the municipality's emphasis on private investment to upgrade Harlem's rundown housing "a large number of outside residents would have to be attracted to the area. "At first," they hypothesized, "most of the newcomers" would be African American, but "as momentum builds a substantial number will be white." That is, of course, if the whites could put aside their fears "of living in a black area that they perceive as a dangerous place." As far as the indigenous population was concerned, the scholars averred that Harlem would remain an "enclave for low-income blacks only if there were subsidized housing programs for the area or a substantial increase in employment."[4]

In the decade that followed, the professors' prognostications began to reach fruition. Leading the charge uptown were, as predicted, people who were akin to the Nortons and Michels, members of a growing black middle-class, who settled in not only because of economics, but to play a "cultural and . . . social role." For some, they were making the statement to those who lived around them that it was possible to become a successful African American professional. Following behind them were whites of comparable or even greater economic station. As of 1990, there were but 672 whites enumerated in the census of Central Harlem (1.5 percent of the total). By 2000, the white population was up to 2,200 (2 percent of the population.) The big spike would take place in the six years that followed. As of 2006, there were almost 13,800 whites in the heart of Harlem, 6.5 percent of the total residents. More indicative of the momentum shift was the fact that, as of 2008, close to a quarter of the white households in Harlem had moved to their present homes within the previous year. By comparison, only 7 percent of the black households had. And in 2010 the reality that the neighborhood was "in the midst of a profound and accelerating shift" was widely noted and discussed when the *New York Times* reported that blacks were "no longer the majority in Harlem." At that point, with African Americans sharing their turf with whites, Latinos, and a variety of foreign-born folks of various races, the 77,000 blacks in Central Harlem were a grouping "smaller than at any time since the 1920s." One sociologist observed that "Harlem has become what it was in the early 1930s—a predominantly black neighborhood but with other groups living there as well."

Those who celebrated about or reacted with equanimity to the change would argue that the transformation was due not only to gentrification with the concomitant forcing of the poor out of their homes. As important was the fact that since "so much of the community was devastated by demolition for urban renewal"—not all of which actually took place—and by the "arson and abandonment" that began in the 1960s, "many newcomers have not so much dislodged existing residents as succeeded them." In other words, "poverty, unemployment and the overpopulation of previous decades, epidemics, and crack had left a territory that was bled out and decayed where many buildings and a great deal of land were unhealthy or vacant." Given these negative sets of circumstances, poor blacks started moving out of Harlem as their buildings decayed or were destroyed as early as the 1970s, when the community's population declined by more than 30 percent.[5]

In 2001, Bill Clinton "put a presidential stamp of approval" on the ongoing forces of transformation when "he chose the 14-story story building at 55 W. 125th Street for his offices after leaving the White House." Even before he spoke to a cheering crowd about his initiative and affection for Harlem, declaring that "no matter how bad it was, people held up their heads . . . and where, when things got good, people were grateful and cared about their neighbors," he had received high marks among community leaders for his administration's designation of Harlem as an "empowerment zone." That meant that hundreds of millions of dollars were earmarked "to develop economic and commercial businesses," ostensibly to benefit the neighborhood's small businesses that had barely hung on over the decades. But while monies did flow their way, larger national chains made their presence felt in Harlem with the aid of government funds and often in competition with the older local outlets. For potential gentrifiers scoping out the neighborhood, the sight of "Starbucks, a multiplex cinema, a Disney stores etc." added to its luster and their interest in settling.[6]

The movement of the upwardly mobile to Harlem was, of course, part of a citywide trend. In fact, the uptown neighborhood was somewhat of a latecomer to Gotham's transformation. The gentrification and revival of other neighborhoods had begun to take place in the bad years of the 1970s. Ironically, at the same time that many of those who had the wherewithal fled to suburbia as the city suffered financial and physical decline, small cohorts of young people reembraced the metropolis and its potentialities. Famed economist John Kenneth Galbraith explained in 1973 that "the suburban movement was the response of the older city dwellers to the poverty and indiscipline of the new arrivals." But, he predicted, "as that shock loses its relevance, the superior quality of city life will naturally reassert itself." As of 1978 it was already observed that "young people who two decades ago would have settled in a Levittown are gravitating towards neighborhoods like Soho and Brooklyn Heights." In some cases, these "trend-setting gentrifiers" or "urban homesteaders" turned once broken-down districts into "delightful neighborhoods." Observers took note that in Manhattan—beginning around 1980 and not too far from Harlem—a once-dreary Columbus Avenue on the Upper West Side now possessed "colorful shops and restaurants."[7]

By the 1990s, with the city's economy revived and offering new job possibilities for the well trained, neighborhood change was in full throttle all over the city. During that decade, those who helped to restore "the Brooklyn Brownstone Belt" of Fort Greene and Dumbo (down under the Manhattan Bridge overpass) could brag that it took only fifteen minutes for them to get to their highly paid jobs in Manhattan. Those who were doing even better took over and upgraded lofts in Soho, while the Meatpacking District, near the Hudson River south of 14th Street, was an attractive alternative for the well-heeled who might like to walk to work.[8]

Arguably, as Harlem joined the movement, it attracted—in addition to those becoming well-off—others who could not as easily "afford to live in the ritzier parts of Manhattan, not to mention the trendier sections of Brooklyn." But for them, too, Harlem was, as it had been for a century, a short commute to work and play downtown. For example, a "free-lance journalist, just out of college" who moved to Harlem in 2013 reported that he was there "out of necessity" and there were, in his accounting, "many more just like him." He and his brother found a sublet on 138th Street off Malcolm X Boulevard, directly across the street from the famous Abyssinian Baptist Church. Perhaps fittingly, as a professional aspirant himself, his place was just a mere block away from the old Strivers' Row.[9]

Just a few years earlier, in 2005, a retired executive who had worked in the hip-hop music business made his way from Yorkville to 116th Street and Lenox Avenue and became the first resident of a remodeled five-story apartment building that had been built in 1910 and undergone "six construction or renovations since 2003." He was also the first white person on the block, or so passersby told him, as he became a fixture on local streets. In time, the other fourteen apartments at 114 West 116th Street would be filled up with both white and black residents. He was attracted by the affordability of housing as well as the vibrant street culture around him. With time on his hands and music in his heart, this self-described "harmonica player extraordinaire" has "played with or sat in" with local bands. And although he has not made a historical connection, he was behaving and indulging himself much like white musicians did generations before when Harlem was an entertainer's place to be.

Given his professed "liberal" background—as a youth in Far Rockaway, he had observed how his parents, staunch integrationists, were friendly with black actor Ossie Davis and other African American entertainers—he was fully comfortable in his new surroundings in Harlem and felt welcomed in the neighborhood. Among his friendly acquaintances was an African American Muslim who sold a black nationalist newspaper across the street from the large Masjid Malcolm Shabazz Mosque.[10]

The freelance writer who lived with his brother on 138th Street also felt accepted in the neighborhood and "confessed" that he had "met with nothing less than kindness" on its now safe streets. Still, he harbored some reservations about his presence as an "intruder . . . with no historical ties" in Harlem. Occasionally, he felt like the tourists who "gawk[ed] at the tremendous scene" on a Sunday morning outside of the Abyssinian Baptist Church. More important, while he admitted "that the causes and effects of gentrification are complicated and I don't purport to fully understand them . . . I know somehow that by living in Harlem, I'm part of a change that will eventually increase property values, raise rents and force out people who've lived here longer." He wondered, "What can I do to grow in this city without hampering someone else?"[11]

Black critics of gentrification both within and without Harlem did not wonder about what the changes meant to their neighborhood. Simply put, for them, it was "a case of the haves and the have–nots." On one side of the avenue, among the privileged newcomers, Harlem had become a "hotspot for high income hipsters attracted by the neighborhood's high quality architecture and by the easy commute to New York City's commercial and business districts downtown." It was also now a mecca for "interlopers eager to experience the urban, uptown African-American experience close up and in person." These are the "swathes of young, white gentrifiers . . . on the march" frequenting "fancy French restaurants, German beer gardens, upscale supermarkets which sell nothing [that] longtime locals," who stand on the other side of the avenue, "can eat or can afford [that] are replacing black bookshops[,] barbershops and soul food joints." So disparate were the two lifestyles on Harlem's streets that "while a select few are enjoying the high life . . . central [*sic*] Harlem has the highest unemployment rate in the city."[12]

In 2014, Brooklyn-born filmmaker Spike Lee, who resides in a palatial townhouse on the Upper East Side, gave articulate, if off-color, voice to those most disturbed about gentrification both where he grew up and in Harlem. He asked rhetorically, with four-letter words punctuating his remarks, "Why does it take an influx of white New Yorkers for the facilities to get better?" Lee complained that until the newcomers came in "the garbage wasn't picked up," the schools were "not good," and "the police weren't around." As a sign of how times had changed, Lee said that "when you see white mothers pushing their babies in strollers, at three o'clock in the morning on 125th Street, that must tell you something."

For Lee, these interlopers suffered from a "Christopher Columbus Syndrome" and were little less than neighborhood imperialists. If these aggressors were not physically destroying "the indigenous people," as is now said about the fifteenth-century explorer and racist, they were acting without "respect" for those for whom Harlem had always been home. In fact, with the collaboration of real estate developers they are changing names of Harlem streets and calling the area from 110th to 125th Street "Stuyvesant Heights."[13]

Meanwhile, less than ten years after he set up his office on 125th Street, Bill Clinton also absorbed his own share of substantive—if less vitriolic—criticism from local residents. There were, reportedly, "strong currents of disappointment and resentment" towards the president "for failing to follow through on projects and promises." For instance, his "pilot small business project" directed at black ownership had not grown as had been pledged. Operation Hope, designed under the Clinton Foundation "to set up financial education programs in local schools," had lost momentum as his organization looked all over the world for worthy projects. One neighborhood leader complained that "the things Bill Clinton has been involved with have taken on an international taste and tone and the Third World is down the block." Most critically, it was said that with Clinton "as the face of gentrification and displacement," neighborhood change had "gotten out of hand." A local Baptist minister openly questioned what "the new Harlem Renaissance" was doing, "bringing in people who are able to pay for these properties, who push people out who can't, like schoolteachers and municipal workers." For him, "the community has been taken over by big business and banks and deep-pocketed entrepreneurs." To cite two housing valuations that greatly distressed the disaffected, when the president moved in to his space, the estimated "top price for a brownstone terrace house in Harlem was $400,000." Just five years later, "a fully renovated townhouse cos[t] as much as $4 million." For more modest accommodations uptown, "a one-bedroom flat which used to rent . . . for $800 a month" in 2000, now was on the market for $1,400.[14]

But perhaps the most pilloried agent of gentrification was an African American real estate operator. In July 2008, *New York* magazine identified Willie Kathryn Suggs as "the most successful and reviled real estate broker in Harlem." Characterized as "a lightning rod in Harlem's larger gentrification debate," she had, according to her opponents, "wantonly driven up real estate prices until no one but the richest Harlemites could afford them and, worse, delivered much of the neighborhood into the hands of wealthy whites." Her activities underscored the tense debate over housing in the neighborhood: "Should Harlem be preserved forever as an affordable haven for blacks? Or should it be sold to the highest bidder?"

Viewing herself as "post-racial or color blind anyway," Suggs readily admitted, "I've sold to people from Israel, Argentina, Egyptians, I sold six properties to a Norwegian. It's clear it is not personal and just business." And she asked rhetorically whether she must, by virtue of her race, sell only to African Americans. For her, such a community-imposed limitation "is called racism. . . . The [black] people whose house I sell and get top dollar love me." On the other hand, her critics strongly believed that "Suggs and others like her are hiding behind principle to their own selfish ends." As one Harlem Tenants Council leader said, "She has reaped the bounty off the backs of poor and working-class people." Suggs's typical rejoinder was that "racism is racism." Besides which, "I don't want my neighborhood to be all black or all white." The question of "Whose Harlem is it?" continues to stir emotions within the uptown black community. But the Jewishness of the white newcomers has not been a consideration.[15]

It is not known when the first groups of Jews began to return to the area. But when population figures from censuses are combined with periodic Jewish communal self-surveys, it appears that Jews, from the 1990s on, have made up a good percentage of white resettlers in Harlem. Although definitive numbers are hard to come by, it seems that Jews were among the first to arrive uptown. For example, in 1990, when it was estimated that less than 700 whites resided in Central Harlem, the 300 Jews noted as in the neighborhood constituted some 45 percent of the white newcomers. And over in East Harlem, some 2,600 Jews were counted—a full 3 percent of the total population.[16]

However, eleven years later, in 2001, it appeared that the Jewish share of the white in-migration was not as robust as before. It appeared that almost the same number of Jews resided in East Harlem as in 1990, a few less than 2,700. Similarly, in Central Harlem, the Jewish population had risen minimally, if at all. But, at that point, the more than 500 Jews in the area apparently constituted at least a quarter of the white residents in the neighborhood.[17]

When demographers looked at the Jewish presence in 2011, it was estimated that even as Jewish numbers had grown over the prior decade they were only a small part of the white community uptown. Approximately 3,800 Jews lived in East Harlem, while 2,700 resided in Central Harlem, where they constituted some 20 percent of the white population. The largest concentration in the latter section was in the streets immediately north of Central Park up to 119th Street—just south of Mt.

Morris Park—and east to west from Fifth Avenue to Morningside Park. In other words, where Jews were most visible was precisely in the area that one hundred years ago had been the center of the affluent Jewish communal presence uptown.

Although a statistical profile of these Jewish settlers' religious identity values is not available—after all, at present Harlem Jewry is a small fraction of Gotham's Jewish polity and flies largely beneath the community's research screen—it may be said that unlike Israel Stone and his fellow founders of Hand-in-Hand a century and a quarter earlier, they did not rush to establish a Jewish communal presence. They more closely resemble the early Harlem Jews who were not especially interested in religious life. Rabbi Gansbourg evidently noticed that reality when he happened upon the area in 2005. For example, that young freelance journalist who sublet near old Strivers' Row, and who it turns out happened to be Jewish, showed no interest in connecting to Jewish life. He defined himself, like so many young Jews of the day, as "more a cultural Jew rather than a religious Jew." His small friendship circle uptown was exclusively gentile. Not incidentally, he did not remain long in Harlem. By the summer of 2015, he had relocated to Brooklyn for reasons that had nothing to do with his ethnic ancestry. Rather, his peregrinations were typical of so many of this social and economic type who frequently move in and out of Gotham's upscale neighborhoods. Similarly, that first Jew back on 116th Street did look for and did not find any Jewish affiliations during his more than a decade in Harlem. This amateur musician who frequents Harlem's haunts is entirely comfortable with his neighbors and they with him. Although Louis Farrakhan might frequent the Mosque across the street and spew anti-Semitism as a latter-day version of Sufi Abdul Hamid of the 1920s and the young Malcolm X of the early 1960s, the statements of this Chicago-based Islamic preacher have not affected life on his block.[18]

Indeed, for the twenty-first-century Jewish residents of Harlem, the last major outbreak of anti-Semitism, and with it a tragic occurrence of violence, was more than a decade in the past. In the fall of 1995, groups of black protestors picketed Freddy's Fashion Mart on 125th Street off Eighth Avenue, taking aim at its owner, Freddy Harari, a Jew who lived in Gravesend, Brooklyn. The battle took place mere steps away from where Blumstein's once stood, the site of neighborhood economic confrontations some seventy years earlier. Only this time, street protest led both to vitriolic racial name calling and ultimately to the murder of seven innocents.

A relative newcomer to the business strip, Harari—who had set up shop in Harlem only three years earlier—was accused of attempting to evict Sikhulu Shange from space that the African record-shop owner had sublet from him. Shange's business had been a fixture in the neighborhood for decades. Unbeknownst to most protestors—at least at the outset of the struggle—the property was owned not by Harari but by a black church, the United House of Prayer, a branch of an evangelical denomination founded by Bishop Charles Manual "Sweet Daddy" Grace in the 1920s. In all events, Shange believed that that he was "double crossed by both" Harari and the church, each of whom, in his view, wanted more space on the block. But the 125th Street Vendors Association saw what was transpiring as a reprehensible example of a Jew imposing his economic will upon a black. As the protest ensued, Rev. Al Sharpton, the controversial head of the National Action Network, rallied to Shange's side and called for a boycott of the Fashion Mart. According to Jewish defense groups, who were keen to monitor Sharpton's activities and statements—as stated in later court papers—demonstrators threatened employees, hurled obscenities at "blood sucking Jews," and talked about burning down the store, whose owner they called an "interloper." Morris Powell, a Sharpton ally and a head of the vendors' group, was recorded as asserting that "these people don't kick back nothing to the community or help do nothing except sponge and parasite off our dollars. . . . And are we going to sit back and allow that to happen? That cracker got to be insane." Interestingly enough, Shange did not see the eviction problem in racial terms, but rather as due to the economics of a changing Harlem. As he saw it, "there are almost no black businesses in Harlem and I'm one of the few. If I go out of business, it's going to be very difficult for me to come back."[19]

On December 8, 1995, the protest turned unquestionably criminal when picketer Roland James Smith Jr. fire-bombed Freddy's Fashion Mart, killing seven black and Latino employees and customers. He died of smoke inhalation during the conflagration, as well. Despite public revulsion over the crime, Powell and others did not desist from their boycott of Harari. For close to three more years, his activists kept their focus both on the site of the tragedy, which was "renovated and renamed" Uptown Jeans, and on the Jewish owner's other 125th Street property,

Showtime. Protestors roamed the shopping street urging those seeking a bargain in the stores to "return fire" because "Freddy's not dead." Finally, late in 1998, Powell's self-declared "unfinished business" ended when Sharpton and Harari's lawyer reached an armistice. Sharpton apologized for calling the business owner an "interloper." In time, Jewish ownership on that once troubled block would end without incident. As of the summer of 2015, the Pretty Girl clothing shop for young adults occupied Uptown Jeans' spot on the street. Next door was the House of Hoops, an offshoot of Foot Locker that "specializes in high end basketball shoes and gear in a contemporary setting." And next to that stood a Gap. Across the street was a branch of Banana Republic and a Red Lobster restaurant, located next door to the world-famous Apollo Theater. And down the block, instead of Showtime, was an Ashley Stewart women's clothing store. The signs of a suburban-like shopping strip mall were all over the inner-city neighborhood.[20]

In the years that followed the struggle over Freddy's, race relations in Harlem rode the crest of the toning down of inter-group tensions citywide. One of the earliest signs that change was afoot took place not in Harlem but in Crown Heights at approximately the same time that peace came to the Harari-Powell-Sharpton affair. Back in 1991, a riot had broken out in that Brooklyn neighborhood—Jews called it a "pogrom"—after a black youngster was run over by a car carrying Hasidim. Subsequently, a revenge murder against a Jewish scholar took place as the neighborhood was torn apart and the town simmered for several crisis-filled days. But in 1998, local African American, Caribbean, and Jewish leaders started working together to head off "potentially volatile" racial confrontations. Although they recognized that great social and cultural differences set the groups apart, there was a common feeling that they did not want their neighborhood perceived as "a war zone torn by racial strife." By a similar token, the destruction of the World Trade Center on 9/11 also produced in its wake a palpable sense among New Yorkers that they all shared a mutual destiny. This unparalleled attack against Gotham raised city residents' awareness that for all of their internecine rivalries and competitions, their enemies were not living next door.[21]

As far as the gentrification of Harlem is concerned, as of the mid-2010s and notwithstanding Spike Lee's screed, reportedly "a culture of political and social resistance has been toned down." Instead, for many others, the issue was how to accept and even embrace the best of the new without ignoring Harlem's past and its people of long-standing. For Ethiopian-born and Swedish-raised Marcus Samuelsson, owner of the Red Rooster, a bistro that caters to a racially mixed crowd, "coming to Harlem has been as much about job creation as anything else." But he is concerned that with the transformation of Harlem, "respect" be shown for "the things that were built here before us." Fittingly, he chose to decorate his establishment to "evoke the Harlem Renaissance." As a colleague of Samuelsson put it, the question was "how do you monetize the cultural experience in a way that remains genuine and authentic." Meanwhile, as has always been the case in Harlem's history—with different classes of people living in proximity to each other—concerns remain about "housing—upholding and expanding affordable housing . . . for those seeking to keep many of Harlem's current residents put."[22]

Renewed Jewish religious and cultural life awaits the moment of its own efflorescence. Still, a noteworthy step towards community building, beyond what Chabad had done in and around its first-floor apartment on Manhattan Avenue between 118th and 119th Street, began in the fall of 2012 with the inauguration of the Harlem Minyan, whose congregational base expanded with the establishment of the Harlem Hebrew Language Academy Charter School. One of its founding leaders, Rabbi David Gedzelman, a top executive at the Steinhardt Foundation for Jewish Life, an organization whose mission includes leading "Jews who are well-integrated into American life to understand the importance of Hebrew and Israel"—and subtly advocating among others for the significance of the Jewish state—had since 2007 been deeply involved in creating Hebrew-language charter schools. While he worked for the presence of "Hebrew in the public spheres in America" for Jews and others alike in Brooklyn and New Brunswick, New Jersey, and contemplated doing likewise in Harlem, Gedzelman and his wife, Judith Turner, a program director at DOROT—a charity that for decades "mobiliz[ed] volunteers of all ages to improve the lives and health of the elderly"—lived on the West Side with their growing family of three children. In the wake of his work with what he perceived as welcoming black community leaders in furthering the Steinhardt initiative, Gedzelman became increasingly comfortable with the neighborhood in transition. So enamored, David and Judith decided to be not only agents of school building but consumers as well. The school that their father's organization was backing would be the school that the children would attend. Harlem unquestionably offered not only better and more affordable housing than their two-bedroom apartment at 697 West End Avenue on the corner of 94th Street, where they had lived since 1995. It also fulfilled their desire to raise their youngsters in a racially, religiously, and culturally diverse environment. Also in the back of David's mind was the fact that his great-grandfather had settled in East Harlem in 1912, when the Gedzelmans came over from Ukraine. Well-nigh one hundred years later, a Jewish family could be identified as having returned to the old neighborhood.

As their new home, the Gedzelmans bought a condominium in a building on the northwest corner of Frederick Douglass Boulevard (Eighth Avenue) and 115th Street, a place that had an interesting real estate history. For many years, 301 West 115th Street had been the home of St. Stephens A.M.E. Church. In an uncommon move that met with community approval, to both upgrade the street while preserving its religious legacy, three real estate developers—two African Americans and an Israeli—convinced the A.M.E.'s leaders to convey their property for a cash payment, with the understanding that the new building to be constructed would rise above the existing church. Reflecting on the deal, Gedzelman observed that the artifact of gentrification that he bought into was "a situation that did not disgrace the legacy of an institution but guaranteed its survival." They moved in May 2011 into a racially diverse building, most of whose residents had never before lived in Harlem.

As observant Jews—atypical of the Jews in the building—there remained for the Gedzelmans the problem of finding a synagogue to their liking and within walking distance on the Sabbath and holidays. In keeping with their adherence to traditional rabbinic ordinances, the family would not travel with the assistance of motorized transportation to services on holy days. For a while, they attended Chabad just two blocks away where they were welcomed, though ultimately that shul was not for them. So they set out to create their own religious space. Thinking ahead, they had to be pleased that the extension of the Manhattan Eruv into Harlem in March 2011, just three months before they moved in, augured that in time more religiously observant families would want to settle near them. An eruv, an unobtrusive wire stretched out around the perimeter of a community, permits people like David and Judith to push baby carriages and carry talises and other religious objects in public domains on the Sabbath without contravening rabbinical rules. In the twenty-first century, an eruv has become a perquisite for the growth of Jewish communities in many locales in America.[23]

Perhaps ironically, for the Gedzelmans it was the secular Hebrew public school that they helped found which would become "the anchor for a Jewish community" in formation. In the summer of 2011, two years before the school was opened, David and Judith met up with and recruited families like theirs who had young children who would become members of the Harlem Minyan. Some had extensive synagogue pedigrees, having attended congregations on the West Side; others had no such backgrounds. In October 2012, they began meeting once a month for a liturgically traditional service in space rented from St. Stephens. With the establishment of the public school, more Jewish families became aware of the Minyan and some joined. As of 2015, on a typical Sabbath some thirty adults and gaggles of children attended services. The congregation's email list consisted of more than one hundred interested parties. They met at rented space in the Dream Center, a storefront community facility on 119th Street between Adam Clayton Powell Boulevard and St. Nicholas Avenue.[24]

Still, according to Jewish journalist Steven I. Weiss who, with his wife and children, was a regular attendee at the Harlem Minyan, "there isn't a single Jewish communal address in the area." There was not one substantial institutional synagogue center, like the many that had been available in Harlem's Jewish heyday. The story of how and why Weiss and his wife, Rachel Feinerman, a professional modern dancer, moved uptown with their two sons paralleled that of the Gedzelmans. They moved to Harlem in 2013 from the Lower East Side. Depicting themselves as "part of a wave of Jewish families priced out of much of Manhattan," they found "Harlem to be an affordable, amiable and safe place to live" and wanted their sons to grow up in a racially diverse environment. They bought a co-op apartment at 1809 Adam Clayton Powell Boulevard on the corner of 111th Street. That six-story building's history mirrored the rise, decline, and revival of Central Harlem. Constructed in 1904 and boasting an elevator, it was initially deemed a luxury multiple-family dwelling. In the middle decades of the twentieth century, it suffered along with most of the structures around it during Harlem's physical nadir. For example, in 1904, each floor had but two large apartments. By the 1960s, six small apartments occupied each floor. Still it survived, albeit in some disrepair, to be part of the neighborhood building rehabilitation movement undertaken with government assistance in the last decades of the 1900s.[25]

Of a traditional religious bent, Weiss—who had studied at Yeshiva College—and Feinerman too recognized that Chabad was the only Jewish outpost within walking distance of their apartment. But since they, like the Gedzelmans, did not find the Gansbourgs' operation to their liking, their only alternative was to trek up the Morningside Park bluff to Orthodox Congregation Ramath Orath on 110th Street, west of Broadway. That is, until they made the acquaintance of a group of other "affiliated" Jews who had also recently made Harlem their homes. They readily joined the Harlem Minyan. [26]

Still, according to Weiss, for Harlem's Jewish community to grow, it needed financial assistance from UJA-Federation of New York to "procur[e] real estate that can incubate Jewish programming." In his view, "even a portion of UJA-Federation $900 million investment portfolio into real estate endowments could have a real impact on the growth potential of a community." But, as of the summer of 2015, this citywide Jewish charity remained uncommitted to Harlem. For Weiss, "the purchase of real estate is not high on the organization's agenda." As a spokesperson for the UJA-Federation explained, "it's got to start from the bottom up. . . . Our experience in Jewish community building has taught us that it requires a combination of indigenous bottom-up grassroots energy coupled with support and guidance from us that sparks the most likely energy to create new communities." In other words, "real estate is the outgrowth of many years of programming, leadership development and many new services and activities."

But the Weiss family, the Gedzelmans, and their friends within and without the Harlem Minyan were impatient, concerned that—like the longtime, indigenous population—they too would become victims of the ever-increasing price of property in this gentrified community. Ironically, as Weiss saw the situation, the "skyrocketed . . . cost of entry" into the new uptown of today, which has welcomed Jews—along with other middle-class whites and blacks—made the reestablishment of a strong Jewish presence problematic. Harlem is now, as it was a century ago, very good for Jews. It remains to be seen whether uptown will witness a second heyday for Judaism.[27]

Conclusion

An Enduring Community History

"The geographical place-name Harlem evokes in most contemporary Americans the imagery of a deteriorated inner-city neighborhood: the metropolitan area's first and most famous black ghetto. Few people are aware that between the close of the Civil War and the end of World War I . . . Harlem was home to a large variety of other ethnic and religious enclaves, including . . . a Jewish community of well over 100,000 people."

Those are the opening words of *When Harlem Was Jewish, 1870–1930*, written forty years ago, when American Jewish community histories were in vogue. Academics rode the crest of social history's popularity. Armed with a commitment to study the inarticulate, and often relying on quantitative sources to tell their stories, my colleagues frequently focused on cities where Jewish immigrants and their children lived in the South, Midwest, and far West. These were venues that scholars had not previously examined. Until then, local Jewish history had been the province of dedicated amateurs and rabbis, chroniclers of events in their locales who were sure to salute their own efforts and institutions. When professionals stepped up to write, there was surely a desire to cover these territories dispassionately. But as important, they were out to move the field away from its endless fascination with the history of the metropolis, specifically the Lower East Side, which had been favored with abundant scholarly and popular treatments.[1]

In counterpoise, I wrote about Harlem, proudly continuing the Jewish New York historiographical tradition. Admittedly, in line with the methods that urban historians were using to study other places and groups, the book turned to census manuscripts and city atlases to tell the tales of men and women who had no time or ability to record their experiences as they tried to advance in America. And back then, the narrative was more about men than it was about women. But, given the work's subject neighborhood, it was not another iteration of immigrant lore and life in downtown New York. Jewish Harlem had its own unique history, worthy of exploration. Still, I discovered that what transpired in the uptown district also contributed to a more nuanced understanding of the Jewish experience in the iconic so-called "ghetto" on the Lower East Side. Exposing the similarities and the differences between the sibling communities provided readers with a greater sense of what life was like for Jews all across Gotham over several generations in world Jewry's largest city.

Over the decades that followed, local Jewish communal histories lost their panache. I sometimes think that the decline in interest had much to do with the number crunching of quantitative sources that limited these works' accessibility to cognoscenti. At the same time, the Lower East Side, as the classic locus of New York Jewry, remained a compelling subject both for what happened there and for what it has represented.[2]

Harlem has had its own enduring transcendent importance, even if it has not been lionized with heroic prose and has only recently become an American Jewish heritage site. It has kept its shelf life and is now worthy of reappraisal because what started among and to Jews in the streets and institutions uptown did not stay in the neighborhood and had crucial implications for Jewish life well beyond the metropolis to this very day. Harlem's Jewish story speaks to the past and present and augurs to presage the future of American Jews. The story of Harlem's Jews has never been, and is not today, a localized saga. Rather, it is a continuing community history with wide resonance. As I told that friendly and intrigued *Times* reporter a decade and a half ago, "there are steps in the evolution of the American synagogue here."

One hundred years after Harlem's Jewish heyday, any American rabbi or educator working within Judaism's multiple streams in the United States who strategizes to bring young people into his or her sanctuary through initial encounters within athletic, artistic, musical, or theatrical portals is picking up on an experiment in promoting what we now call "Jewish continuity" that was first tried out on 116th Street. The Harlem Jewish "retrieval" effort, as this work was called back then, shows that this sort of creativity was not the province of any one easily categorized religious expression. The assignment of denominational labels to activists who make their marks upon their communities obscure rather than enlighten understandings of religious phenomena. Significant too is that the struggles over the legitimacy of religious innovation and who might be the change makers that took place in Harlem before World War I remind us of the long history of American Jews' diverse opinions over what should be done to ensure group continuity. Just like in Harlem, leaders and those whom they hope will follow them often harbor and act on very different visions of how to guarantee a future for American Judaism.

But how certain is the guarantee of American Judaism's survival? Here the up-to-date Harlem story will continue to be important because it delivers a challenging and perhaps a dystopian message about the future of this faith and community in the United States in the twenty-first century. The scene on uptown streets today surely evidences that Jews, as middle-class gentrifiers, comfortable in Gotham, and ready to take advantage of the city's social and cultural treasures, are returning to a community where their people were once the majority. However, notwithstanding some religious leaders' efforts, Judaism has been very slow to make its mark again in Harlem. In some respects, Jewish history uptown is repeating itself, as the founders of Congregation Hand-in-Hand way back in the 1870s had their own difficulties in convincing their fellow Jews that the faith was worth perpetuating through a shul and a school for themselves and their youngsters. Today, however, the dilemma of affiliation is even more profound. So many of the young people who make the uptown bistros and cafés the places where they like to congregate dissociate themselves from anything more than an ephemeral "cultural" Jewish connection. Given these circumstances, the question of whether Judaism will grow again in Harlem will merit continued observation. Once again, what is happening in this locale underscores the issues of Jewish identification in America.

Harlem's Jewish history, likewise, has enduring relevance for contemplations of the course of black-Jewish relations yesterday, today, and tomorrow. Unquestionably, if the Lower East Side was, and is, for Jews, their consummate touchstone, Harlem looms largest in actuality and memory for African Americans. In that environment, as residents, entrepreneurs, property owners, and patrons, Jews found, in some eras, welcomed places and in other times very unfavorable feelings towards them in what was, and is, America's black mecca. Some Jews were seen as exploiters, others as collaborators. There were Jews who were outspoken in not wanting to have blacks live next door to them and did their utmost to stifle African American entrepreneurship. Yet at the same time, others came into the neighborhood as early advocates of civil rights for an oppressed minority. Still others settled without comment within the African American section of uptown. These Jews persisted in that part of Northern Harlem until the 1920s. Most important, what transpired in the neighborhood between Jews and African Americans after World War I bespeaks their differing financial fates and social statuses within the life of the metropolis. Simply put, Jews generally did much better than African Americans in the economic sphere. And it is axiomatic that racism held blacks back from integration to a degree far more injurious to their advancement than anti-Semitism did in undermining Jewish mobility and acceptance. It is ironic that in a racist society where Jews very often wanted to be categorized as "white"—and did not always succeed in that integrationist quest—they surely achieved that status among black observers of controversies within the uptown scene. These crucial variances in fates continued well into the post-war decades, when Harlem was in steep decline and even Jewish memory of their time uptown was receding as they lived in different urban and suburban spheres from most blacks.

But even more significantly, in this context of African American–Jewish relations, what started in the streets of Harlem did not stay there. The diversity of opinions and behaviors that were manifested in the uptown area—from friendly and collegial to antagonistic and downright angry—have not only been replicated elsewhere but have been the hallmarks of how Jews have looked at African Americans and vice versa to this present day.

Finally, the contemporary beginning of Jewish return to the old neighborhood, arm in arm with many middle-class African Americans—and other whites, as well—and the concomitant displacement of the poor residents of Harlem reminds us that Gotham itself is ultimately a work in progress. Such was the case with the incipient urban-renewal efforts of a century ago and their attendant consequences both for poor Jews and their early gentrified, all-rightnik fellows both downtown and uptown. This book, with its historical and present-day perspective, provides a teaching moment regarding how a city revitalizes itself, and at whose expense, as different classes of residents attempt to live and advance in this nation's largest and very complex metropolis.

NOTES

ABBREVIATIONS

The following abbreviations are used in the notes:

AH: American Hebrew

AN: Amsterdam News

F: Forward

HS: Hebrew Standard

JCR: The Jewish Communal Register of New York City, 1917–1918 (New York: Kehillah [Jewish Community] of New York City, 1918)

JM: Jewish Messenger

JMJ: Jewish Morning Journal

NYT: New York Times

RERBG: Real Estate Record and Builders Guide

YT: Yiddishes Tageblatt

INTRODUCTION

1 For a full explication of the contributions that this book made to American Jewish, African American, and urban historiography, see Jeffrey S. Gurock, *When Harlem Was Jewish, 1870–1930* (New York: Columbia University Press, 1978), 157–68.
2 Joseph Berger, "New Documentary Follows Leading Yiddish Writer's Life in New York City," *NYT* (July 24, 2011), www.nytimes.com.
3 David W. Dunlap, "Vestiges of Harlem's Jewish Past," *NYT* (June 7, 2002), www.nytimes.com. See also Dunlap, *From Abyssinian to Zion: A Guide to New York's Houses of Worship* (New York: Columbia University Press, 2004), 44.
4 Paul Radensky, "To the Editor," *NYT* (June 14, 2002), www.nytimes.com.
5 Francine Parnes, "Religion Journal: A Synagogue Steeped in Harlem History Defies the Odds, but Still Struggles to Survive," *NYT* (November 1, 2003), www.nytimes.com.
6 "Revive: The Baptist Temple Church on 116th," *Harlem Bespoke* (December 8, 2010), http://harlembespoke.blogspot.com.
7 Jeffrey S. Gurock, *Jews in Gotham: New York Jews in a Changing City, 1920–2010* (New York: NYU Press, 2012), 1–4.

8 Carly Silver, "Jews Gradually Reclaiming Place in Harlem's History," *Columbia Daily Spectator* (October 29, 2008), http://columbiaspectator.com.; Mindi Hecht, "Centered around a College, Family Guides Harlem's Jewish Renaissance," *Chabad.org* (December 19, 2007), www.chabad.org.
9 There seems to have been, between 2005 and 2008, an ephemeral "egalitarian, independent minyan that met monthly for Friday night services in private homes within a specified geographical radius [in Harlem]." My informant, who lived on 117th Street and Lenox Avenue, could not recall precisely where the group met. There is no record of their continuing to meet beyond 2008, when the Borgenichts moved in. Email correspondence with Amanda Melpolder, September 16 and 23, 2014.
10 Sharon Otterman, "Underwriting Abraham," *NYT* (December 2, 2012). See also my comments in Simone Weichselbaum, "Harlem Is Getting Its Own Torah after Seven Decades without a Scroll," *Daily News* (October 24, 2013), www.nydailynews.com; Karen Schwartz, "Harlem Gives Birth to First Torah Scroll in 75 Years," *Chabad.org* (November 23, 2011), www.chabad.org.
11 Dovid Zaklikowski, "Rabbi Led Jewish Revival in Harlem," *Chabad.org* (February 18, 2013), www.chabad.org.
12 Daniel Bretton Tisdale, "Chabad of Harlem," *Harlem World Magazine* (March 14, 2012), www.harlemworldmagazine.com.
13 Debra E. Katz, "Led by Chabad, Diverse Group of Jews Make Up New Presence in Harlem," *Daily News* (September 13, 2008), www.nydailynews.com. See also Hecht, "Centered around a College."
14 Phone interview with Yoel Borgenicht, September 23, 2014. On Jackson Heights and Forest Hills residential anti-Semitism, see Gurock, *Jews in Gotham*, 18–20.
15 Simone Weichselbaum, "Hebrew—in Harlem, It's Not Just for Jews Anymore, Thanks to a New Language Academy," *Daily News* (August 14, 2013), www.nydailynews.com. See also Julie Wiener, "Harlem Hebrew Charter Gearing Up," *Jewish Week* (December 11, 2012), www.thejewishweek.com.

CHAPTER 1. A JEWISH OUTPOST IN HARLEM, 1870–1880

1 The information on the Stone family was derived from data contained in the 1850 and 1870 United States Census of Population available through ancestry.com. On the social and cultural life of central European Jews in the downtown neighborhood, see Annie Polland and Daniel Soyer, *Emerging Metropolis: New York Jews in the Age of Immigration, 1840–1920* (New York: NYU Press, 2012), 30–31.
2 On the economic life of first and second generation German Christian and German Jewish immigrants in Kleindeutschland, see Stanley Nadel, *Little Germany: Ethnicity, Religion and Class in New York City, 1845–1880* (Urbana and Chicago: University of Illinois Press, 1990), 46.
3 On dry goods stores and German immigrants, see Nadel, *Little Germany*, 81. On the growth of the area around 50th Street in Manhattan during this period, see

Andrew S. Dolkart, *Central Synagogue in Its Changing Neighborhood* (New York: Central Synagogue, 2001), 23–24, 28–29.

4 Herbert Manchester, *The Story of Harlem and the Empire City Savings Bank* (New York: n.p., 1929); "Old Timer's Tales of Harlem's Growth," *Harlem Magazine* (December 1914): 18. See Maurice H. Harris, *A Forty Years Ministry* (New York, n.p., 1925), 2; Charles H. White, "In Uptown New York," *Harper's Monthly* (June,1906): 220–28, quoted in Gilbert Osofsky, *Harlem: The Making of a Ghetto* (New York: Harper, 1966), 74. On the location of Stone's business, see *Trow's New York [City] Directory*, vol. 82 (1872).

5 For what it was like to ride the omnibuses, see Clifton Hood, *722 Miles: The Building of the Subways and How They Transformed New York* (New York: Simon & Schuster, 1993), 41; Jonathan Gill, *Harlem: The Four Hundred Year History from Dutch Village to Capital of Black America* (New York: Grove Press, 2010), 95, 104. See also "Old Timer Writes of Days When East Harlem Was a Salt Marsh," *Harlem Home News* (February 6, 1916): 6.

6 For a comprehensive history of peddling among Jews both in the United States and many other places around the world, see Hasia Diner, *Roads Taken: The Great Jewish Migrations to the New World and the Peddlers Who Forged the Way* (New Haven, CT: Yale University Press, 2015).

7 On the family background and activities of the Stone and Zabinskie families, see data from the 1870 United States Census of Population available through ancestry.com. As far as their being neighbors is concerned, the *New York City Directory* for 1872 indicates that Zabinskie was a seller of shoes and either his home or business was located at 2318 Third Avenue, where the Stones lived. Israel Stone's business was at 2355 Third Avenue. Hence it is reasonable to say that they were neighbors.

8 The first reference to the existence of this synagogue dates from 1869. See *JM* (October 17, 1869), n.p. Hand-in-Hand was renamed Temple Israel of Harlem in 1877. Its own tradition is that the congregation was established in 1873. On the reasons for establishing the synagogue in a remote Harlem, see *Temple Israel: Seventy-Fifth Anniversary Journal* (New York: n.p., 1949), n.p. See also "Temple Israel of Harlem: History of the Congregation," *AH* (May 20, 1898): 68.

9 Harold Heft, "A South Carolinian among the Mormons: Photographer Solomon Carvalho's Transcontinental Adventure," *F* (January 20, 2012), http://forward.com/articles/149954/a-south-carolinian-among-the-mormons/#ixzz3G3Efbat1; "Solomon Nunes Carvalho: Early Jewish Community Pioneer, Artist & Photographer," *Jewish Museum of the American West* (August 21, 2012), www.jmaw.org.

10 On the founding, operation, and leadership of the Jewish school see *JM* (January 30, 1898), n.p.; *AH* (May 20, 1898): 69. See also *Constitution and School Regulations of the Shangarai Limud Society of Harlem* (New York, n.d).

11 *AH* (March 14, 1880): 180; *AH* (March 26, 1880): 61.There were various estimates in the Anglo-Jewish press of the day as to how many children were enrolled as of 1880, ranging from 150 to 200.

12 On the mission of the early YMHAs, see Jeffrey S. Gurock, *Judaism's Encounter with American Sports* (Bloomington: Indiana University Press, 2005), 37. On the early location of the downtown Y, see www.92y.org/timeline.

13 "Congregation Hand-in Hand," *JM* (June 18, 1880), n.p.; *JM* (August 19, 1881), 2. A simple comparison of Hand-in-Hand's membership as listed in the Anglo-Jewish press of the day with that of Harlem's Jewish social organizations indicates clearly that religiously oriented members joined the social organizations, but that not all members of the Harlem Y—or, for that matter, the Harlem B'nai B'rith—belonged to the synagogue.

14 For information on Reform Jewish theology and attitudes towards its mission in the late nineteenth century, see Marc Lee Raphael, *Profiles in American Judaism: The Reform, Conservative, Orthodox, and Reconstructionist Traditions in Historical Perspective* (San Francisco: Harper and Row, 1984), 20–30. On Schickler's background, see *New York City Directory* (1879), available through ancestry.com. On Rubin's short tenure at Hand-in-Hand and his replacement by Lindner, see *JM* (August 23, 1879), n.p.; *JM* (August 13, 1880), n.p. See also *AH* (May 20, 1898): 68.

15 On the original service at the synagogue, see Harris, *Forty Years*, 1. On the splits and diversity in the membership see *JM* (September 14, 1877), n.p; *JM* (September 20, 1878), n.p.; *JM* (June 21, 1876), n.p.

16 *JM* (August 13, 1880), n.p.

17 Col. Alonzo B. Caldwell, *A Lecture: The History of Harlem: A Historical Narrative Delivered at the Harlem Music Hall* (New York: n.p., 1882), 29–31.

18 The information on the Stone family was derived from data contained in the 1880 United States Census of Population, available through ancestry.com. The information about the Stones' homes in the 1870s and 1880s was derived from E. Robinson, *Atlas of the City of New York, 1885* (New York: n.p., 1885), made available by the Map Room, New York Public Library.

CHAPTER 2. BROWNSTONE JEWISH BOURGEOISIE AND WORKERS IN TENEMENTS, 1880–1900

1 Clifton Hood, *722 Miles: The Building of the Subways and How They Transformed New York* (New York: Simon & Schuster, 1993), 42; Real Estate Record Association, *A History of Real Estate Building and Architecture in New York City During the Last Quarter of a Century* (New York: n.p., 1898), 77, 78.

2 On the background of the Panic of 1873 and its impact on New York City, see Edwin G. Burrows and Mike Wallace, *Gotham: A History of New York City until 1898* (New York: Oxford University Press, 2000), 1020–23.

3 Polland and Soyer, *Emerging Metropolis*, 58, 62. For an account of Hand in-Hand's financial difficulties, see *AH* (June 4, 1880): 33.

4 Real Estate Record Association, *History of Real Estate*, 76–79. See also *RERBG* (August 7, 1886): 955; *YT* (February 12, 1900): 4.

5 For the patterns of early 1880s construction in Harlem, see *RERBG* (October 8, 1881): 941; *RERBG* (October 22, 1881): 987; *RERBG* (May 14, 1881): 489–90. On the

nature of dumbbell and other forms of tenement house life, see Moses Rischin, *The Promised City: New York Jews, 1870–1914* (Cambridge, MA: Harvard University Press, 1963), 81–83. On the reaction of Olmstead to the appearance of tenements in Harlem, see Gill, *Harlem*, 117.

6 On Howells's remarks, see Hood, *722 Miles*, 54. See also *RERBG* (November 13, 1883): 851.

7 On the problems of overcrowding in the wake of the Panic of 1873 and the relief that came with the new rapid transit system, see *RERBG* (November 6, 1880): 961.

8 On this better type of housing, see the promotional articles "Houses for the Middle Class," *RERBG* (January 3, 1880): 3; "Houses on 116th Street," *RERBG* (November 8, 1879): 896; "Houses in Harlem," *RERBG* (October 1, 1881): 927.

9 Rischin, *The Promised City*, 9–10; United States Industrial Commission, *Reports of the Industrial Commission on Immigration*, vol. 1: *Immigration and Education* (Washington, DC: U.S. Govt. Printing Office, 1901), 470–71.

10 United States Census Office (John S. Billings), *Vital Statistics of New York City and Brooklyn Covering a Period of Six Years Ending May 31, 1890* (Washington, DC: U.S. Govt. Printing Office, 1894), 100ff. On a downtown amateur historian's take on the neighborhood becoming Russian Jewish, see J. D. Eisenstein, "The History of the First Russian-American Jewish Congregation: The Beth Hamedrosh Hagodol," *Publications of the American Jewish Historical Society* (1901): 63.

11 U.S. Industrial Commission, *Reports* 1, 470–71; U.S. Census Office, *Vital Statistics*, 100ff.

12 *Harlem Local Reporter* (May 2, 1891), noted in Osofsky, 237, n. 61. See also *Harlem Local Reporter* (April 16, 1890), quoted in Osofsky, *Harlem*, 80. For a memoirist's recollection of Harlem life, see Frederic A. Birmingham, *It Was Fun While It Lasted* (Philadelphia and New York: J.B. Lippincott, 1960), 13–14, 39.

13 Osofsky, *Harlem*, 79; Birmingham, *It Was Fun*, 41, Gill, *Harlem*, 111.

14 For biographical information on Peixotto, see his obituary in *NYT* (September 9, 1890): 4. See also Lloyd P. Gartner, "Roumania, America and World Jewry: Consul Peixotto, 1870–76," *American Jewish Historical Society Quarterly* 58 (1968–69): 25–117.

15 For the family background of the Sulzberger and Hays families and their connection through marriage to the Ochs clan, see Susan E. Tifft and Alec S. Jones, *The Trust: The Private and Powerful Family behind The New York Times* (Boston, New York, and London: Little, Brown, 1999), 109–11. See also David de Sola Pool, *Portraits Etched in Stone: Early Jewish Settlers, 1682–1826* (New York: Columbia University Press, 1952), 268, 329; Susan Roth, "Rachel Hays Sulzberger," *Jewish Women's Archive* (March 1, 2009), http://jwa.org.

16 Gill, *Harlem*, 110.

17 Vincent Sheean, *Oscar Hammerstein I: The Life and Exploits of an Impresario* (New York: Simon & Schuster, 1956), 29, 41. Subsequent to his work on building an entertainment center in Harlem, the ambitious Hammerstein looked southward and was instrumental in making Times Square the entertainment capital of

America. He built seven theaters in that district and also funded the construction of theaters in Philadelphia and London. See Gill, *Harlem*, 113–114, 122–25.

18 Independence Day Association of Harlem, *Celebration, 1886* (New York: n.p., 1887), 9, 16.

19 Harlem Republican Club, N.Y., *By-Laws and List of Members* (New York: n.p., 1888); Harlem Democratic Party, N.Y., *Constitution, By-Laws, House Rules, Members* (New York: n.p., 1892), On Hays's possible judgeship, see *AH* (October 23, 1891).

20 For the cost of initiation, see Osofsky, *Harlem*, 80. On Cantor's difficulties, see *YT* (July 1, 1889): 1. On the disbanding of the Harlem Club, see Michael Henry Adams, *Harlem Lost and Found: An Architectural and Social History, 1765–1915* (New York: Monacelli Press, 2002), 58.

21 "Temple Israel of Harlem: History of the Congregation," *AH* (May 20, 1898): 68–69.

22 For a source that indicates that Harris graduated from the Emanu-El Theological Seminary, see "Temple Israel of Harlem": 69. On the history of the school and the fact that it did not ordain, see Bertram W. Korn, "The Temple Emanu-El Theological Seminary of New York City," in Jacob Rader Marcus, ed., *Essays in American Jewish History* (New York: KTAV Publishing House, 1975), 367–70. For a source that contends that Gottheil ordained Harris, see Temple Israel, *Seventy-Fifth Anniversary Journal* (New York: n.p., 1949), n.p. See also a short biographical sketch of Harris's career published in the *American Jewish Year Book* 5 (1903–4): 61–62, which indicates that the Temple Emanu-El Theological Seminary ordained Harris.

23 Tifft and Jones, *The Trust*, 136.

24 Harris, *Forty Years*, 3. On the theological basis of the Jastrow prayer book, see Moshe Davis, *The Emergence of Conservative Judaism: The Historical School in the Nineteenth Century* (Philadelphia: Jewish Publication Society of America, 1963), 302.

25 *JM* (June 27, 1884): 2.

26 Harris, *Forty Years*, 3.

27 *AH* (January 24, 1890): 266.

28 *AH* (May 20, 1898): 90–92; *AH* (March 3, 1899): 627. See also Temple Israel Sisterhood, New York, "Minutes of Meetings, 1891–1893" (American Jewish Archives).

29 Congregation Ansche Chesed, "Minutes of Congregational Meetings, 1876–1893" (Congregation Ansche Chesed Archive); *AH* (February 15, 1887), n.p.; *JM* (May 25, 1889): 2; *AH* (July 6, 1888): 140; *AH* (January 11, 1907): 250–51.

30 On the chronology of Shaare Zedek's founding, see Hyman B. Grinstein, *The Rise of the Jewish Community of New York, 1654–1860* (Philadelphia: Jewish Publication Society of America, 1946), 472.

31 On Galewski's background and success in America, see Burton J. Hendrick, "The Great Jewish Invasion," *McClure's Magazine* (January 1907): 314.

32 *JM* (August 20, 1897): 2; *JM* (July 21, 1897): 2; *JM* (July 21, 1899): 347; Congregation Shaare Zedek, "Minutes of the Meetings of the Board of Trustees," meeting of May

28, 1899 (Congregation Shaare Zedek Archive); Congregation Shaare Zedek, *One Hundredth Anniversary* (New York: n.p, 1937).

33 For information on the distribution of east Europeans who settled in Harlem as of 1890, see U.S. Census Office, *Vital Statistics*, 234–37. For examples of ads that appeared in the Yiddish newspaper, see *YT* (March 30, 1892): 2; *YT* (April 22, 1892): 2; *YT* (May 13, 1892): 2; *YT* (November 2, 1892): 2.

34 For an example of Rabbi Distillator's self-promotion, see *YT* (September 5, 1888): 4. On his difficulties with the Health Department, see *Harlem Local Reporter* (October 1, 1892): 1. On the founding of the Uptown Talmud Torah, see *YT* (May 5, 1892): 2. See also the Incorporation Papers of Congregation Nachlath Zvi and the Uptown Talmud Torah on file at the Office of the New York County Clerk.

CHAPTER 3. UPTOWN HOMES FOR JEWISH IMMIGRANTS, 1895–1917

1 Hendrick, "The Great Jewish Invasion," 308–9, 318.

2 Ibid., 318–19.On the status of the Stone family in 1990 and 1905, see the data derived from the 1900 U.S. Census of Population and the 1905 New York State Census of Population, available through ancestry.com.

3 For Abraham Cahan's description of Jewish involvement in real estate, see his autobiography, *Bleter fun Mein Leben* (New York: Forward Association, 1926–31), especially volume 3, 428–29. Similar descriptions are to be found in his classic immigrant novel *The Rise of David Levinsky* (New York: Harper, 1917), 464.

4 Cahan, *Rise of David Levinsky*, 464. Edward A. Steiner, "The Russian and Polish Jew in America," *Outlook* (November 1, 1902): 532. For a reference to a study of Harlem in 1913, see Osofsky, *Harlem*, 88.

5 For a brief biography of Cohen, see *JMJ* (April 21, 1911): 1. On his involvement with the Eldridge Street Synagogue, see Annie Polland, *Landmark of the Spirit: The Eldridge Street Synagogue* (New Haven, CT, and London: Yale University Press, 2009), 71.

6 On Cohen's negotiations with Congregation Ansche Chesed, see Congregation Ansche Chesed, "Minutes of Board of Trustees Meetings," meeting of October 4, 1907. See *HS* (February 24, 1905): 4 for the location of the Cohen's residence.

7 On Elias A. Cohen's involvement with Congregation Ansche Chesed and the Harlem Federation, see *HS* (October 19, 1906): 3; *HS* (October 25, 1906): 13.

8 For a reference to the complexity of the lifestyle of the "all-rightnik," see Robert Zecker, *Metropolis: The American City in Popular Culture* (Westport, CT: Praeger, 2000), 62.

9 For a full treatment of the battle between Cohen and his cohort against the leadership of the Eldridge Street Synagogue, see Jeffrey S. Gurock, "Synagogue Imperialism in New York City: The Case of Congregation Kehal Adath Jeshurun, 1909–1911," *Michael* 15 (2000): 95–108. For the *Forward*'s view of the proceedings, see *F* (April 14, 1911): 1. On Cohen's plans for moving the Yeshiva Rabbi Isaac Elchanan to Harlem, see Gilbert Klaperman, *The Story of Yeshiva University: The First Jewish University in America* (London: Macmillan, 1969), 128–29.

10 For Rabbi Sossnitz's ad, see *YT* (May 22, 1892): 2.

11 Alter Landesman, *Brownsville: The Birth, Development and Passing of a Jewish Community in New York* (New York: Bloch, 1971), 40–47, 67–77.

12 Ibid., 40. On the relative paucity of needle trades workers in Harlem as opposed to the Lower East Side and elsewhere in the city, see Ben Morris Selekman, Henreitte Rose, and Walter J. Couper, *The Clothing and Textile Industries of New York and Environs* (New York: Regional Plan of New York and Environs, 1925), 67–68.

13 As of 1892, of some 724 cigar manufacturers in the city only 139, or 19 percent, were situated north of 59th Street; 43, or 5 percent, were in Harlem. See *Trow's Business Directory of Greater New York, 1892*, 227–37.

14 Gaylord S. White, "The Upper East Side-Its Neglect and Needs," *Charities* (July 16, 1904): 748–51.

15 *Harlem Local Reporter* (November 27, 1890): 4.

16 New York State Public Service Commission, First District, *History and Description of the Rapid Transit Routes in New York City* (Albany, NY: Public Service Commission for the First District, 1910), 16–27.

17 "Rapid Transit Progress," *Harlem Local Reporter* (April 18, 1893): 4.

18 Hood, *722 Miles*, 67.

19 *RERBG* (September 16, 1899): 401. The description of the building up of parts of Harlem was derived from an examination of the area's land-use maps of the time period. See George Washington Bromley, *Atlas of the City of New York, 1894. 1898–99* (Philadelphia: n.p., 1894, 1898–1899).

20 *RERBG* (October 18, 1899): 759. On the weakness of this early building code in addressing the problems of tenement life, see Roy Lubove, *The Progressive and the Slums* (Pittsburgh: University of Pittsburgh Press, 1962), 121.

21 Hood, *722 Miles*, 75–76, 85; *RERBG* (October 22, 1898): 572.

22 *RERBG* (August 25, 1900): 235.

23 *RERBG* (September 2, 1899): 336.

24 *YT* (April 19, 1896): 3.

25 New York State Bureau of Labor Statistics, *16th Annual Report* (Albany, 1898), 1046.

26 Ibid., 1051.

27 New York State Legislature, Assembly, *Tenement House Committee, Report of the Tenement House Committee of 1894 as Authorized by Chapter 479 of the Laws of 1894* (Albany, 1894), 250–52.

28 *RERBG* (September 16, 1899): 40; *RERBG* (January 19, 1900): 93.

29 On efforts to control immigrant youngsters' play through playgrounds, see Cary Goodman, *Choosing Sides: Playground and Street Life on the Lower East Side* (New York: Schocken Books, 1979), 7.

30 Citizens' Union of New York, *Small Parks and Public Piers for the People* (New York: n.p., 1897): 2.

31 *Map of Public Parks, Boroughs of Manhattan and Richmond* (New York: n.p., 1902).

32 *RERBG* (August 4, 1900): 144.

33 In 1902, the newly formed New York City Tenement House Department published a study of the tenement house population of Manhattan based on the 1900 U.S. Census of Population manuscripts. A study of these statistics indicates that 3,404 Russian Jewish families lived in Harlem. My own study of 275 Russian Jewish families enumerated in the same source reveals that their average family size consisted of 4.9 people. Projecting that figure for 3,404 families results in a total Russian Jewish population of approximately 16,680. These numbers do not include east European Jews from Galicia or Romania, who would be listed under their national origins but would not be as easily identifiable as Jews. See New York City Tenement House Department, *First Report, 1902–03*, vol. 2 (1902–3).

34 The aforementioned Tenement House Department report indicates that of the 3,404 Russian Jewish families living in Harlem in 1900, 1,953 (57 percent) resided south of 110th Street and east of Fifth Avenue. Within that area, they constituted some 12 percent of the population, while north and west of 110th Street they comprised but 5 percent of the population.

35 For more complete statistical data on Jewish economic distribution in Harlem as of 1900 see Gurock, *When Harlem Was Jewish*, 38–39, 182–83. See also *F* (November 10, 1907): 7 for a discussion of the Jewish Market. On the movement of the tobacco industry, see Lucy W. Killough, *The Tobacco Industry in New York and its Environs* (New York: Regional Plan of New York and Its Environs, 1924), 12–13.

36 See Gurock, *When Harlem Was Jewish*, 38, 174 table A.2 for information on this occupational distribution.

37 Ibid.

38 For the newspaper report on migration, see *JMJ* (August 16, 1907): 6.

39 Robert De Forest and Lawrence Veiler, *The Tenement House Problem* (New York: Macmillan, 1903), vol. 1, xiv–xvi.

40 *RERBG* (November 7, 1903): 824.

41 Ibid.

42 *RERBG* (July 27, 1901): 110.

43 *RERBG* (January 5, 1901): 4–5.

44 For the number of Jews entering New York City during this period, see Samuel Joseph, *Jewish Immigration to the United States, 1881–1910* (New York: Columbia University Press, 1914), 195.

45 For a comprehensive study of many relocation schemes, see Jack Glazier, *Dispersing the Ghetto: The Relocation of Jewish Immigrants Across America* (Ithaca, NY: Cornell University Press, 1998).

46 Union Settlement, *Annual Report of the Headworker* (New York: n.p., 1907), 8. See also "Communal Work in Harlem," *AH* (February 10, 1905): 353.

47 *YT* (March 25, 1906): 8. For a reference to workers in Harlem who advanced economically to become real estate people and builders, see Cahan, *Bleter*, 433.

48 *RERBG* (January 6, 1906): 1; *RERBG* (January 19, 1907): 145; *RERBG* (January 4, 1908): 8. For a study of the land-use patterns of that era derived primarily from city atlases, see Gurock, *When Harlem Was Jewish*, 183.

49 *YT* (February 17, 1904): 8; *JMJ* (July 11, 1906): 4.

50 On the attitudes of newly affluent Jews to the better accommodations that were made available after 1900 downtown, see Andrew R. Heinze, *Adapting to Abundance: Jewish Immigrants, Mass Consumption and the Search for American Identity* (New York: Columbia University Press, 1990), 46. On predictions that downtown would continue improving and Harlem would decline into a slum, see *JMJ* (February 25, 1914): 3. For a vision of what fancy Harlem looked like to potential affluent migrants, see "About Town," *YT* (March 25, 1906): 8. For an analysis based on 1905 census data of the patterns of economic mobility which indicates that this new Central Harlem neighborhood was an elite enclave with its Jewish residents enjoying a degree of economic advancement greater than elsewhere in the city, see Gurock, *When Harlem Was Jewish*, 185, notes 63, 66, 67.

51 "The New Jewish Quarter of Harlem," *American Israelite* (February 10, 1904): 8.

52 Cahan, *Bleter*, 431–32.

53 *F* (March 6, 1904): 4.

54 *F* (March 20, 1904): 4; *F* (March 19, 1904): 1. See also Cahan, *Bleter*, 434.

55 For a Jewish organizational census of the Jewish population of New York City as of 1917, see *JCR*, 84.

56 "Rabbi Samuel Greenfield Interviewed," *HS* (January 28, 1910), n.p.

57 On the arrival and settlement of Ladino-speaking Jews in Harlem, see Aviva Ben-Ur, *Sephardic Jews in America: A Diasporic History* (New York: NYU Press, 2009), 37. Ben-Ur suggests that these "upwardly mobile" Jews were in the neighborhood "by the 1920s." However, the area in which they appear to have settled—as we have seen—included tenements for the poor as well as housing for the upwardly mobile. Her work also suggests that while there were instances of "rapprochement" between Ashkenazim and Sephardim in Harlem (140–42), generally these two Jewish groups lived separate existences. Finally, Ben-Ur has correctly bemoaned the lack of attention histories of this immigrant period in New York have given to Sephardic experiences. One of the reasons for this oversight is the relative paucity of Ladino press coverage of the late-nineteenth- and early-twentieth-century communal experience. Hence, for example, the paucity of what is known about Congregation Moses Montefiore. See on its short recorded history in Harlem, *JM* (February 3, 1888): 2; *JM* (June 15, 1888): 2; *AH* (March 31, 1993): 8.

CHAPTER 4. SIBLING COMMUNITIES

1 H. Lang, "A Few Recollections," *Branch No. 2 Arbeter Ring Thirtieth Anniversary Journal, 1899–1929* (New York: Arbeter Ring Branch No. 2, 1929), 29–33.

2 Joseph Anapol, "The History of Branch No. 2 Arbeter Ring," *Anniversary Journal*, 2–8; Abraham Baroff, "On the Occasion of the Thirtieth Anniversary," *Anniversary Journal*, 19–20. See also, on the commutation problem, Maximillian Hurwitz, *The Workmen's Circle: Its History, Ideals, Organizations and Institutions* (New York: Workmen's Circle, 1936), 17.

3 Lang, "A Few Recollections," 31.

4 Lang, "A Few Recollections," 29–31. See also *F* (May 3, 1901): 4.
5 Hurwitz, *Workmen's Circle*, 36–37; Anapol, "History," 2; R. Ash, "Greetings," *Anniversary Journal*, 15–16.
6 Tony Michels, *A Fire in Their Hearts: Yiddish Socialists in New York City* (Cambridge, MA: Harvard University Press, 2005), 205–07.
7 Ash, "Greetings," 15–16; Anapol, "History," 2–8; Hurwitz, *Workmen's Circle*, 167–68.
8 Michels, *A Fire*, 205–15.
9 *Lodzer Almanac, 25th Anniversary Jubilee of Branch No. 324 Arebeter Ring (1909–1934)* (New York: Lodzer Branch #24 A.R., 1934), 6–7.
10 Michels, *A Fire*, 210–11. On the location of these various Jewish socialist organizations in Harlem, see *JCR*, 373, 962, 1262, 1384.
11 Michels, *A Fire*, 214–16.
12 For an important study of this women-initiated form of customer protest that focuses on developments on the Lower East Side, see Paula E. Hyman, "Immigrant Women and Consumer Protest: The New York City Kosher Meat Boycott of 1902," *American Jewish History* (September, 1980): 91–105. For early developments in Harlem, see *F* (May 17, 1902): 1.
13 *F* (May 18, 1902): 1.
14 *F* (May 19, 1902): 2; *F* (May 20, 1902): 1–2.
15 *F* (June 13, 1902): 4. See also Nathan Ausubel, *The Jewish Labor Movement in New York* (New York: Works Progress Administration, n.d), 2–8.
16 Moses Rischin, *The Promised City: New York's Jews, 1870–1914* (Cambridge, MA: Harvard University Press, 1963), 190; B. A. Weinrebe, *Jewish Suburban Movement, Jewish Cooperative Movement* (New York: Works Progress Administration, Historical Records Survey, Federal Writers Project, n.d), 3.
17 *F* (December 11, 1902): 2; *F* (December 12, 1902): 5.
18 On the founding and early activities of the Bakers Union, see Hertz Burgin, *Die Geschichte fun die Yiddishe Arbayter Bevegung in Amerika, Rusland and England* (New York: United Hebrew Trades, 1915), 873; H. K. Blatt, *Trade Unions and Labor Movement* (New York: Works Progress Administration, Historical Records Survey, Federal Writers Project, n.d.), 38–39; Yosel Cohen, *Jewish Bakers' Union* (New York: Works Progress Administration, Federal Writers Project, n.d), 3–5.
19 Burgin, *Die Geschichte*, 872; *F* (June 12, 1903): 5.
20 *F* (July 15, 1903): 2.
21 Weinrebe, *Jewish Suburban*, 4–5.
22 *F* (January 26, 1904): 2; *F* (June 13, 1904): 1. Two smaller cooperative ventures were started in Harlem in the immediate pre–World War I period. In March 1915, a cooperative lodging house was established at 52 East 106th Street. One month later, the Industrial and Agricultural Cooperative Association founded a second uptown boarding house at 111th Street and Lexington Avenue. See *The Day* (March 18, 1915): 3; *The Day* (April 23, 1915): 3.
23 Burgin, *Die Geschichte*, 872.

24 Ibid.; Cohen, *Jewish Bakers' Union*, 3–5.
25 Archibald A. Hill, "Rental Agitation on the East Side," *Charity* (April 16, 1904): 387. See also Jenna W. Joselit, "The Landlord as Czar: Pre–World War I Tenant Activity," in Ronald Lawson, ed., *The Tenant Movement in New York City, 1904–1984* (New Brunswick, NJ: Rutgers University Press, 1986), 40–43.
26 *F* (March 28, 1904): 1; *F* (May 18, 1904):1.
27 *F* (April 18, 1904): 2; *F* (April 26, 1904): 1; *F* (April 29, 1904): 1.
28 *F* (January 1, 1908): 1; Joselit, "Landlord as Czar," 42–43.
29 *F* (December 31, 1907): 1; *F* (December 29, 1907):1; *F* (January 4, 1908): 8; *F* (January 5, 1908): 1.
30 *F* (January 6, 1908): 1; *F* (January 4, 1908): 8; *F* (December 29, 1907): 1.
31 *F* (January 10, 1908): 1, 8; *F* (January 11, 1908): 1, 8; *F* (January 15, 1908): 8.
32 Rischin, *Promised City*, 188–89.
33 Ausubel, *Jewish Labor Movement*, 44; *F* (September 30, 1907): 16; *F* (June 4, 1912): 4.
34 Ausubel, *Jewish Labor Movement*, 43–44; *F* (June 21, 1913): 3; *F* (July 27, 1913): 8.
35 *F* (August 20, 1913): 8; *F* (August 31, 1913): 1; *F* (September 8, 1913): 8.
36 *F* (August 29, 1913): 8; *F* (March 20, 1914): 3; *F* (November 27, 1914): 3.
37 *JMJ* (April 23, 1915): 8.
38 For a cogent argument about the Jewish socialist radicals' control of downtown streets, see Michels, *A Fire*, 69–71, 122–23. For examples of the myriad of journals, magazines, and the like published in the neighborhood, see Rischin, *Promised City*, 117–22.
39 Harry Rogoff, *An East Side Epic: The Life and Times of Meyer London* (New York: Vanguard Press, 1930), 16.
40 For Miller's remarks, see Rischin, *Promised City*, 227. For the understanding that a "discipline commitment" was necessary to be a full-hearted member of the movement, see Irving Howe, *The World of Our Fathers: The Journey of the East European Jews to America and the Life They Found and Made* (New York: Random House, 1976), 289.
41 On Tammany philo-Semitism, see Polland and Soyer, *Emerging Metropolis*, 181–83.
42 On the larger question of debates in immigrant households between husbands and wives over religious versus secular concerns, see Polland, "'May A Freethinker Help a Pious Man?' The Shared World of the 'Religious' and the 'Secular' among Eastern European Jewish Immigrants to America," *American Jewish History* (December, 2007): 403–4.
43 Polland and Soyer, *Emerging Metropolis*, 182.
44 For a comprehensive examination of the 1908–1910 congressional elections, see Arthur Gorenstein, "A Portrait of Ethnic Politics: The Socialists and the 1908 and 1910 Congressional Elections on the East Side," *Publications of the American Jewish Historical Society* (March 1961): 202–227. See especially, 203, 207, 211, 223–24. See also on Hillquit's stance, Rischin, *Promised City*, 223–24; Howe, *World of Our Fathers*, 313–14. On the technique of "straddling" on the immigration question,

see David Shannon, *The Socialist Party in America: A History* (New York: Macmillan, 1955), 47–50.

45 It should be remembered that, in 1912, progressivism reached its political apogee as four candidates spoke for social reform—Wilson, Taft, Theodore Roosevelt, and the socialist Eugene V. Debs. Thus, at that point, for a Jewish immigrant to vote for a Socialist was quite close to being within the American political mainstream and not regarded as an unpatriotic act as it might have been earlier and certainly was during and after World War I.

46 For voting statistics, see *The City Record Official Canvass of the County of New York*, vols. 28–42 (1900–1914).

47 For voting statistics on the 1914 election, see *The City Record Official Canvass of the County of New York*, vol. 42, pt. 12 (December 31, 1914). See also Rischin, *Promised City*, 235; *F* (February 20, 1916): 2.

48 *F* (January 23, 1916): 7.

49 *F* (February 20, 1916): 2; *F* (July 10, 1916): 2.

50 *American Jewish Chronicle* (July 27, 1916): 377; *F* (September 9, 1916): 1; *F* (October 19, 1916): 9. See also Rischin, *Promised City*, 235.

51 *YT* (April 16, 1916): 4; Naomi W. Cohen, *Not Free to Desist: the American Jewish Committee, 1906–1966* (Philadelphia: Jewish Publication Society, 1972), 53.

52 *American Jewish Chronicle* (September 15, 1916): 603–13; *American Jewish Chronicle* (November 3, 1916):787.

53 *American Jewish Chronicle* (November 3, 1916): 787.

54 *YT* (November 8, 1916): 1; *The Day* (March 28, 1916): 609.

55 *YT* (October 26, 1916): 4; *JMJ* (November 3, 1916): 4.

56 *The Day* (March 28, 1916): 4; Louis Marshall to Isaac Siegel, November 2, 1916 (Marshall Papers, American Jewish Archives).

57 *JDF* (October 27, 1917): 1; *The Day* (October 27, 19156): 4; *American Jewish Chronicle* (November 3, 1916): 787; *JMJ* (November 3, 1916): 4; *F* (October 26, 1916): 1; *F* (November 6, 1916): 1.

58 For the voting statistics, see *The City Record Official Canvass of the County of New York*, vol. 44, pt. 12 (December 31, 1916).

59 For the voting statistics, see *The City Record Official Canvass of the County of New York*, vol. 46, pt. 12 (December 31, 1918); *The City Record Official Canvass of the County of New York*, vol. 48, pt. 12 (December 21, 1920).

60 Arthur Mann, *La Guardia: A Fighter against His Times, 1882–1933* (Chicago and London: University of Chicago Press, 1959), 45–46, 156–57.

61 On the patterns of decline of observance among these Jews both in eastern Europe and upon arrival in the United States, see Jeffrey S. Gurock, *Orthodox Jews in America* (Bloomington: Indiana University Press, 2005), 84–108. For a contemporaneous source that contrasts observance in shtetls and cities, see Kimmy Caplan, "Rabbi Isaac Margolis: From Eastern Europe to America," *Zion* (1992–93): 225.

62 See Rischin, *Promised City*, 145, for the understanding of religion at half-mast on the Lower East Side. On the early history of these schools that were the forerunner of Yeshiva University, see Jeffrey S. Gurock, *The Men and Women of Yeshiva: Orthodoxy, Higher Education and American Judaism* (New York: Columbia University Press, 1998), 8–42.

63 On the founding of Yeshiva Elijah Gaon M'Vilna and its mission, see *JMJ* (December 12, 1907): 5; *YT* (January 19, 1908): 8; *JMJ* (October 8, 1915): 2. On the history of the Beth Hamidrash Ha-Godol in Harlem, see *YT* (October 11, 1901): 8; *HS* (November 20, 1903): 4.

64 On the split that led to two yeshivas in Harlem, see *JMJ* (October 8, 1915): 2.

65 *JMJ* (May 16, 1909): 7; *JMJ* (April 4, 1912): 8.

66 *JMJ* (May 29, 1913): 5; *JMJ* (November 21, 1911): 8. After World War I, as Yeshiva Chaim Berlin and Mesivta Torah Vodaath matured and expanded their outreach in their respective Brooklyn neighborhoods, both became far more separatist than previously with outlooks comparable to that of Harlem's Yeshiva Toras Chaim.

CHAPTER 5. PARTNERS AND PROTESTS

1 Much of the information for this depiction of the established American Jewish leadership to the arrival of masses of east European Jews—including a reference to Emma Lazarus's classic poem "The New Colossus"—is derived from the chapter "Germans vs. Russians" in Rischin, *Promised City*, 97–103. On Radin's background and activities, see *AH* (February 12, 1908): 409; Rischin, *Promised City*, 102–3.

2 On the founding of these east European alternatives, see Rischin, *Promised City*, 106–7.

3 *AH* (December 25, 1903): 3; *AH* (January 8, 1904): 273. For other examples of missionary threats in Harlem, see *AH* (December 4, 1905): 633; *AH* (December 28, 1906): 189.

4 *JM* (August 2, 1896): 2; *AH* (December 31, 1896): 257.

5 *HS* (June 21, 1901): 4; *AH* (February 11, 1904): 1.

6 *AH* (January 29, 1904): 359. On Cowen's efforts, see Philip Cowen, *Memories of an American Jew* (New York: International Press, 1932), 106.

7 *AH* (February 5, 1904): 392; *AH* (February 28, 1904): 480; *HS* (January 1, 1904): 8; *AH* (February 17, 1905): 387; *AH* (February 10, 1905): 353–54.

8 *AH* (April 7, 1906): 616; *AH* (July 7, 1905): 160.

9 *HS* (October 19, 1906): 3; *AH* (October 25, 1906): 13. On Lucas's activities, see Jeffrey S. Gurock, "Jewish Communal Divisiveness in Response to Christian Influences on the Lower East Side, 1900–1910," in Todd Endelman, ed., *Jewish Apostasy in the Modern World* (New York: Holmes and Meier, 1987), 255–71. On Temple Israel's newly reestablished presence in East Harlem, see also *AH* (February 5, 1904): 392. On the creation of a Jewish Centre uptown, see *AH* (July 19, 1907): 273.

10 *AH* (July 7, 1905): 160; *AH* (April 26, 1907): 661.

11 On the image of second-generation Jewish estrangement in Harlem, see *American Israelite* (February 11, 1904): 1.

12 For a comprehensive study of *landsmanshaften*—including the religious aspect—see Daniel Soyer, *Jewish Immigrant Associations and American Identity* (Cambridge, MA: Harvard University Press, 1997), especially 56–61. For a listing of *landsmanshaften* in New York, including Harlem, see *JCR*, 145–286.

13 For an example of the many critiques of this form of Jewish institutional life, see *JMJ* (September 7, 1917): 5.

14 *YT* (February 5, 1903): 7; *HS* (September 15, 1916): 1, 3. For a sharp critique of the *cheders* by one of the leading Jewish educators of the early twentieth century, see Alexander Dushkin, *Jewish Education in New York City* (New York: Bureau of Jewish Education, 1918), 67.

15 On the reputation of the Talmud Torah in eastern Europe, see Alexander M. Dushkin, *Jewish Education in New York City* (New York: Bureau of Jewish Education, 1918), 66.

16 *YT* (May 22, 1892): 2; *AH* (November 16, 1894): 69; *HS* (January 12, 1894):1; *YT* (January 3, 1896): 2. For the activities of the downtown Hebrew Free School Association, see Rischin, *Promised City*, 100–101.

17 *AH* (August 19, 1904): 348. On the early curriculum of the school, see also Zvi Scharfstein, ed. *Sefer Ha-Yovel shel Agudat Ha-Morim Ha-Ivriim B'New York* (New York: Modern Linotype, 1944), 156.

18 Hutchins Hapgood, *The Spirit of the Ghetto: Studies of the Jewish Quarter of New York* (New York: Funk & Wagnalls, 1902), 53.

19 Ibid., 55–58; *YT* (April 5, 1903): 1.

20 On the origins of this modern approach to Hebrew-language training, see Jonathan Krasner, *The Benderly Boys and American Jewish Education* (Waltham, MA: Brandeis University Press, 2011), 23.

21 *YT* (March 27, 1905): 4; *HS* (March 2, 1906): 4; *HS* (March 30, 1906): 4.

22 *YT* (February 25, 1904): 4.

23 *YT* (February 24, 1905): 4.

24 *HS* (February 24, 1905): 4; *YT* (May 15, 1905): 8.

25 *YT* (May 15, 1905): 8; *YT* (May 23, 1905): 4.

26 *HS* (April 26, 1907): 4; *MJ* (June 4 1907): 4; *AH* (February 28, 1908): 444; *HS* (October 29, 1909): 4; *JCR*, 1396, 1404–9.

27 *YT* (March 16, 1906): 8; *AH* (February 28, 1908): 44.

28 The intriguing and idiosyncratic career and postures of Margolies and his relationships with leading New York rabbis, lay leaders, and institutions have been studied. See Jeffrey S. Gurock, *American Jewish Orthodoxy in Historical Perspective* (Hoboken, NJ: KTAV Publishing House, 1996), 19–21; Jeffrey S. Gurock, *The Men and Women of Yeshiva: Higher Education, Orthodoxy and American Judaism* (New York: Columbia University Press, 1988), 32–34; Jeffrey S. Gurock and Jacob J. Schacter, *A Modern Heretic and a Traditional Community: Mordecai M. Kaplan, Orthodoxy, and American Judaism* (New York: Columbia University Press, 1997), 49–52.

29 Elias A. Cohen to Louis Marshall (March 31, 1908) (Marshall Papers, American Jewish Archives).

30 Elias A. Cohen to Louis Marshall (December 7, 1909) (Marshall Papers, American Jewish Archives).

31 Ibid.
32 Jacob Schiff to Henry Glass of the Uptown Talmud Torah Association (January 7, 1910); Jacob Schiff to the Board of Directors of the Uptown Talmud Torah Association (February 14, 1910) (Marshall Papers, American Jewish Archives).
33 On the involvement of Schiff with the Seminary, see Jack Wertheimer, ed., *Tradition Renewed: A History of the Jewish Theological Seminary of America*, vol. 1 (New York: Jewish Theological Seminary of America, 1997), 48–53, 573, 576, 661. See also Jacob Schiff to Isidor Hershfield, Hon. Secretary, Uptown Talmud Torah (February 24, 1910) (Marshall Papers, American Jewish Archives).
34 Louis Marshall to Jacob Schiff (March 5, 1910); Jacob Schiff to Isidor Hershfield (February 28, 1910) (Marshall Papers, American Jewish Archives).
35 *JMJ* (February 6, 1911), n.p.; *AH* (March 22, 1912): 609; *HS* (April 11, 1913): 4.
36 Herbert S. Goldstein, ed., *Forty Years of Struggle for a Principle: The Biography of Harry Fischel* (New York: Bloch Publishing Company, 1928), iii, 12–13.
37 Ibid., 31, 66–71.
38 *JMJ* (August 11, 193): 5; *JMJ* (October 12, 1913): 4.
39 *HS* (October 3, 1913): 10.
40 Kehillah of New York, Minutes of Meetings of the Executive Committee of the Jewish Community (Kehillah) of New York City, meeting of October 10, 1911 (Israel Friedlander Papers, Library of the Jewish Theological Seminary of America). See also Arthur A. Goren, *New York Jews and the Quest for Community: The Kehillah Experiment, 1908–1922* (New York: Columbia University Press, 1970), 96–99, 111–19; Dushkin, *Jewish Education*, 107–9.
41 *AH* (December 5, 1913): 152; Alexander Dushkin to Jeffrey S. Gurock (August 4, 1978).
42 *JMJ* (February 24, 1913): 2. A copy of the editorial in translation was preserved in the Louis Marshall Papers (American Jewish Archives).
43 *AH* (February 27, 1914): 502. See also Harry Fischel to Jacob Schiff (February 27, 1914) (Schiff Papers, American Jewish Archives).
44 Harry Fischel to Jacob Schiff (February 27, 1914) (Schiff Papers, American Jewish Archives).
45 *HS* (March 5, 1915): 11.
46 *JMJ* (August 7, 1908): 5; *JMJ* (August 14, 1908): 7–8.
47 *JMJ* (June 5, 1911): 2.
48 *JMJ* (June 3, 1910): 2.
49 S. Benderly, "The Present Status of Jewish Education in New York City," *JCR*, 349–50.

CHAPTER 6. ATTRACTIVE SYNAGOGUES

1 On the early policies of the YMHAs in New York, including Harlem, see Benjamin Rabinowitz, "Y.M.H.A.'s (1851–1913)," *Publications of the American Jewish Historical Society* 37 (1947): 280–82. On Unterberg's background, see *JCR*, 564.
2 On the problem of white slavery, see Rischin, *Promised City*, 61; Howe, *World of Our Fathers*, 96–97.

3 On the origins and mission of the YWHA, see David Kaufman, *Shul with a Pool: The "Synagogue-Center" in American Jewish History* (Hanover, NH, and London: Brandeis University Press, 1999), 76–81.
4 On the needs that called these "Young People's Synagogues" into existence, see Jeffrey S. Gurock, "Consensus Building and Conflict over Creating the Young People's Synagogue of the Lower East Side," in Norman J. Cohen and Robert Seltzer, eds., *The Americanization of the Jews* (New York: NYU Press, 1995), 230–46.
5 On Kehal Adath Jeshurun's history and services before the Cohen issue, see Jeffrey S. Gurock, "A Stage in the Emergence of the Americanized Synagogue among East European Jews, 1890–1910," *Journal of American Ethnic History* (spring 1990): 7–25.
6 On Ohab Zedek's early history, see Chaim Sternberger, *First Hungarian Congregation Ohab Zedek* (New York: First Hungarian Congregation Ohab Zedek, 2005), 5–6.
7 *HS* (February 7, 1908): 9.
8 *HS* (January 17, 1908): 8.
9 *HS* (January 31, 1908): 13.
10 On Klein's background, see Nancy Isaacs Klein, *Heritage of Faith: Two Pioneers of Judaism in America* (Hoboken, NJ: KTAV Publishing House, 1987), 23. On the lack of interest with Klein's style of sermonic, see Ira Eisenstein, *Reconstructing Judaism: An Autobiography* (New York: Reconstructionist Press, 1986), 11–12.
11 Bernard Drachman, *The Unfailing Light: Memoirs of an American Rabbi* (New York: Rabbinical Council of America, 1948), 148–63, 167, 183–84, 208–11, 276–78. See also Jeffrey S. Gurock, "From Exception to Role Model: Bernard Drachman and the Evolution of Jewish Religious Life in America, 1880–1920," *American Jewish History* (June 1987): 456–84. On the Ramaz-Kaplan relationship, see Gurock and Schacter, *Modern Heretic*, 31–54.
12 On Drachman's views of cantors, see Drachman, *Unfailing Light*, 281–84. See also Eisenstein, *Reconstructing Judaism*, 5. On Rosenblatt's background and his views of Drachman's abilities, see Samuel Rosenblatt, *Yossele Rosenblatt: The Story of His Life as Told to His Son* (New York: Farrar, Straus and Young, 1954), 31–90, 121.
13 On the change of leadership at Ansche Chesed see *HS* (April 28, 1911): 4; *HS* (May 12, 1911): 4. See also Congregation Ansche Chesed, Minutes of Meetings of the Congregation, meetings of November 30, 1911, and December 29, 1913. Comparable personnel changes also took place in 1910 at Congregation Anshe Emeth of West Harlem, which engaged Jewish Theological Seminary graduate Rabbi Julius J. Price, and in 1911 when Rabbi Benjamin A. Tintner, son of Rabbi Morris Tintner, one of Harlem's earliest Reform rabbis, became spiritual leader of Temple Mount Zion.
14 On the ritual and seating patterns at the women's Y synagogue, see Kaufman, *Shul with a Pool*, 80–81.
15 *HS* (April 28, 1905): 4; *HS* (May 25, 1905): 4; *HS* (April 14, 1905): 4.
16 Two women, Mrs. Rivka Banner and Miss Irene Stern, were members of the synagogue's original board of directors. See the Incorporation Papers of Congregation

Mikveh Israel on file at the New York County Clerk's Office. See also *YT* (March 25, 1906), n.p. On female participation in the leadership of downtown youth synagogues, see Gurock, "Consensus Building," 230–46.

17 *HS* (June 6, 1906): 4; Kaufman, *Shul with a Pool*, 80. See also Archibald McClure, *Leadership of the New America* (New York: George H. Doren, 1916), 171–72.

18 *YT* (January 6, 1916): 4.

19 *AH* (January 15, 1901): 431; *YT* (January 6, 1916): 8: Goren, *New York Jews*, 77–78.

20 *HS* (January 7, 1916): 19; *YT* (January 6, 1916): 8.

21 *HS* (June 18, 1915): 1, 24.

22 *YT* (September 20, 1915): 8; *YT* (February 10, 1916): 8; *HS* (February 11, 1916): 16.

23 *YT* (September 18, 1916): 8; *AH* (January 29, 1915): 343; *YT* (February 26, 1915): 8. See also YMHA of New York, Meetings of Special Joint Committee Consisting of Members of the Social, Finance and Membership and Neighborhood Committees, meeting of March 14, 1915, for a discussion of the reticence of the 92nd Street Y to involve itself directly in Harlem activities. On the mission of the Harlem Y, see *JCR*, 484.

24 *HS* (September 15, 1916): 24.

25 *HS* (September 15, 1916): 1, 3, 24.

26 *HS* (September 15, 1916): 1, 24.

27 On the expansion of the women's Y activities, see Kaufman, *Shul with a Pool*, 81.

28 On Kaplan's activities at the 92nd Street Y and his problems with it, see Mel Scult, *Judaism Faces the Twentieth Century: A Biography of Mordecai M. Kaplan* (Detroit: Wayne State University Press, 1993), 132. See also *YT* (September 18, 1916): 8; *AH* (January 29, 1915): 343.

29 Isaac B. Berkson, *Theories of Americanization: A Critical Study with Special Reference to the Jewish Group* (New York: Columbia University Teachers College, 1921), 183, 189.

30 Gurock and Schacter, *Modern Heretic*, 93.

31 *JMJ* (September 7, 1917): 5; Herbert S. Goldstein to Jacob H. Schiff, April 11, 1917 (Schiff Papers, American Jewish Archives).

32 Goldstein to Schiff, April 11, 1917; Isaac Siegel to Goldstein, April 3, 1917 (Schiff Papers, American Jewish Archives).

33 Institutional Synagogue, Synagogue Constitution, art. 3, sec. 2, art. 6, sec. 1 (Yeshiva University Archive).

34 Aaron I. Reichel, *The Maverick Rabbi: Rabbi Herbert S. Goldstein and the Institutional Synagogue—"A New Organizational Form"* (Virginia Beach, VA: Donning, 1984), 123–24, 220.

35 *HS* (April 27, 1917): 10; *HS* (June 11, 1917): 12; *AH* (June 11, 1917): 29; *American Jewish Chronicle* (June 18, 1917): 56.

36 *JMJ* (September 7, 1917): 5; *AH* (January 18, 1918): 322; *HS* (February 8, 1918): 5; *HS* (October 18, 1918): 5.

37 *AH* (January 18, 1918): 322.

38 *YT* (February 19, 1917): 8.

39 Ibid.

40 *American Jewish Chronicle* (June 15, 1917): 163. On Sunday's activities and persona, see William G. McLoughlin Jr., *Billy Sunday Was His Real Name* (Chicago: University of Chicago Press, 1955).

41 *American Jewish Chronicle* (June 15, 1917): 324.

42 Gurock and Schacter, *Modern Heretic*, 89–92; Gurock, *Judaism's Encounter with American Sports*, 63, 69–71.

CHAPTER 7. THE SCATTERING OF THE HARLEM JEWISH COMMUNITY, 1917–1930

1 *Anniversary Journal*, 21, 22, 24–25; Federal Writers' Project, Yiddish Writers Group, *Die Yiddishe Landmanshaften fun New York* (New York: I.L. Peretz Writers Union, 1938), 114–15.

2 Information on the Stone and Spitz families was derived from the 1915, 1925, 1930 and 1940 U. S. Census manuscripts, available through ancestry.com. Information on the history and structure of the buildings and houses they lived in was derived from ny.curbed.com, realtor.com, and Harlembespoke.blogspot.com. For Israel Stone's death certificate, see *State of New York, Department of Health of The City of New York, Bureau of Records, Standard Certificate of Death*, January 21, 1923.

3 These population estimates are all derived from the survey of the "Jewish Population of New York City" that the New York Kehillah conducted in 1917. See *JCR*, 83–87.

4 On the growth of the Bronx and its connection to rapid transit improvements, see Hood, *722 Miles*, 94, 108–9, 136. See also Lloyd Ultan and Gary Hermalyn, *The Bronx in the Innocent Years, 1890–1925* (New York: Harper and Row), xvii–xix, xxv. On the growth before World War I of Brownsville and East New York, see Alter F. Landesman, *Brownsville: The Birth, Development and Passing of a Jewish Community in New York* (New York: Bloch,1969), 85–86, 101–2.

5 New York City Tenement House Department, *Seventh Report, 1912–14* (New York: Martin Brown Press, 1912–14), 65, 121.

6 New York City Tenement House Department, *Eighth Report, 1915–16* (New York: Marion Brown Press, 1915–16), 18; New York City Tenement House Department, *Ninth Report, 1917* (New York: Martin Brown Press, 1917), 11.

7 Walter Laidlaw, ed., *Population of the City of New York 1890–1930* (New York: City Census Committee, 1932), 82.

8 Tenement House Department, *Ninth Report*, 11; New York State Reconstruction Commission, *Housing Conditions: Report of the Housing Committee of the Reconstruction Commission of the State of New York* (Albany: J.B. Lyon, 1920), 9.

9 New York State Commission on Housing and Regional Planning, *Report of Commission of Housing and Regional Planning to Governor Alfred E. Smith and to the Legislature of the State of New York on the Present Housing Emergency, December 12, 1923* (Albany: J.B. Lyon, 1924), 14; Reconstruction Commission, *Housing Conditions*, 21.

10 Reconstruction Commission, *Housing Conditions*, 10–11.

11 Walter Laidlaw, ed., *Statistical Sources for Demographic Studies of Greater New York* (New York: New York City 1920 Census Committee, 1923).

12 Commission on Housing, *Report*, 14.

13 *JMJ* (February 25, 1913): 4; *YT* (May 9, 1916): 8.

14 Commission on Housing, *Report*, 38.

15 Gurock, *When Harlem Was Jewish*, 140–41. On post–World War I racial tensions in American cities, see Arthur I. Waskow, *From Race Riot to Sit-In: 1919 and the 1960s* (Garden City, NY: Doubleday, 1966), 2, 21–22, 304–8.

16 On the tax exemption law, see *RERBG* (March 5, 1921), n.p.

17 *RERBG* (September 3, 1921), n.p.; *RERBG* (March 18, 1922), n.p. On the citywide patterns during the 1920s, see New York City Tenement House Department, *Tenth Report, 1918–1929* (New York: Martin Brown Press, 1929), 36–49.

18 *Population, Land Values and Government: Studies of the Growth and Distribution of Population and Land Values and of Problems of Government, Regional Survey of New York and its Environs* (New York: Regional Plan of New York and its Environs, 1929), 62; *RERBG* (September 21, 1921), n.p.; *RERBG* (February 26, 1927), n.p.

19 *RERBG* (September 21, 1921). n.p.; Edwin Harold Spengler, *Land Values in New York in Relation to Transit Facilities* (New York: Columbia University Press, 1930), 19–24; Hood, *722 Miles*, 158–61, 174.

20 Leon Wexelstein, *Building Up Greater Brooklyn with Sketches of Men Instrumental in Brooklyn's Amazing Development* (New York: Brooklyn Biographical Society, 1925), xvii–xx, quoted in Deborah Dash Moore, *At Home in America: Second-Generation New York Jews* (New York: Columbia University Press, 1981), 42.

21 Moore, *At Home in America*, 44–53.

22 Richard Plunz, *A History of Housing in New York City: Dwelling Type and Social Change in the American Metropolis* (New York: Columbia University Press, 1990), 151–57; Andrew S. Dolkart, "Homes for People Cooperatives in New York City, 1916–1929," *Sites* 30 (1989): 33–35.

23 For statistics on Jewish out-migration from older neighborhoods and resettlement elsewhere in the city, see *JCR*, 82, 85; C. Morris Horowitz and Lawrence J. Kaplan, *The Jewish Population of the New York Area, 1900–1975* (New York: Federation of Jewish Philanthropies, 1959), 22, 133, 157, 209, 239.

24 Jewish Welfare Board, *Preliminary Study of the Institutional Synagogue* [typescript] (New York: Jewish Welfare Board, 1924).

25 Bureau of Jewish Social Research, *First Section: Studies of the New York Jewish Population: Jewish Communal Survey of Greater New York* (New York: Bureau of Jewish Social Research, 1928), 8.

26 Jewish Welfare Board, *Study of the Institutional Synagogue in Relation to Harlem, N.Y.C.* (New York: Jewish Welfare Board, 1928), 33; Horowitz and Kaplan, *Jewish Population*, 156–61.

27 On relocation destinations, see Leo Grebler, *Market Behavior in a Declining Area: Long Term Changes in Inventory and Utilization of Housing on New York's Lower East Side* (New York: Columbia University Press, 1952), 124–25. On the differing

fates of Jews and African Americans in Harlem, circa 1920–1930, see Osofsky, *Harlem*, 130, 248.

28 Marcy S. Sacks, *Before Harlem: The Black Experience in New York City before World War I* (Philadelphia: University of Pennsylvania Press, 2006), 72–74.

29 Ibid., 76, 79, 81, 82. See also National League on Urban Conditions among Negroes, *Housing Conditions among Negroes in Harlem, N.Y.C.* (New York: Poole Press Association, 1915), 8, 13.

30 "Real Estate Race War Is Started in Harlem," *NYT* (December 17, 1905): 12.

31 "The Negro Invasion," *NYT* (December 17, 1911): 14.

32 Seth M. Scheiner, *Negro Mecca: A History of the Negro in New York City, 1865–1920* (New York: NYU Press, 1965), 30.

33 *AH* (December 16, 1911): 168.

34 Lang, "A Few Recollections," 29–33. See also Samuel Golden, "Some Days Are More Important: A Memoir of Immigrant New York, 1902–1913," in Ronald Dotterer, Deborah Dash Moore and Steven M. Cohen, eds., *Jewish Settlement and Community in the Modern Western World* (Selinsgrove, PA: Susquehanna University Press, 1991), 178–79. For examples of the newspapers' outrage at Jews supporting attacks against blacks, see *YT* (August 16, 1900): 1, 4; *YT* (September 7, 1900): 1; *YT* (May 11, 1906): 1; *F* (July 7, 1905): 1.

35 "Race Riot Rages in Harlem Streets," *NYT* (August 5 1907): 1.

36 Shannon King, *Whose Harlem Is This Anyway?: Community Politics and Grassroots Activism during the New Negro Era* (New York: NYU Press, 2015), 34.

37 "Store Rentals in New York," *New York Age* (October 19, 1911): 4; "Lenox Avenue and Its Trade," *New York Age* (April 6, 1916): 1.

38 Laidlaw, *Statistical Sources*, 70ff; National League on Urban Conditions, *Housing Conditions*, 8, 13.

39 For a statistical breakdown of the Jewish and black presence in this region of Harlem as of 1920 see the discussion in Gurock, *When Harlem Was Jewish*, 148.

40 Scheiner, *Negro Mecca*, 20.

41 Osofsky, *Harlem*, 128–30.

42 On Jewish settlement patterns in the 1920s and the problems of anti-Semitism in Queens, see Gurock, *Jews in Gotham*, 15, 19–20. On relocation destinations, see Grebler, *Market Behavior*, 124–25.

43 Osofsky, *Harlem*, 151–58. On the problems Jews had in the Bronx co-ops, see Richard Plunz, *A History of Housing in New York City: Dwelling Type and Social Change in the American Metropolis* (New York: Columbia University Press, 1990), 161–62.

44 Osofsky, *Harlem*, 130; Commission on Housing, *Report*, 16.

45 The explanation about the variation in the cost of housing in East Harlem as opposed, for example, to working-class sections of the Bronx in the early 1930s is derived from an examination of the *New York City Market Analysis* (New York: New York Herald Tribune, Daily News and New York Times, 1933). On the beginnings of the Puerto Rican presence in East Harlem, see Lawrence Royce Chenault, *The Puerto Rican Migrant in New York* (New York: Columbia University Press, 1938).

46 Howard M. Brotz, *The Black Jews of Harlem: Negro Nationalism and the Dilemmas of Negro Leadership* (New York: Schocken Books, 1964), 12–13; "The Black Jews of Harlem," *BlackPast.org* (n.d.), www.blackpast.org; Roberta S. Gold, "The Black Jews of Harlem: Representation, Identity and Race, 1920–1939," *American Quarterly* (June 2003): 184–86, 215.

47 Gold, "Black Jews," 180, 194; Hasia Diner, *In the Almost Promised Land: American Jews and Blacks, 1915–1935* (Westport, CT: Greenwood Press, 1977), 69. See also Edward Wolf, "Negro 'Jews': A Social Study," *Jewish Social Service Quarterly* (June 1933): 319; "Who Are We?," *Black Jews* (n.d.), http://blackjews.org.

48 Gold, "Black Jews," 180–82, 215–16. See also "The Black Jews of Harlem."

49 *HS* (August 17, 1917): 12.

50 Hebrew Tabernacle, Minutes of Congregational Meetings, 1908–1919 (American Jewish Archives).

51 Ibid.

52 Hebrew Tabernacle, Minutes of Meetings of the Board of Trustees, meetings of March 24, 1919, October 27, 1919, and November 14, 1919 (American Jewish Archives).

53 Hebrew Tabernacle, Minutes of Meetings of the Board of Trustees, meeting of December 5, 1920 (American Jewish Archives).

54 Hebrew Tabernacle, Minutes of Congregational Meetings, meeting of April 27, 1920 (American Jewish Archives).

55 Harris, *Forty Years*, 1–4.

56 Works Progress Administration, Historical Records Survey, Inventory of Records of Churches, Jewish Synagogues, New York City, 1939 (Municipal Archives).

57 On the agreement between the synagogue and the Board of Education, see an untitled document, apparently a bill of sale or foreclosure between the Institutional Synagogue and the Bank of New York, dated April 12, 1943, which reviews in great detail the history of the agreement and the reasons for the present sale (Institutional Synagogue Records, Yeshiva University Archives). On Rabbi Goldstein's movement out of Harlem and the rise of the West Side Institutional Synagogue, see Reichel, *Maverick Rabbi*, 305–19.

58 Works Progress Administration, Historical Records Survey. On the fate of the UTT's building, see "Our History, 1873–1973: The First Hundred Years," *St. Cecilia's Parish* (n.d.), http://saint-cecilia-parish.org.

59 The deed from Congregation Kehal Adath Jeshurun (Grantor) to Sharon Baptist Church (Grantee), November 15, 1930, is on file in the Department of Buildings, Borough of Manhattan. See also Ellen Levitt, *The Lost Synagogues of the Bronx and Queens* (Bergenfield, NJ: Avoteinu, 2011), 52.

60 Ben-Ur, *Sephardic Jews in America: A Diasporic History*, 140, 274 n. 22.

61 The family's history in Harlem and ultimate migration out of the neighborhood is documented through the 1910, 1920, and 1940 U.S. Census records available through ancestry.com.

CHAPTER 8. JEWS IN AFRICAN AMERICAN HARLEM BY DAY AND BY NIGHT, 1920–1945

1 Irving Louis Horowitz, *Dreams and Nightmares*, 2nd rev. ed. (New Brunswick, NJ, and London: Transactions, 2012), 1, 4. For population estimates of the various sections of Harlem, see Horowitz and Kaplan, *Jewish Population*, 157–61.

2 Horowitz, *Dreams and Nightmares*, 58, 94.

3 Ibid., 4; Ben-Ur, *Sephardic Jews*, 155, 157. See also Gill, *Harlem*, 218.

4 Horowitz, *Dreams and Nightmares*, 4–5, 93.

5 Vivian Morris, "Thursday Girls," in Lionel C. Bascom, ed., *A Renaissance in Harlem: Lost Voices of an American Community* (New York: Amistad, 1999), 114–45; Vivian Morris, "Slave Market," in Bascom, *Renaissance*, 146–50. Vivian Morris, "Domestic Price Wares," in Bascom, *Renaissance*, 157–60. See also Ruth Edmonds Hill, ed., *The Black Women History Project*, vol. 8 (Westport, CT, and London: Meckler, 1991), 127.

6 Vivian Morris, "Domestic Workers Union," in Bascom, *Renaissance*, 155–56.

7 Cheryl Lynn Greenberg, *Troubling the Waters: Black-Jewish Relations in the American Century* (Princeton, NJ: Princeton University Press, 2006), 107–8.

8 Cheryl Lynn Greenberg, *Or Does It Explode?: Black Harlem in the Great Depression* (New York: Oxford University Press, 1997), 116, 120–22, 125. See also Winston C. McDowell, "Keeping Them 'In the Same Boat Together'?," in V. P. Franklin, Nancy L. Grant, Harold M. Kletnick, and Genna Rae McNeil, eds., *African Americans and Jews in the Twentieth Century* (Columbia and London: University of Missouri Press, 1998), 226.

9 McDowell, "'In the Same Boat,'" 226.

10 Greenberg, *Or Does It Explode?*, 126–27; McDowell, "'In the Same Boat,'" 228.

11 It is not possible to quantify with any precision what proportion of the Communists active in Harlem during the Depression were Jews. Party records did not break down the religious or ethnic background of comrades. However, it has been argued by a scholar of these radicals during this time and at this place—based on interviews with both blacks and whites who were active then—that the "majority of those active in the black neighborhoods of Harlem may have been of Jewish ancestry." For a discussion of radical activity in Harlem and Jewish involvement in the 1930s, see Mark Naison, *Communists in Harlem during the Depression* (Urbana, Chicago, and London: University of Illinois Press, 1983), 118–21, 214–15, 321–23.

12 Allen D. Grimshaw, *Racial Violence in the United States* (Chicago: Aldine Publishing Company, 1969), 127. See also Greenberg, *Troubling the Waters*, 109.

13 Greenberg, *Troubling the Waters*, 109, 112.

14 Wallace Thurman, "The Blacker the Berry," in Rafia Zafar, ed., *Harlem Renaissance: Five Novels of the 1920s* (New York: Library of America, 2011), 797.

15 For background information on Brecher and Schiffman and affirmative views of their efforts in Harlem, see Ted Fox, "The Apollo Theater before 125th Street Was the Black Main Street," *Huffington Post* (February 20, 2014), www.huffington-

post.com. See also Ted Fox, *Showtime at the Apollo: The Story of Harlem's World Famous Theater*, rev. ed. (Clinton Corners, NY: Mill Road, 2003); David Hinckley, "Top of the World: The Apollo, 1934," *Daily News* (May 12, 1998), www.nydaily-news.com; "Frank Schiffman, Co-Founder of Harlem's Apollo, Dies at 80," *NYT* (January 17, 1974): 35.

16 Fox, "The Apollo Theater." See also Nathan Irvin Huggins, *Harlem Renaissance* (London, Oxford, and New York; Oxford University Press, 1971), 291–92.

17 *AN* (July 1, 1925): 10, noted in King, *Whose Harlem*, 84.

18 *AN* (September 22, 1926): 10, noted in King, *Whose Harlem*, 87.

19 Harold Cruse, *The Crisis of the Negro Intellectual* (New York: William Morrow, 1967), 77.

20 Ibid., 78.

21 "About Things Theatrical," *AN* (July 1, 1925): 10.

22 King, *Whose Harlem*, 90. It may be noted that the absence of characterization of the labor issue as a Jewish versus black concern is reflected both in the press of the day and books that have discuss the events of 1925–1927. The polemical work of Harold Cruse, which has much to say about Jewish-black relationship in Harlem over an extended time period, does not mention the owners' religious background in the motion picture operators boycott. Similarly, in his scholarly treatment of these events and other issues in Harlem in 1920–1930, King always refers to whites and not Jews as in conflict or in dialogue with African Americans.

23 Hinckley, "Top of the World."

24 Robert Palmer, "Lights Go On at the Apollo," *NYT* (May 5, 1978): C10; Edward Rothstein, "The Apollo: Uptown's Showbiz Incubator," *NYT* (February 8, 2011): C1.

25 Hinckley, "Top of the World." See also Ami Eden, "Remembering Jackie Robinson's Fight With Black Nationalists Over Anti-Semitism," *Jewish Week* (April 13, 2013), www.thejewishweek.com.

26 Lewis A. Ehrenberg, *Steppin' Out: New York Nightlife and the Transformation of American Culture, 1890–1930* (Westport, CT: Greenwood Press, 1981), 255.

27 Ann Douglas, *Terrible Honesty: Mongrel Manhattan in the 1920s* (New York: Farrar, Straus and Giroux, 1995), 75–79; Ronald Sanders, "The American Popular Song," in Douglas Villiers, ed., *Next Year in Jerusalem: Portraits of the Jew in the Twentieth Century* (New York: Viking, 1976), 198; Wallace Thurman, *Negro Life in New York's Harlem* (Girard, KS: Haldeman-Julius Publications, 1928), 24; Ehrenberg, *Steppin' Out*, 255.

28 Sophie Tucker, *Some of These Days: The Autobiography of Sophie Tucker* (Garden City, NY: Doubleday, Doran and Company, 1945), 27–34, 38.

29 Ann Borden, "Sophie Tucker, 1884–1966," in Paula Hyman and Deborah Dash Moore, eds., *Jewish Women in America: An Historical Encyclopedia*, vol. 2 (New York and London: Routledge, 1997), 1416–19. See also June Sochen, "Fanny Brice and Sophie Tucker: Blending the Particular and the Universal," in Sarah Cohen Blacher, ed., *From Hester Street to Hollywood: The Jewish-*

American Stage and Screen (Bloomington: Indiana University Press, 1983), 45; Gill, *Harlem*, 162–63.

30 Ehrenberg, *Steppin' Out*, 195–97.

31 Herbert G. Goldman, *Fanny Brice: The Original Funny Girl* (New York: Oxford University Press), 12, 17, 31, 36–37. See also Michael Alexander, *Jazz Age Jews* (Princeton, NJ: Princeton University Press, 2001), 145; Gill, *Harlem*, 163–64. On the inability of the composers to enter the clubs where she was performing, see Seth Berkman, "Harlem's Good Ol' Days," *F* (January 18, 2003),http://forward.com.

32 Thaddeus Russell, *A Renegade History of the United States* (New York: Simon & Schuster, 2011), 169; Herbert G. Goldman, *Jolson: The Legend Comes to Life* (New York and London: Oxford University Press, 1988), 58; William G. Hyland, *George Gershwin: A New Biography* (Westport, CT, and London: Praeger, 2003), 24–25. See also Robert F. Moss, "Was Al Jolson 'Bamboozled'?," *Los Angeles Times* (October 20, 2006), www.latimes.com.

33 Howe, *World of Our Fathers*, 563. See also, Ehrenberg, *Steppin' Out*, 195.

34 Eric L. Goldstein, *The Price of Whiteness: Jews, Race, and American Identity* (Princeton, NJ: Princeton University Press, 2006), 154–55; Michael Rogin, "Black Sacrifice, Jewish Redemption: From Al Jolson's *Jazz Singer* to John Garfield's *Body and Soul*," in Franklin et al., *African Americans and Jews*, 86–89; Jeffrey Melnick, *A Right to Sing the Blues* (Cambridge, MA: Harvard University Press, 1999), 12. See also Alexander, *Jazz Age Jews*, 172–73. Alexander posits that "blackface is a symptom of confusion about Jewish identity in America. Confusion is not abandonment."

35 Moss, "'Bamboozled'?" See also Eddie Deezen, "Al Jolson—Misunderstood Hero or Villain?," *Today I Found Out* (October 9, 2014), www.todayifoundout.com. On Anderson's play, see Garland Anderson, *Uncommon Sense: The Law of Life in Action* (London: L.N. Fowler and Com., 1933).

36 On Gershwin's family background and his early interest in music, see, for example, Hyland, *George Gershwin*, 3, 9; Gill, *Harlem*, 164. See also Isaac Goldberg, *George Gershwin: A Study in American Music* (New York: Simon & Schuster, 1931), 54. On pianos as a sign of affluence, see Andrew Heinze, *Adapting to Abundance: Jewish Immigrants, Mass Consumption and the Search for Jewish Identity* (New York: Columbia University Press, 1990), 139–41.

37 Hyland, *George Gershwin*, 16–18; Maurice Peress, *From Dvorak to Duke Ellington: A Conductor Explores American Music and Its African-American Roots* (Cary, NC: Oxford University Press, 2004), 68; Stanley Crouch, "Gershwin Is Still Cause for Rhapsody: An Inspired Borrower of a Black Tradition," *NYT* (August 30, 1998), www.nytimes.com; Goldberg, *George Gershwin*, 75, 275. On Jewish families having problems with their children becoming part of the black music scene, see Berkman, "Harlem Good Ol' Days."

38 Hyland, *George Gershwin*, 135, 160; Peress, *Dvorak to Duke Ellington*, 70–71. See also Mike Oppenheim, "The Harlem Renaissance and American Music,"*All About Jazz* (March 3, 2013), www.allaboutjazz.com.

39 Crouch, "Gershwin."

40 For a positive vision of Jewish entrepreneurship in black music, see Stephen J. Whitfield, "From Patronage to Pluralism: Jews in the Circulation of African American Culture," *Modern Judaism* (February 2013): 2.

41 Melnick, *Right to Sing*, 36; Thurman, *Negro Life*, 33; Whitfield, "Patronage to Pluralism," 1. See also Berkman, "Harlem's Good Ol' Days."

42 Grimshaw, *Racial Violence*, 117. On the damage done during the 1935 riot, see Greenberg, *Troubling the Waters*, 54. On the decline of slumming after the riots, see Gill, *Harlem*, 303, 321. On the decline in slumming, see also Berkman, "Harlem's Good Ol' Days."

43 On the relationship between Jewish entrepreneurs and black music, see Jonathan Karp, "Blacks, Jews, and the Business of Race Music, 1945–1955," in Rebecca Kobrin, ed., *Chosen Capital: The Jewish Encounter with American Capitalism*, (New Brunswick, NJ, and London: Rutgers University Press, 2012), 141, 146, 155, 160.

CHAPTER 9. HARLEM'S NADIR FOR BLACKS AND JEWS, 1950–1980

1 Horowitz and Kaplan, *Jewish Population*, 156–57, 160–61. On the paltry numbers of Jews resident in Central and East Harlem in 1981, see "The Low Income Jewish Population of New York City: A Report Prepared for the Metropolitan New York Coordinating Council on Jewish Poverty" [typescript] (New York: Nova Institute,1984), 12–13, 16. The data reported in 1984 was based on statistics as of 1981.

2 *Manhattan Communities: Summary Statements of Population Characteristics* (New York: Research Department Community Council of Greater New York, 1955), n.p. (see sections on Central Harlem and East Harlem). See also Gill, *Harlem*, 334.

3 Joshua M. Zeitz, *White Ethnic New York: Jews, Catholics and the Shaping of Postwar Politics* (Chapel Hill: University of North Carolina Press, 2007), 148–49.

4 On middle-class out-migration from Harlem, see Emily Rosenbaum and Samantha Friedman, *The Housing Divide: How Generations of Immigrants Fare in New York's Housing Market* (New York: NYU Press, 2007), 105.

5 "The Root of the Trouble," *NYT* (July 23, 1964): 26; Layhmond Robinson, "Negroes View of Plight Examined in Survey Here," *NYT* (July 27, 1964): 1.

6 Fred Powerledge, "Negro Riots Reflect Deep-Seated Grievances," *NYT* (August 2, 1964): 13.

7 Lenora E. Berson, *The Negroes and the Jews* (New York: Random House, 1971), 338–40. On Malcolm X's reference to Jewish storeowners as "colonialists," see Dan Cohn-Shebok, *Anti-Semitism: A History* (Sparkford: Sutton Publishers, 2002), 310.

8 Jewish Telegraphic Agency, *Daily News Bulletin* (July 23, 1964): 1; *Jewish Press* (July 3, 1964): 1; *Jewish Press* (July 10, 1964): 1; *Jewish Press* (July 31, 1964): 1.

9 For a comprehensive examination of the texture of Jewish life in New York City and suburban locales in the two decades after World War II—along with some references to Jews moving to sun-belt regions as well as statistics and analyses of the segregated nature of Gotham—see Gurock, *Jews in Gotham*, chapters 4–5.

Details on what became of the Spitz-Stone family decades after they left Harlem from phone interview with Marilyn Spitz Maxwell, June 26, 2015.

10 Jerald E. Podair, *The Strike That Changed New York: Blacks, Whites and the Ocean Hill–Brownsville Crisis* (New Haven, CT, and London: Yale University Press, 2002), 34–36. On press coverage of the protests, see, for example, Lawrence Buder, "Harlem Negroes Plan a 'School-In,'" *NYT* (August 27, 1964): 30; M. A. Farber, "I.S. 201 Play Site Stirs New Dispute," *NYT* (December 24, 1966): 9.

11 Podair, *The Strike*, 115–24. See also Jonathan Kaufman, *Broken Alliance: The Turbulent Times between Blacks and Jews in America* (New York: Scribner, 1988), 142–43, 148–49.

12 Matthew Israel, "As Landmark: An Introduction to 'Harlem on My Mind,'" *Art Spaces Archive Project* (August 5, 2010), www.as-ap.org; Bridget R. Cooks, "Black Artists and Activism: *Harlem on My Mind* (1969)," *American Studies* 48:1 (spring 2007): 5–40, especially 5–6, 9, 14, 16, 17. See also Steven C. Dubin, *Displays of Power: Memory and Amnesia in the American Museum* (New York and London: NYU Press, 1999), 25–27.

13 On Van Ellison's essay and excerpts from the text, see Cooks, "Black Artists," 19–20. On young blacks' attitudes towards the sentiments expressed in the essay, see Louis Harris and Bert E. Swanson, *Black-Jewish Relations in New York City* (New York, Washington, and London: Praeger, 1970), 153.

14 Cooks, "Black Artists," 20–21. See also Kaufman, *Broken Alliance*, 157–58; Robert G. Weisbord and Arthur Stein, *Bittersweet Encounter: The Afro-American and the American Jew* (New York: Schoken Books, 1970), 180–82. On the views of the leader of the Synagogue Council of America, see Henry Siegman, "Negro Anti-Semitism," in Herbert A. Strauss, ed., *Conference on Anti-Semitism, 1969*, (New York: American Federation of Jews from Central Europe, 1969), 42.

15 Weisbord and Stein, *Bittersweet Encounter*, 181. Interestingly, the more moderate *Amsterdam News* (February 1, 1969), while quick to call the Met issue "an overblown black-Jewish confrontation," was concerned that "the present hysteria over an exploited introduction by a teenage girl causes the whole community to be branded, by some as, anti-everything but Black." Quoted in Weisbord and Stein, *Bittersweet Encounter*, 181, n. 50.

16 For statistics on Jewish attitudes towards the Met controversy, see Harris and Swanson, *Black-Jewish Relations*, 153. Their report notes that by a "narrow 37–31 percentage . . . Jews familiar with the controversy" felt that Van Ellison's remarks "were not typical of the way other young blacks felt about the Jews." For an opinion by a leading Jewish intellectual who believed that the Jewish communal response was disproportionate to the significance of the essay, see Nathan Glazer, "Blacks, Jews and the Intellectuals," *Commentary* (April 1969): 38. See also Ismar Schorsch, "Reflections on a Jewish Dilemma," in Strauss, *Conference*, 48–49. On different perspectives on race among Jews depending on where they lived in the city, see Gurock, *Jews in Gotham*, 140–49.

17 Andy A. Beveridge, "Harlem's Shifting Population," *Gotham Gazette* (September 2, 2008), www.gothamgazette.com; "Low Income Jewish Population," 12–13, 16.

18 Matthew P. Drennan, "The Decline and Rise of the New York Economy," in John Hull Mollenkopf and Manuel Castells, eds., *Dual City: Restructuring New York* (New York: Russell Sage Foundation, 1991), 29–33; Thomas Bailey and Roger Waldinger, "The Changing Ethnic/Racial Division of Labor," in Mollenkopf and Castells, *Dual City*, 43. See also Charlayne Hunter, "Recession Adds to Problems of Jobless Blacks: What Figures Show Recession Hits Jobless Blacks Harder," *NYT* (December 16, 1974): 35.

19 Charlayne Hunter, "Population, Housing and Jobs Declining," *NYT* (November 21, 1974): 49. See also Selwyn Raab, "Crime Rate Down in Perilous Areas, Up in Rest of the City," *NYT* (December 2, 1974): 69.

20 Hunter, "Population," 49, 53; Frederick M. Binder and David M. Reimers, *All Nations under Heaven: An Ethnic and Racial History of New York City* (New York: Columbia University Press, 1995), 220; Joshua Freeman, *Working-Class New York: Life and Labor since World War II* (New York: New Press, 2000), 274–75.

21 Raab, "Illegal Narcotics Traffic Is Worst Here in Five Years," *NYT* (December 8, 1975): 1, 49; Roger Wilkins, "Stemming Flow of Street Drugs Eludes Harlem," *NYT* (June 25, 1979): D1. See also Bruce D. Johnson et al., *Taking Care of Business: The Economics of Crime by Heroin Abusers* (Lexington, MA, and Toronto: Lexington Books, 1985), 17.

22 C. Gerald Fraser, "People Are Gloomy on Future in Area," *NYT* (November 21, 1974): 49; Orde Coombs, "Three Faces of Harlem," *NYT* (November 3, 1974): E32, E35.

23 Roger Wilkins, "Crime and the Streets," *NYT* (February 18, 1975): 29.

24 On the physical state of Morningside Park, see Edith Evans Asbury, "Youths Pitching In to Save Parks," *NYT* (August 10, 1976): 29; Deirdre Carmody, "A Preservationist Group Enters Long Battle of Morningside Park," *NYT* (May 2, 1983): B1; Gill, *Harlem*, 402. On Columbia University's fears of visitors hopping on the wrong train, see "Columbia Presses for Transit Signs on IRT Platform," *NYT* (February 8 1975): 5. For a report on a visitor who took the wrong train, see "Patrolling of Morningside Park Increases after Stabbing There," *NYT* (September 8, 1973): 35. See also Charles Kaiser, "Scaling Morningside Heights," *NYT* (October 1, 1976): 71.

25 Edward C. Burks, "The A Train, a Loser, May Cut Express Runs," *NYT* (May 26, 1975): 17.

26 Lena Williams, "Once-Hailed Subway Is Scorned in East Harlem," *NYT* (June 24, 1977): 29.

27 "Youths, Denied 25c by Medical Student, Shoot Him in Back," *NYT* (October 12, 1971): 45.

28 Steven Schleifer to Gurock, email, July 2, 2015; phone interview with Schleifer, July 8, 2015.

CHAPTER 10. THE BEGINNINGS OF RETURN

1 Lena Williams, “Middle-Class Blacks Return to Harlem,” *NYT* (August 21, 1976): 47. See also Thurman, *Negro Life*, 11.

2 Charleyne Hunter, “Harlem Brownstone Lures New Generation of Blacks,” *NYT* (October 2, 1973): 90.

3 Sheila Rule, “Signs of Harlem Rebirth Seen in Construction Spurt,” *NYT* (March 1, 1980): 25. See also Lee A. Daniels, “Gateway Area on Verge of Major Redevelopment,” *NYT* (February 19, 1984): R1.

4 “Migration of Affluent Whites to Harlem Forecast,” *NYT* (May 28, 1984): 23.

5 Sam Roberts, “No Longer Majority Black, Harlem Is in Transition,” *NYT* (January 5, 2010), www.nytimes.com; Andy A. Beveridge, “Harlem's Shifting Population,” *Gotham* (September 2, 2008), http://gotham-magazine.com.. See also Charlotte Recoquillon, “Neoliberalism and Spatial (in) Justice: The Gentrification of Harlem,” *Spatial Justice* (June 6, 2014): 5, 8.

6 Christy Smith-Bloman, “A New Harlem: A New Renaissance,” *Cooperator* (February 2012), http://cooperator.com; Recoquillon, “Neoliberalism,” 5.

7 Andrew Hacker, “The City's Comings, Goings,” *NYT* (December 2, 1973): 26; Blake Fleetwood, “The New Elite and an Urban Renaissance,” *NYT* (January 14, 1979): SM26, SM34.

8 Fred Siegel, *The Prince of the City: Giuliani, New York and the Genius of American Life* (New York: Encounter Books, 2005), 268–69.

9 Jordan G. Teicher, “Confessions of a Harlem Gentrifier,” *Salon* (August 19, 2013), www.salon.com.

10 Interview with Henry “Harp” Blaukopf, July 14, 2015. On the building's history, see its listing in addressreport.com.

11 Teicher, “Confessions.”

12 “The Harlem Gentrification: From Black to White,” *New African Magazine* (June 25, 2014), http://newafricanmagazine.com.

13 Joe Coscarelli, ”Spike Lee's Amazing Rant Against Gentrification: ‘We Been Here,’” *New York* (February 25, 2014), http://nymag.com.

14 John Freeman Gill, “Cold Shoulders,” *NYT* (July 27, 2008), www.nytimes.com; Cybz, “Gentrification in Harlem Is Getting Out of Hand,” Just Realeyez (August 11, 2007), https://justrealeyez.wordpress.com; Nicholas Wapshott, “Harlem to Clinton: You're Ruining Us,” *Independent* (July 23, 2006), www.independent.co.uk.

15 Robert Kolker, “Whose Harlem Is It,” *New York* (July 6, 2008), http://nymag.com. See also “The Harlem Gentrification: From Black to White.”

16 *The New York Jewish Population Study: Profile of Counties, Boroughs and Neighborhoods* (New York: UJA-Federation of New York, 1995): table 7.

17 *Jewish Community Study of New York: 2002* (New York: UJA-Federation of New York, 2004): exhibit 12A. It must be noted that the statistics for Jews are broken down by zip codes. In the case of Harlem, zip code 10027, where 876 Jews were found, includes Morningside Heights and Harlem Heights. Although it is likely

that most of that cohort lived in the Columbia University area—above Harlem—some of those counted undoubtedly lived in the western part of Harlem, east of Morningside Park. Hence the number is estimated as "more than 500." I am grateful for the zip code data provided both for 2001 and, as we will immediately see, for 2011 by the Berman Jewish Data Bank of the Jewish Federation of North America and the assistance of Professor Ronald Miller. The interpretation of the data is mine alone.

18 Jordan G. Teicher to Gurock, email, July 14, 2015.

19 Dan Berry, "Plans to Evict Record-Shop Owner Roiled Residents," *NYT* (December 9, 1995): 31; Don Van Natta Jr., "Inquiry Is Focusing on Protests," *NYT* (December 13, 1995): B1.

20 Peter Noel, "Freddy's Not Dead," *Village Voice* (December 29, 1998), www.villagevoice.com. The information on the stores in Harlem as of the summer of 2015 was derived by the author from a walk along 125th Street on July 22, 2015.

21 Jim Yardley, "Jews and Blacks Try to Avoid Reprise of '91 in Crown Heights," *NYT* (April 4, 1998): A1, B6. For the argument that 9/11 changed New Yorkers' attitudes towards inter-group relations in the city, see Gurock, *Jews in Gotham*, 219–20.

22 Rose Hackman, "What Will Happen When Harlem Becomes White," *Guardian* (May 16, 2015), www.theguardian.com/us.

23 On the history of eruvs in New York, see Jeffrey S. Gurock, "Eruv: A Gateway into Orthodoxy in Gotham in the 20th–21st Centuries," in Adam Mintz, ed., *It's a Thin Line: Eruv from Talmudic to Modern Culture* (New York: Scharf Publications/Yeshiva University Press, 2014), 91–105.

24 Interview with Rabbi David Gedzelman, July 31, 2015. For the mission of the Steinhardt Foundation, see Steinhardtfoundation.org. For DOROT's mission see, doorotusa.org.

25 On the history of 1807 Seventh Avenue, see streeteasy.com.

26 Interview with Steven I. Weiss, July 15, 2015. As of the summer of 2015, Romemu, a nondenominational "Jewish renewal" congregation, had a tangential connection to Harlem. This congregation, in existence since 2006 on the Upper West Side of Manhattan, has held its Sabbath and holiday services in rented quarters in a church on 105th Street and Amsterdam Avenue. But its administrative offices, its rabbis' offices, and some of its educational programming have taken place since 2013 in Harlem at 110th Street and Central Park North. Of its some six hundred family units, only thirty-seven reside in Harlem. Its Hebrew school has an enrollment of some forty students and meets twice a week in Harlem. Interestingly, most of the pupils do not live in the neighborhood. As of the summer of 2015, the congregation had yet to determine whether Harlem would be the location of its hoped-for permanent synagogue. See romemu.org; congregational promotional and activities documents provided by David Cavil of Romemu and interviews with Cavil and Rabbi Dianne Cohler-Esses, July 22, 2015.

27 Steven Weiss, "Missed Opportunities for Jewish Life in Renewed Urban Neighborhoods," *Contact* (winter 2015): 3–7.

CONCLUSION

1 Among the more important community studies of that era that relied appreciably upon quantitative sources were Marc Lee Raphael, *Jews and Judaism in a Midwestern Community: Columbus, Ohio, 1840–1975* (Columbus: Ohio Historical Society, 1979); Stephen Hertzberg, *Strangers within the Gate City: The Jews of Atlanta, 1845–1915* (Philadelphia: Jewish Publication Society, 1978); and William Toll, *The Making of an Ethnic Middle Class: Portland Jewry over Four Generations* (Albany: State University of New York Press, 1982). In the decades before the rise of social history, Lloyd Gartner produced a number of institutionally based and nonquantitative community histories that were a number of steps up from the amateur work described. See, for example, his *The History of the Jews of Los Angeles* (San Marino: Huntington Library, 1970), written with Max Vorspan; *The History of the Jews of Milwaukee* (Philadelphia: Jewish Publications Society, 1963); and *The History of the Jews of Cleveland* (Cleveland: Western Reserve Historical Society, 1978).

2 Among the most important histories of New York Jews are Deborah Dash Moore, *At Home in America: Second Generation New York Jews* (New York: Columbia University Press, 1981), written at approximately the same time as my Harlem book; Beth S. Wenger, *New York Jews and the Great Depression: Uncertain Promise* (New Haven, CT: Yale University Press, 1996); and Eli Lederhendler, *New York Jews and the Decline of Urban Ethnicity* (Syracuse, NY: Syracuse University Press, 2001). Noteworthy also is the first comprehensive history of New York Jewry from its seventeenth-century inception to the present era, Deborah Dash Moore, ed., *City of Promises: A History of the Jews of New York*, 3 vols. (New York: NYU Press, 2012).

INDEX

ABOUT THE AUTHOR

Jeffrey S. Gurock is Libby M. Klaperman Professor of Jewish History at Yeshiva University. He is the author or editor of eighteen books, including the prize-winning *Jews in Gotham: New York Jews in a Changing City, 1920–2010* (NYU Press). He lives with his family in the Riverdale section of the Bronx.